"*A Heart Aflame for God* is one of the most edifying and spiritually insightful books I have ever read. While confessional Protestants often look to other traditions for guidance in spiritual formation, Matthew Bingham is like a miner uncovering the rich, life-giving treasures of the Reformed tradition. I wish I could travel back in time and hand this book to my younger self. Highly recommended!"

Hans Madueme, Professor of Theological Studies, Covenant College

"In our current historical moment, rife as it is with digital noise, doctrinal shallowness, and irreverent worship, some professing Christians have moved away from the biblical faith in search of ostensibly soul-satisfying alternatives. Turning to denominations like Roman Catholicism or Eastern Orthodoxy, many crave the stillness, theological intricacy, and spiritual gravitas that are promised by those traditions but that, when weighed in the balances, are found wanting. Matthew Bingham returns to the old paths by examining the sound doctrine and experiential piety of the Reformed tradition, a faith whose theologians of previous centuries—whether the English Puritans, the Dutch *Nadere Reformatie* divines, or the Old Princeton theologians—were masters of the craft of vibrant spiritual formation. Bingham examines how the Reformed tradition promotes spiritual growth through the disciplines of Scripture reading, meditation, and prayer, as well as through self-examination, worship, and Christian fellowship. This is a very helpful exposition and affirmation of Reformed experiential piety."

Joel R. Beeke, Chancellor and Professor of Homiletics and Systematic Theology, Puritan Reformed Theological Seminary; Pastor, Heritage Reformed Congregation, Grand Rapids, Michigan

"In a time when many evangelicals are experiencing great spiritual anxiety and discontentment, Matthew Bingham retrieves a distinctively Reformed account of spiritual formation. This book is like food in a time of hunger. Many are leaving evangelicalism in search of a greater depth of spiritual practice. Bingham helps us see how this need can be met within the resources of our own tradition. Drawing especially from the Puritans, he builds a robust theology of prayer, Scripture reading, meditation, self-examination, relationship, and even nature and the human body. Rich in both theology and spiritual insight, *A Heart Aflame for God* will serve and edify readers at multiple levels. Highly recommended!"

Gavin Ortlund, President, Truth Unites; Theologian in Residence, Immanuel Church, Nashville, Tennessee

"Matthew Bingham calls us to leave the experiential shallows of modern evangelicalism and to plunge into the deeper understanding of Christian formation that was developed by the Reformers and Puritans from their sustained reflection on the word and works of God. This is an incredibly important new book—a word in season to those who are weary."

Crawford Gribben, Professor of History, Queen's University Belfast; author, *An Introduction to John Owen*

"This book on spiritual formation by Matthew Bingham is just the tonic for this age, in part because it relies on many 'ages' throughout church history. To address contemporary concerns, while also offering a positive approach to how to live as a Christian, Bingham has marshaled some of the best in this delightful treatise. A Reformed approach to living a spiritual life is not an oxymoron but rather part and parcel of how Reformed theologians, including many of the illustrious Puritan divines, did theology. This is a modern 'Puritan' work addressing a present need in the hopes that evangelicals will embrace the tools readily available to them to make them mature, deep-thinking Christians."

Mark Jones, Senior Minister, Faith Reformed Presbyterian Church, Vancouver, British Columbia

"This work stands as a guiding light, showing us that a heart aflame for God can thrive within a Reformed understanding of spiritual formation. I highly recommend Matthew Bingham's insightful and accessible book to anyone yearning for a stronger connection to the Reformed faith and a deeper walk with God. Protestant readers will discover that the resources for profound spiritual growth can be found within their tradition."

Karin Spiecker Stetina, Associate Professor of Biblical and Theological Studies, Talbot School of Theology, Biola University

"One of the major effects for evangelical Christians living in the modern West with its ahistorical ethos and *mentalité* is an ignorance of the spiritual riches of their tradition. Matthew Bingham's work on spiritual formation and what have traditionally been called the means of grace is a fabulous remedy for this dire situation. Drawing especially on the Puritan writings of our evangelical heritage (he even includes quotes from that relatively unknown star of the Puritan firmament Brilliana Harley!), Bingham charts a way for modern Christians to benefit from that notable era of spiritual wisdom and so walk worthy of their calling. It is a book, I trust, that will bring much good to God's people and glory to the God of the Puritans!"

Michael A. G. Haykin, Professor of Church History and Biblical Spirituality, The Southern Baptist Theological Seminary

"Matthew Bingham helps the sons and daughters of the Reformation feel no shame for the origin story of their piety. He displays the rich fare of spiritual formation passed down to us by the Reformers, even as he strongly resists the modern trend of adopting spiritual and mystical practices from other traditions. This book outlines the contours of a truly healthy spirituality that is inseparably connected to healthy doctrine—with the 'Reformation triangle' at its foundation and with Christ at its center."

    A. Craig Troxel, Robert G. den Dulk Professor of Practical Theology, Westminster Seminary California; author, *With All Your Heart*

"Oh to have 'great souls' like the early modern saints. Our inner persons today have shriveled so small. We are fragile and weak of heart. We are in desperate need of enlarged, deepened, conditioned souls that glory in real glories, fear real threats, and keep Godward balance in the tides of unbelief, decadence, and trivial distraction. Bingham has collected many Puritan treasures in one chest, arranged them in order, and made them accessible for use today. The health of your soul in the late modern world—and perhaps, through you, the healing of others—may await a slow, attentive engagement with this book. The more I read, the better it got. I've already made plans to reread this book."

    David Mathis, Senior Teacher and Executive Editor, Desiring God; Pastor, Cities Church, Saint Paul, Minnesota; author, *Habits of Grace*

"In Galatians 4:19, the apostle Paul expressed his longing to see that 'Christ is formed' in believers. From this verse, the term *spiritual formation* has arisen to describe the biblical process of molding the mind, heart, and life of a Christian into conformity to Christ. Books related to this theme have appeared for as long as Christian books have been written, but I cannot recommend many of them because they rely heavily on writers who hold to a different gospel than the one taught in Scripture. They may say wonderful things about how a Christian should pray, for example, but behind those commendations is false teaching about how a person becomes a Christian in the first place. I cannot encourage the reading of some books on the subject because they advocate spiritual formation by means of practices not found in Scripture at all. But *A Heart Aflame for God* rightly contends for a *sola Scriptura* spirituality. Those unfamiliar with the Reformed tradition on spiritual formation (which seems to be true of some of the bestselling contemporary authors on spiritual formation) will be surprised by the depth and breadth of the riches uncovered by Bingham. He carefully considers the views of other traditions, but he maintains that all true spirituality must be founded on the Bible and the gospel it proclaims. As Jesus prayed, 'Sanctify them in the truth; your word is truth' (John 17:17)."

    Donald S. Whitney, Professor of Biblical Spirituality and John H. Powell Professor of Pastoral Ministry, Midwestern Baptist Theological Seminary; author, *Spiritual Disciplines for the Christian Life*; *Praying the Bible*; and *Family Worship*

A Heart Aflame for God

A Heart Aflame for God

A Reformed Approach to Spiritual Formation

Matthew Bingham

CROSSWAY®

WHEATON, ILLINOIS

Library of Congress Cataloging-in-Publication Data
Names: Bingham, Matthew C., 1983– author.
Title: A heart aflame for God : a reformed approach to spiritual formation / Matthew Bingham.
Description: Wheaton, Illinois : Crossway, 2025. | Includes bibliographical references and index.
Identifiers: LCCN 2024022134 (print) | LCCN 2024022135 (ebook) | ISBN 9781433592621 (hardcover) | ISBN 9781433592638 (pdf) | ISBN 9781433592645 (epub)
Subjects: LCSH: Reformed Church. | Christian life.
Classification: LCC BX9422.3 .B544 2025 (print) | LCC BX9422.3 (ebook) | DDC 248.088/2842—dc23
    /eng/20241207
LC record available at https://lccn.loc.gov/2024022134
LC ebook record available at https://lccn.loc.gov/2024022135

Crossway is a publishing ministry of Good News Publishers.

SH			34	33	32	31	30	29	28	27	26	25
15	14	13	12	11	10	9	8	7	6	5	4	3	2	1

For Amelia, John, James, and David—
olive shoots around the table,
who I pray will grow up well (Ps. 128:3).

Contents

Acknowledgments

IT IS A PRIVILEGE to thank those who helped shape this book and bring it to fruition. First and foremost, I am grateful to all my students at Oak Hill College, especially those who took my elective courses on spiritual formation and Puritanism. Much of the material developed in this book began in those class sessions, and both the content and form of what follows has been sharpened and strengthened by the many thoughtful comments and questions shared in the classroom. Likewise, I owe a huge debt to my colleagues at Oak Hill and Phoenix Seminary, whose support and interest has been a wonderful source of encouragement. In particular, I am grateful to Matthew Sleeman, a mentor, prayer partner, and friend who championed this project from the beginning and always had time for a chat along the way.

In addition, I am indebted to the entire team at Crossway, all of whom have been a joy to work with. In this connection, I must extend a special word of appreciation to David Barshinger, whose keen editorial sensibility has considerably strengthened this book.

I am grateful to Crawford Gribben for continuing to be a constant source of wisdom and good advice. I owe many thanks to my good friends in ministry Reagan Marsh and Joshua DeLong, who read portions of the manuscript and offered tremendously helpful feedback. And I am so thankful to Gareth Burke, who models godliness and faithfulness in all that he does and whom I will always consider a mentor and friend. I am also blessed to have Christian parents and parents-in-law—Gordon, Lisa, Gary, and Nancy—all four of whom model faithfulness, generosity, and love.

This book could never have happened without the support of my beautiful wife, Shelley. Walking alongside me at every stage of the writing process, she has provided encouragement and enthusiasm, reading the manuscript from start to finish and improving it at every turn. She is the love of my life *and* my best critic!

Finally, I am thankful for my children—Amelia, John, James, and David—who bring me joy each day and to whom this book is dedicated.

Introduction

YOU CAN LEARN A LOT about the state of twenty-first-century evangelicalism by talking to those who leave it. This isn't always true, of course—some ex-evangelicals leave with such a bitter taste that their subsequent commentary feels more vindictive than insightful—but many offer useful lessons to those of us who remain within the fold.

Consider, for example, the case of Joel and Stephanie Dunn, a married couple who left their Southern Baptist roots to convert to Eastern Orthodoxy. As described in an article in the *Christian Post*, the Dunns were drawn to Orthodoxy because they believed it offered spiritual resources that were absent from the evangelical churches they were familiar with. After Joel came "face-to-face" with a sense of his own "depravity," he arrived at the conclusion that in his Baptist tradition, "there was nothing . . . to help [him] through it other than" advice to "pray harder and have faith." Convinced that "there's got to be more than that," the Dunns went looking for a church that would provide "more tools" to help them on their Christian journey. The article's author writes, "The Orthodox Church had the tools, they soon discovered, and not only were they helpful resources but they helped create saints."[1] In converting from evangelicalism to Eastern Orthodoxy, the Dunns were not alone. A May 2023 piece in the *Wall Street Journal* reported

---

1 Brandon Showalter, "Why This Evangelical Couple Became Eastern Orthodox (Part 1)," *Christian Post*, October 24, 2020, https://www.christianpost.com/.

on a surge of new converts swelling the ranks of Orthodox parishes, many coming from evangelical backgrounds.[2] What is it exactly that draws them? At least in the case of Joel and Stephanie Dunn, it seems that what they were really after was spiritual formation.

To be perfectly honest, I can relate to their feelings. I grew up in a vibrant evangelical church. The people in the pews were almost all friendly, well meaning, and generous. My pastors were passionate about ministry and genuinely concerned for their congregations. We had no shortage of events on the church calendar; from weekly youth group and vacation Bible school to short-term summer missions trips, my days and nights were full of well-run, thoughtfully constructed activities. If there was any scandal or impropriety in our church, I didn't know about it. In other words, I enjoyed a happy evangelical upbringing for which I am genuinely thankful to God.

And yet for all this exposure to a seemingly healthy contemporary evangelical culture, something was missing from my Christian life, or at least underdeveloped. For a long time, I felt confused by what should be, from one angle, the most basic aspect of my faith: my own spiritual formation. Though I remember a desire to deepen my spiritual life in theory, I often felt confused about how exactly to pursue such an aim in practice. Beyond a simple commitment to some sort of daily "quiet time," I would have struggled to articulate what it actually might look like to "grow in the grace and knowledge of our Lord and Savior Jesus Christ" (2 Pet. 3:18) and to "work out [my] own salvation with fear and trembling" (Phil. 2:12).

I suspect that I was not alone in this feeling. I have spoken to many Christians with a background like mine who would express a similar sense that the evangelical busyness in which they participated left gaps in their understanding of Christian growth. Some of these people, like Joel and Stephanie Dunn, have left evangelicalism altogether and now

---

2   Francis X. Rocca, "Eastern Orthodoxy Gains New Followers in America," *Wall Street Journal*, May 17, 2023, https://www.wsj.com/.

claim to have found a more satisfying faith within Eastern Orthodoxy or Roman Catholicism. Others have left not just evangelical Christianity but Christianity full stop. And among those who have remained within the evangelical fold, a lack of clarity about how they ought to pursue the spiritual life is often paired with a troubling openness to spiritual techniques and methods that owe more to nonevangelical, non-Protestant, and even non-Christian traditions than to the Reformation heritage that ostensibly ought to be theirs. This is deeply unfortunate because evangelicalism actually has a rich biblical tradition of spiritual formation, and yet, somehow, it often gets ignored.

To a large extent, the particularities described here reflect a long-standing impulse within evangelical Christianity, namely, a preference for outward expansion and growth at the expense of inward development and depth. Considered on its own terms, of course, this outward impulse points toward something very good: extending and fulfilling Christ's charge to his first disciples "You will be my witnesses in Jerusalem and in all Judea and Samaria, and to the end of the earth" (Acts 1:8). Whether it's George Whitefield (1714–1770) barnstorming up and down the American colonies, Hudson Taylor (1832–1905) charging into the interior of China, or Billy Graham (1918–2018) filling up Madison Square Garden for an evangelistic rally, the picture of evangelicals at their best has typically involved men and women relentlessly pressing onward, seeking the lost wherever they might be found, and advancing the kingdom of God in all directions.

And yet even as we celebrate the positive side, keen observers of evangelical culture, both from within and without, have long sensed that the drive for outward expansion has sometimes seemed to come without any accompanying pursuit of greater depth. The vine has spread with marvelous speed, but the roots below have not always gone very deep. "To put it most simply," writes historian Mark Noll, "the evangelical ethos is activistic, populist, pragmatic, and utilitarian." The result of this restless energy, argues Noll, is that evangelical culture "allows little space for broader or deeper intellectual effort because it is dominated by the urgencies of the moment."[3]

And though Noll's concern is largely with "the weaknesses of evangelical intellectual life," these trends raise larger questions about our more basic theological commitments and spiritual health.[4] Richard Lovelace (1931–2020) drew attention to the problem in his 1979 book *Dynamics of Spiritual Life*, in which he coined the term "sanctification gap" to describe evangelicalism's "peculiar conspiracy . . . to mislay the Protestant tradition of spiritual growth" in favor of "frantic witnessing activity." In particular, Lovelace lamented his discovery during seminary that "most Protestants were ignorant of the body of tradition which seemed . . . to be the living heart of the Reformation heritage."[5] Among twenty-first century evangelicals, real progress has been made on this score, thanks in part to Lovelace's own work. But his criticism struck a chord that still resonates with many today. Commenting on Lovelace's "sanctification gap," John Coe and Kyle Strobel note that the "critique remains as accurate now as it did nearly four decades ago." Moreover, they go on to helpfully observe that despite a growing evangelical interest in spiritual growth, "there has not always been a recovery of a distinctively evangelical understanding of formation."[6] This latter point is a crucial one. As we explore further in chapter 1, the decades since the publication of Lovelace's book have seen a flood of titles dedicated to spiritual formation, but many of these works do not consistently align their vision of Christian growth with the Reformation heritage evangelicalism arose out of.

The need, then, is not simply to address spiritual growth per se but to do so in a way that takes seriously the foundational Protestant theo-

---

3   Mark A. Noll, *The Scandal of the Evangelical Mind* (Grand Rapids, MI: Eerdmans, 1994), 13, 12.

4   Noll, *Scandal*, 13.

5   Richard F. Lovelace, *Dynamics of Spiritual Life: An Evangelical Theology of Renewal*, expanded ed. (1979; repr., Downers Grove, IL: IVP Academic, 2020), 232, 231.

6   John H. Coe and Kyle C. Strobel, "Introduction: Retrieving the Heart of the Christian Faith," in *Embracing Contemplation: Reclaiming a Christian Spiritual Practice*, ed. John H. Coe and Kyle C. Strobel (Downers Grove, IL: IVP Academic, 2019), 2–3.

logical commitments that motivated the Reformation in the first place. The purpose of this book is to do just that: to explore and commend a distinctively Reformed Protestant vision of Christian growth for twenty-first-century evangelicals. In so doing, I hope to address not only committed evangelicals desiring deeper roots but also those within evangelical circles who are feeling the pull of nonevangelical traditions. Often, as in the case of Joel and Stephanie Dunn, that pull is predicated less on intellectual agreement and more on the perceived allure of the opportunities for spiritual formation that these other communions offer. Alongside such stories of ordinary people questioning evangelicalism, high-profile converts to Roman Catholicism (e.g., Christian Smith) and Eastern Orthodoxy (e.g., Hank Hanegraaff) serve to highlight and further a growing sense of religious discontent among many. Increasing numbers of Christians reared in evangelical churches are disillusioned and frustrated by a religious culture that, at its worst, can seem superficial, shallow, and almost wholly disconnected from the ancient faith that once inspired men and women to bravely go to the lions. They are seeking a deeper, more serious Christian expression, a quest that often leads to methods and techniques beyond the boundaries of Reformation Protestantism.

A chief goal of the present volume is to speak to what Kenneth Stewart has described as an "evangelical identity crisis" by pointing readers to the rich Reformation heritage that is already theirs.[7] While guarding against an uncharitable "anti-Catholicism" or an unattractive and pinched parochialism, the book aims to demonstrate to evangelical readers that the spiritual depth and seriousness they rightly long for can be found without having to look to Rome or Constantinople.

Locating Our Reformation Heritage

If the main burden of this book is to retrieve a Reformed approach to spiritual formation for the benefit of contemporary Christians, then

---

7 Kenneth J. Stewart, *In Search of Ancient Roots: The Christian Past and the Evangelical Identity Crisis* (Downers Grove, IL: IVP Academic, 2017).

we need to be clear on just what it is we are attempting to retrieve. To that end, we need to plot something of the historical territory—exactly who and what are we talking about? When we refer to "our Reformation heritage," we are focusing our attention mostly on the sixteenth-century Protestant Reformers and their seventeenth-century post-Reformation successors. Within these pages we often use the label "early modern" to refer to this period of history (ca. 1500–1800). Early modern Protestants are our primary focus because it was these men and women who recovered the distinctively word-centered approach to the spiritual life we are concerned with and faithfully preserved, advanced, and elaborated its legacy in subsequent centuries.

And though we sometimes speak more broadly of "Reformation Christianity," we should note at the outset that our primary touch-point is the Reformed tradition, which represents one important and distinctive strand within the larger Protestant Reformation. Typically, historians have divided the Protestant Reformation into three such distinctive strands: the Lutheran, the Reformed, and the Radical. The first two, the Lutheran and Reformed traditions, are often grouped together and described as constituting the "magisterial Reformation." This term is used because both Lutheran and Reformed churches worked in cooperation with the state, enjoying the official sanction of the various "magistrates" under whose protection they operated. This contrasts with the so-called Radical Reformation, a label popularized in 1962 by historian George Huntston Williams and used as a sort of catchall term to describe various Protestants who broke away from Rome but were also at odds with the magisterial Reformers.[8]

---

8   George Huntston Williams, *The Radical Reformation*, 3rd ed. (Kirksville, MO: Truman State University Press, 2000). The term Radical Reformation is widely used and generally understood. We should, however, mention in passing that the term is also deeply problematic because it lends a sense of unity and coherence to what was, in fact, a widely dispersed and ideologically variegated group of people who often had no real connections to one another. See Kat Hill, "The Power of Names: Radical Identities in the Reformation Era," in *Radicalism and Dissent in the World of Protestant Reform*, ed. Bridget Heal and Anorthe Kremers (Göttingen: Vandenhoeck & Ruprecht, 2017), 53–68.

All three of these Reformation expressions rejected the authority of the Roman Catholic Church, and all three sought to reform the church in a manner consistent with the principles of *sola Scriptura* and justification by faith alone.[9] For this reason, it is appropriate to group them all under the common banner of the Protestant Reformers, and yet this common identification should not obscure the fact that the three branches have their own distinctive qualities as well.[10] Many of these characteristic emphases represent the varying degrees to which the three streams sought to either preserve or reject the medieval Catholic doctrine and religious culture that preceded the Reformation. In key respects, especially on issues relating to liturgy and worship, Lutheranism was the most conservative of the three—in the sense of wishing to "conserve" traditional inherited forms—while the Radical Reformers, as the name suggests, were the most eager to wipe the inherited slate clean and start afresh.[11] The Reformed tradition landed somewhere in the middle, happy to retain and preserve a catholic inheritance wherever possible while also looking to boldly follow Scripture even when it led to sharp breaks with the medieval past. And while most of what is said in the present volume would apply to all evangelical Protestants, it is also true that the sources I draw on and some of the distinctive ideas I defend come specifically from the Reformed tradition.

In terms of its starting point, the Reformed tradition began with the Protestant churches of sixteenth-century Switzerland, a group led

---

9   Given the extreme range of individuals comprehended under the label Radical Reformation, one would hesitate to state that absolutely *all* of them agreed about anything beyond, perhaps, their desire to break from the bishop of Rome. But with that caveat in place, the statement above stands as a useful general observation.

10   One classic work that introduces these distinctions well is Timothy George, *The Theology of the Reformers*, 25th anniversary ed. (1988; repr., Nashville: B&H Academic, 2013).

11   On Lutheranism as conservative, see Scott H. Hendrix, *Recultivating the Vineyard: The Reformation Agendas of Christianization* (Louisville: Westminster John Knox, 2004), 95–96. On the meaning of *radical*, the word comes from the Latin *radix*, meaning "root." To speak of "radical" change thus suggests change that goes all the way down to the very roots of an issue, the opposite of a change that was merely superficial or surface level.

by men such as Huldrych Zwingli (1484–1531), Heinrich Bullinger (1504–1575), who succeeded Zwingli in Zurich, and, of course, the Genevan Reformer John Calvin (1509–1564). Because of Calvin's international reputation and tremendous literary output, he is sometimes equated with Reformed Protestantism itself, a trend reflected in and bolstered by the use of the term Calvinism. And yet while the Calvinist label is long-standing and widely used, it's important to recognize that the Reformed tradition extends well beyond the theology and legacy of any one individual, however significant he might be.[12] Indeed, while originating in Switzerland with Zwingli as "the father of Reformed Protantism," this particular flavor of Christianity quickly spread throughout France, Germany, the Netherlands, Poland, Hungary, England, Scotland, Ireland, and eventually North America.[13]

And as the tradition spread geographically, it also became increasingly varied theologically, admitting greater variation in its approach to subjects like church government, the sacraments, the proper role of the civil magistrate, and the precise relationship between the biblical covenants, all while retaining an identifiable core that would continue to differentiate Reformed Protestantism from its alternatives. Through the production of confessional documents like the Belgic Confession (1561), the Heidelberg Catechism (1563), the Westminster Confession (1646),

---

12 For caution regarding the use of the term Calvinism, see Willem J. van Asselt, "Calvinism as a Problematic Concept in Historiography," *International Journal of Philosophy and Theology* 74, no. 2 (2013): 144–50. Examples of recent scholarly literature making prominent use of the term include Philip Benedict, *Christ's Churches Purely Reformed: A Social History of Calvinism* (New Haven, CT: Yale University Press, 2002); D. G. Hart, *Calvinism: A History* (New Haven, CT: Yale University Press, 2013); Crawford Gribben and Graeme Murdock, eds., *Cultures of Calvinism in Early Modern Europe* (New York: Oxford University Press, 2019). Bruce Gordon and Carl Trueman strike a helpful balance by acknowledging both that Calvin was not "a singularly authoritative source for all that came after him" and that "he was, and remains, arguably first among equals as a source for Reformed thought." Bruce Gordon and Carl R. Trueman, "Introduction," in *The Oxford Handbook of Calvin and Calvinism*, ed. Bruce Gordon and Carl R. Trueman (New York: Oxford University Press, 2021), 2.

13 Peter Opitz, "Huldrych Zwingli," in *The Cambridge Companion to Reformed Theology*, ed. Paul T. Nimmo and David A. S. Fergusson (Cambridge: Cambridge University Press, 2016), 117.

and the Second London Baptist Confession (1677/1689), the substance of the Reformed tradition was codified in forms that still guide churches around the world right up to the present day.[14] And though these confessional statements do not agree in every detail, they are all connected by common themes and emphases and a distinctive doctrinal consensus on key issues. As Paul Nimmo and David Fergusson explain, across its various representative texts, "the Reformed tradition sets forth a particular agenda of theological discourse in a remarkably symphonic way" and is marked by "an identifiable set of theological instincts, of doctrinal impulses—a certain Christian sensibility."[15]

And while Protestant evangelicals today express a wide range of opinions regarding the Reformed tradition, all of us are indebted to it whether we continue to identify with it or not. "From one point of view," writes Sinclair Ferguson, "most evangelical theology in the English-speaking world can be seen as an exposition of, deviation from or reaction to Reformed theology."[16] Of the three major Reformation divisions we discussed earlier, the Reformed stream represents something of a majority report among those who would go on later to identify with the evangelical movement. This analysis applies across the spectrum of evangelical theology, but for those of us who identify with one of the Reformed confessions named above or even for those who see themselves fitting in more loosely with a more general

---

14 For the complete text of these and many other Reformed confessions, see James T. Dennison, *Reformed Confessions of the 16th and 17th Centuries in English Translation*, 4 vols. (Grand Rapids, MI: Reformation Heritage Books, 2008–2014). Although in this book we will adopt a relatively broad understanding of what constitutes "the Reformed tradition," we should note that the question of just how broadly the label should be applied has been a subject of some debate among scholars. For a range of views on this topic, see Matthew C. Bingham, Chris Caughey, R. Scott Clark, Crawford Gribben, and D. G. Hart, *On Being Reformed: Debates over a Theological Identity*, Christianities in the Trans-Atlantic World (Cham, Switzerland: Palgrave Macmillan, 2018).

15 Paul T. Nimmo and David A. S. Fergusson, "Introduction," in Nimmo and Fergusson, *Cambridge Companion to Reformed Theology*, 4–5.

16 Sinclair B. Ferguson, "The Reformed View," in *Christian Spirituality: Five Views of Sanctification*, ed. Donald L. Alexander (Downers Grove, IL: InterVarsity Press, 1988), 47.

"Calvinism," looking to the Reformed tradition to take our historical bearings makes good sense.[17]

In exploring how that tradition has approached spiritual formation, I of course take an interest in what John Calvin had to say, but I also draw on a range of other Reformed voices. This includes movements such as the Dutch *Nadere Reformatie,* or Further Reformation, a movement of renewal within the Netherlands that featured profound explorations of spirituality from writers such as Willem Teellinck (1579–1629), Wilhelmus à Brakel (1635–1711), and Campegius Vitringa (1659–1722).[18] It includes soundings from the eighteenth-century North American Jonathan Edwards (1703–1758), a pastor-theologian described by one near contemporary as both "the possessor of a mighty mind" and "one of the most holy, humble and heavenly minded men, that the world has seen, since the apostolic age."[19] One particularly rich source for Reformed reflection on spiritual growth comes from the so-called "Old Princeton" theologians, a group including Archibald Alexander (1772–1851), Charles Hodge (1797–1878), and B. B. Warfield (1851–1921). While these individuals have long been recognized for their contributions to Reformed scholarship, in recent years they have been increasingly appreciated for their sustained attention to "the formation of Christian character and the cultivation of 'vital piety.' "[20] But among all the varied

17   For that more general Calvinism, I'm thinking here of the contemporary religious subculture described in Collin Hansen, *Young, Restless, Reformed: A Journalist's Journey with the New Calvinists* (Wheaton, IL: Crossway, 2008); Flynn Cratty, "The New Calvinism," in Gordon and Trueman, *Oxford Handbook of Calvin and Calvinism,* 641–55.

18   Joel R. Beeke, *Puritan Reformed Spirituality: A Practical Theological Study from Our Reformed and Puritan Heritage* (Darlington, UK: Evangelical Press, 2006), 289–94; Hart, *Calvinism,* 169–72.

19   Ashbel Green, *Discourses Delivered in the College of New Jersey* (Philadelphia: E. Littell, 1822), 317. For Edwards and spiritual growth, see John Piper, *God's Passion for His Glory: Living the Vision of Jonathan Edwards* (Wheaton, IL: Crossway, 2006); Dane C. Ortlund, *Edwards on the Christian Life: Alive to the Beauty of God,* Theologians on the Christian Life (Wheaton, IL: Crossway, 2014); George M. Marsden, *An Infinite Fountain of Light: Jonathan Edwards for the Twenty-First Century* (Downers Grove, IL: IVP Academic, 2023).

20   James M. Garretson, ed., *Princeton and the Work of the Christian Ministry* (Edinburgh: Banner of Truth, 2012), 1:xix; see W. Andrew Hoffecker, *Piety and the Princeton Theologians: Archibald Alexander, Charles Hodge, and Benjamin Warfield* (Phillipsburg, NJ: Presbyterian and Reformed,

pools of Reformed thought from which we draw in the pages that follow, perhaps no single source is as significant as that of the English Puritans.

Defining just what exactly constituted "Puritanism" has been a long-standing source of historical controversy and debate.[21] For our purposes here, we can happily understand the English Puritans as a group of sixteenth- and seventeenth-century English Protestants who wanted to bring the Church of England into closer alignment with the Reformed tradition that we've just been describing.[22] Beginning under the reign of Queen Elizabeth I (r. 1558–1603) and continuing into the second half of the seventeenth century, these men and women wanted to "purify" the English national church of any remaining inappropriate attachments to Roman Catholicism and thus to reform it "according to the word of God, and the example of the best reformed Churches."[23] In so doing, they developed a religious culture that thrived across English, Scottish, Irish, and North American contexts, producing some of the finest pastor-theologians that the church has yet seen.[24] Names

---

1981); Mark A. Noll, "Charles Hodge as an Expositor of the Spiritual Life," in *Charles Hodge Revisited: A Critical Appraisal of His Life and Work*, ed. John W. Stewart and James H. Moorhead (Grand Rapids, MI: Eerdmans, 2002), 181–216; Fred G. Zaspel, *Warfield on the Christian Life: Living in Light of the Gospel* (Wheaton, IL: Crossway, 2014).

21 Patrick Collinson, "A Comment: Concerning the Name Puritan," *Journal of Ecclesiastical History* 31, no. 4 (1980): 483–88, https://doi.org/10.1017/S0022046900044791; John Coffey, "The Problem of 'Scottish Puritanism,' 1590–1638," in *Enforcing Reformation in Ireland and Scotland, 1550–1700*, ed. Elizabethanne Boran and Crawford Gribben (Aldershot: Ashgate, 2006); Ian Hugh Clary, "Hot Protestants: A Taxonomy of English Puritanism," *Puritan Reformed Journal* 2, no. 1 (2010): 41–66.

22 For a relatively brief and accessible historical introduction to Puritanism, see Francis J. Bremer, *Puritanism: A Very Short Introduction*, Very Short Introductions 212 (New York: Oxford University Press, 2009). For a wonderful treatment of Puritanism's rich spirituality and theology, it is still hard to top J. I. Packer, *A Quest for Godliness: The Puritan Vision of the Christian Life* (Wheaton, IL: Crossway, 1990). For those looking for something more substantial, the best scholarly survey of Puritanism is David D. Hall, *The Puritans: A Transatlantic History* (Princeton, NJ: Princeton University Press, 2019).

23 This phrase comes from the 1643 Solemn League and Covenant, a document through which Scottish and English leaders expressed their shared vision for church reform across the three kingdoms of England, Scotland, and Ireland. Reformed Presbyterian Church of Scotland, "The Solemn League and Covenant (1643)," accessed May 15, 2024, https://www.rpcscotland.org/.

24 Although this book focuses primarily on Puritanism as it developed in England and North America, for Puritanism within Scottish, Welsh, and Irish contexts, see Margo Todd, *The Culture*

like Richard Sibbes (1577–1635), John Owen (1616–1683), Thomas Watson (1620–1686), and John Flavel (ca. 1627–1691) were steady-selling authors in their day and continue to draw appreciative readers in our own.

There are at least four good reasons to give the Puritans the sustained attention they receive in this book. First, for English-speaking Christians looking to retrieve a Reformed Protestant heritage, the Puritans are a logical center point for the simple reason that they were early modern Reformed Christians who spoke and wrote primarily in English, making their enormous body of theological and pastoral writings much more accessible to English speakers today. If one wants to discover what early modern Reformed Christianity looked like in an English-speaking context, then one is necessarily looking to Puritan authors to do so. Indeed, when historian David Hall is asked the question "What was Puritanism?" his answer is "to emphasize everything the movement inherited from the Reformed and how this inheritance was reshaped in Britain and again in early New England—as it were, the Reformed tradition with a Scottish, English, or colonial accent."[25] This linguistic proximity to us means that English-speaking Christians today can enjoy reading Puritan authors in their own words and without the need for translation.

Second, moving beyond this linguistic continuity, a deeper and more substantive thread connects early modern Protestants with contemporary evangelicals. The eighteenth-century Great Awakening that birthed the evangelical movement can be credibly interpreted as taking up the theological and spiritual mantle of the Puritan movement that preceded it. While evangelicalism was shaped by several key streams, none were as singularly significant as Puritanism for influencing its priorities, theo-

---

of Protestantism in Early Modern Scotland (New Haven, CT: Yale University Press, 2002); Crawford Gribben, "Puritanism in Ireland and Wales," in *The Cambridge Companion to Puritanism*, ed. John Coffey and Paul C. H. Lim (Cambridge: Cambridge University Press, 2008), 159–73.

25 Hall, *Puritans*, 1–2.

logical emphases, and inner logic.[26] Key figures like Jonathan Edwards, George Whitefield, and Gilbert Tennent (1703–1764) embodied and advanced the warm Calvinist piety that characterized the Puritans before them. Even John Wesley (1703–1791), whose Arminian theology put him out of step with the aforementioned evangelical leaders, had great admiration for Puritan devotional writing, including many Puritan extracts in his fifty-volume *Christian Library*, a collection of abridged devotional works intended to help itinerant Methodist ministers.[27] Such observations lend force to the conclusions of historian John Coffey:

> The terms "Puritanism" and "evangelicalism" force us to chop the history of the tradition into separate slices, breaking up the flow of the story. But again and again, one finds that it is simply impossible to account for key features of modern evangelicalism without reference to their roots in the sixteenth and seventeenth centuries.[28]

For contemporary evangelicals, then, if we want to better understand how our theological forebears understood spiritual formation, we cannot ignore our Puritan inheritance.

Third, the Puritans devoted an incredible amount of time and attention to the subject of spiritual formation. "At its heart," writes historian

---

26 Some historians have emphasized the discontinuity between Puritanism and evangelicalism, often stressing the theopolitical nature of Puritanism, pointing out that the Puritan dream was to reform the national church, something that was never on the Great Awakening's agenda. This is, of course, correct as far as it goes. But when one views Puritanism from the perspective of the broader religious culture it fostered, its continuities with the subsequent evangelical movement become more obvious and compelling. On the case for continuity, see John Coffey, "Puritanism, Evangelicalism, and the Evangelical Protestant Tradition," in *The Emergence of Evangelicalism: Exploring Historical Continuities*, ed. Michael A. G. Haykin and Kenneth J. Stewart (Nottingham, UK: Apollos, 2008), 252–77. On the case for discontinuity between Puritanism and evangelicalism, see Mark A. Noll, *The Rise of Evangelicalism: The Age of Edwards, Whitefield and the Wesleys*, vol. 1 in *A History of Evangelicalism: People, Movements and Ideas in the English-Speaking World* (Downers Grove, IL: IVP Academic, 2003), 49.

27 It should be noted, though, that Wesley often edited Reformed authors, "chopping out the Calvinist bits." Hall, *Puritans*, 347.

28 Coffey, "Evangelical Protestant Tradition," 273.

Charles Hambrick-Stowe, "Puritanism was a devotional movement, rooted in religious experience."[29] Whether using the language of "keeping the heart" or "practicing piety," Puritan authors wrote at length on what it means to live and grow as a Christian. "Insofar as Protestantism experienced an era of consolidation in the late sixteenth and seventeenth centuries," writes historian Dewey Wallace, "Puritanism can be seen as an important (perhaps the most important) phase in the development of a distinctly Reformed piety and spirituality."[30] In part, this prodigious output of devotional literature flowed from their reflexive understanding that Christian living and Christian theology were mutually reinforcing and in no way at odds with one another. When the Puritan theologian William Ames (1576–1633) sought to define theology, he drew on precisely this connection, writing that "theology is the doctrine or teaching of living to God."[31] Among other verses quoted in support of this definition, Ames drew his readers' attention to Acts 5:20, where the angel, after freeing the apostles from prison, instructs them, "Go and stand in the temple and speak to the people all the words of this Life." The apostolic preaching and teaching about God and Christ and the Holy Spirit was not mere information transfer but was instead the God-appointed means through which real spiritual life is conveyed. The Puritans were deeply impressed by this reality, and it led them to produce an enormous body of devotional literature still unrivaled in its quality and fidelity to Scripture.

Finally, the fourth reason for this book to give a disproportionate share of its attention to the Puritans is that Puritan authors wrote with a biblically grounded spiritual intensity that twenty-first-century evangelicals sorely need. Sinclair Ferguson has observed that "for those

29 Charles E. Hambrick-Stowe, *The Practice of Piety: Puritan Devotional Disciplines in Seventeenth-Century New England* (Chapel Hill: University of North Carolina Press, 1982), vii.

30 Dewey D. Wallace Jr., "Introduction," in *The Spirituality of the Later English Puritans: An Anthology*, ed. Dewey D. Wallace Jr. (Macon, GA: Mercer University Press, 1987), xii.

31 William Ames, *The Marrow of Theology*, ed. John Dykstra Eusden (Grand Rapids, MI: Baker, 1997), 77.

unacquainted with their writings, a first encounter with Puritan literature can be like entering a world where people seem bigger, wiser, and years older."[32] Similarly, J. I. Packer (1926–2020) has argued that when we measure modern evangelicals against the Puritans, we discover, to our shame, that "the Puritans, by contrast, as a body were giants. They were great souls serving a great God."[33] Others have made similar observations, noting a sense of contrast between the depth and power of the Puritan vision and the relative shallowness and weakness of our own. Whatever reasons we might posit for this contrast, it seems that what the Puritans had is what we now desperately require.[34]

As taste-making voices in pop culture, academia, and the corporate world conspire to make the thought world of Scripture seem ever more implausible, remote, and offensive to contemporary, post-Christian sensibilities, the temptation for evangelical Christians will always be toward a sort of reverse discipleship in which the claims of Christ are accommodated ever more to the claims of culture and in which believers become conformed to this world rather than being "transformed by the renewal of [their] mind" (Rom. 12:2). This is, of course, a perennial temptation in every age, but given that we in the West are now witnessing the collapse of many heretofore foundational societal assumptions about morality, sexuality, and what constitutes real human flourishing, the urgency of our need for countercultural biblical formation feels especially pressing.[35]

Under such conditions, the Puritans offer real help. Where we doubt and lack confidence in the authority and relevance of Scripture across

---

32 Sinclair B. Ferguson, *Some Pastors and Teachers: Reflecting a Biblical Vision of What Every Minister Is Called to Be* (Edinburgh: Banner of Truth, 2017), 167.

33 Packer, *Quest for Godliness*, 22.

34 Insightful recent attempts to explain the shallowness of modern evangelicalism include Michael Horton, *Christless Christianity: The Alternative Gospel of the American Church* (Grand Rapids, MI: Baker, 2008); David F. Wells, *The Courage to Be Protestant: Truth-Lovers, Marketers, and Emergents in the Postmodern World* (Grand Rapids, MI: Eerdmans, 2008).

35 For a powerful analysis of our current cultural moment and how we got here, see Carl R. Trueman, *The Rise and Triumph of the Modern Self: Cultural Amnesia, Expressive Individualism, and the Road to Sexual Revolution* (Wheaton, IL: Crossway, 2020).

all areas of life, they speak with vigor and conviction. Where we feel tempted to water down the biblical worldview to bring it more in step with the spirit of the age, they double down. Where we seek refuge in a therapeutic Christianity that appeals to our wounded pride but is ultimately foreign to a scriptural worldview, the Puritans remind us afresh that sin before a holy God is our most serious problem and that Christ and his gospel are our only solution. In a word, the Puritans speak with a freshness and fire that can correct some of the characteristic weaknesses of our present cultural moment, and this makes them most excellent conversation partners as we look to retrieve a Reformed approach to spiritual formation.

The Shape of What Is to Come

Before we go any further, three caveats should be made to set expectations for what this book is and is not. First, in presenting a "Reformed approach" to spiritual formation, this book is not trying to suggest that everything that follows belongs exclusively to the Reformed tradition. Certain ideas, of course, are genuinely definitional for Reformation Christianity and are not easily found elsewhere. And yet all three historic branches of Christianity—Protestantism, Roman Catholicism, and Eastern Orthodoxy—are indeed branches from a common trunk, sharing core concepts, convictions, and sensibilities. At many points throughout this book, then, you will find ideas, practices, and attitudes ascribed to the Reformed tradition that surely admit numerous parallels and continuities with other Christian traditions. The point is not to argue that Reformed spirituality represents a hermetically sealed capsule unto itself but rather to recognize both that there is a characteristic shape to how Reformed Christians have pursued spiritual formation and that its distinctive contours are well worth our patient attention.

Second, the reason this book pays so much attention to Reformed spirituality is because I am persuaded that a Reformed approach to spiritual formation is consistent with what the Bible itself teaches. In focusing on a particular Christian tradition, then, we are not attempting to recommend tradition for tradition's sake. Reformation-minded Christians want to pursue a faith that takes the Bible alone as the ultimate authority for life and doctrine and do not wish to accept an idea simply because that is what has been taught before. We want to listen to and learn from those who went before us, and we should think long and hard before dismissing theological insights that have nurtured the faith of many, but ultimately, our doctrine must derive from Scripture.

Third, scanning the table of contents, readers might note what could appear to be a glaring omission: there is no chapter on the church. Though I talk about Christian relationships in chapter 8, this is not equivalent to a proper treatment of the local church's role in our spiritual formation. Note that this omission is intentional and should not be taken to imply that the church is unimportant. In fact, the reality is precisely the opposite: the role of the church and the questions it raises in terms of polity, the sacraments, church discipline, the Lord's Day, and the role of ordained ministers are, collectively, too deep and too wide for the current volume. Our focus here is on the individual Christian and how he or she ought to think about spiritual formation in light of the wisdom offered by our Reformation forebears. That should in no way diminish the significance of the local church, but it is to signal at the outset that this is not our purpose here. For a bit more on this topic, please see the appendix, "A Brief Note on Spiritual Formation, Individualism, and the Church."

With those caveats out of the way, let's briefly preview what's to come and how it fits together. This book is divided into four main parts. In part 1, "Foundations," we lay the groundwork for all that follows. If our overarching purpose is to set forth a "Reformed approach" to "spiritual formation," consider the two chapters of part 1 as an attempt to unpack both of those key terms—chapter 1 considering what we mean by spiritual formation and then chapter 2 looking more specifically at how that concept fits with a commitment to Reformed theology.

Part 2 presents what I am calling the "Reformation triangle," a nexus of Scripture intake, meditation, and prayer that represents the heart of both Reformed piety and this book. In part 3, "Widening Our Scope," we take the three Reformation triangle disciplines and apply them more broadly to three additional means of grace: self-examination, an appreciation of the natural world, and Christian relationships. Finally, part 4 addresses two challenging topics: the role of the body in spiritual formation and what to do when our pursuit of spiritual formation doesn't proceed according to plan.

PART 1

———————

FOUNDATIONS

1

Spiritual Formation

A Simple Concept with a Complicated History

THIS BOOK IS ABOUT living the Christian life. And a basic biblical assumption about the Christian life is that it ought to be a growing life. When the Bible describes walking with God, the expectation is that it will never be a static, settled affair but rather a journey characterized by continual development, increase, and forward movement. The Christian "press[es] on toward the goal for the prize of the upward call of God in Christ Jesus" (Phil. 3:14). Indeed, an expectation of growth is built into the very idea of being "born again" (John 3:3). Birth marks the beginning of new life, which will be characterized by subsequent maturation and growth. Thus we read that having been "born again to a living hope through the resurrection of Jesus Christ from the dead," Christians are like "newborn infants" who "long for the pure spiritual milk" of God's word "that by it [they] may *grow up* into salvation" (1 Pet. 1:3; 2:2).

Such growth in Christ is, first and foremost, the work of the Holy Spirit in the lives of believers. When the apostle Paul writes that Christians are "being transformed . . . from one degree of glory to another," he describes the transformation in passive terms, as something that is happening *to* the people of God as the gracious result of the Spirit's work in their lives: "For this comes from the Lord who is the Spirit" (2 Cor. 3:18). And yet while the overarching transformation is God's work in us and not ultimately our work in ourselves, the Bible also makes clear that growth in the Christian life involves our active, intentional effort and energy. Shortly after Paul attributes our spiritual growth to the Spirit's work in us, he urges believers, without any embarrassment or sense of tension, to work for spiritual growth themselves: "Since we have these promises, beloved, let us cleanse ourselves from every defilement of body and spirit, bringing holiness to completion in the fear of God" (2 Cor. 7:1).

Clearly, then, the Bible portrays Christian growth as both God's work and, in some lesser but no less real sense, our work. The question of how these two ideas relate to each other in harmony rather than contradiction has been the subject of much controversy throughout the history of the church, and in chapter 2, we examine more closely how Reformation-minded Protestants have understood that relationship. But for now, let's simply note that the Bible puts both ideas forward and that in this book we are primarily concerned with the second idea, that believers must be actively involved in Spirit-wrought Christian growth.

In recent decades, the term *spiritual formation* has been adopted by many as a helpful way of referring to the active role we take in pursuing godliness. As we see in this chapter, the term has a somewhat complicated history and is not without its critics. Yet when properly contextualized, it's a term that can still helpfully communicate what we are interested in here. What distinguishes our interest in spiritual formation from other books discussing the same is that here we are working to understand what spiritual formation sounds like when set in a distinctly Reformed-evangelical key.[1] To do that, as mentioned in the introduction, we are drawing on the work of early modern

---

1 We will say more about this Reformed-evangelical tradition in chap. 2.

(ca. 1500–1800) Protestant theologians, pastors, and devotional writers, looking to understand how they brought "holiness to completion in the fear of God" (2 Cor. 7:1) so that we might better do the same today.

What Is *Keeping the Heart*?

When we think specifically of the active role that believers are called to play in their own spiritual growth, one of the Bible's loveliest exhortations comes from Proverbs 4:23:

> Keep your heart with all vigilance,
>   for from it flow the springs of life.

This verse was a favorite of the English Puritans, who used it during the sixteenth and seventeenth centuries to capture and communicate a sense of the Christian's overarching spiritual task. If you are a Christian, your main business before God and other people is to "keep your heart" in and through all life's varying circumstances. The Puritan pastor John Flavel expounded this verse at some length in his work *A Saint Indeed: or, The Great Work of a Christian, Opened and Pressed* (1668). "The greatest difficulty in conversion," wrote Flavel, "is to win the heart to God; and the greatest difficulty after conversion is to keep the heart with God." He described keeping the heart as "the very pinch and stress of religion" and "the great business of a Christian's life."[2] Flavel's writing on this theme is perhaps the best known, but other Puritan authors such as Stephen Marshall (ca. 1594–1655) and Richard Alleine (1610–1681) appealed to the verse as well, finding in it a pleasing distillation of the Bible's approach to godliness and growth.[3] Marshall, for example, suggested that "there is not one Pearl of greater price, one sentence of more divine use than" Proverbs 4:23.[4] The English Puritan theologian John Owen

---

2   John Flavel, *The Works of John Flavel* (London: Banner of Truth, 1968), 5:423, 425.

3   Richard Alleine, *Instructions about Heart-Work* (London, 1681).

4   Stephen Marshall, *The Works of Mr. Stephen Marshall* (London, 1661), 128.

insisted that "watching or keeping of the heart" is that "which above all keepings we are obliged unto." Elsewhere, appealing directly to Proverbs 4:23, Owen stressed that among a person's various "keepings" or concerns—for family, for possessions, for reputation—one must "attend to that of the heart" above all else. "There is no safety without it," wrote Owen, for if you "save all other things and lose the heart, . . . all is lost."[5]

But what exactly does it mean to keep the heart, and why did these early modern pastors find it such a helpful concept? Flavel explained it like this:

> To keep the heart . . . is nothing else but this constant care and diligence of such a renewed man, to preserve his soul in that holy frame to which grace hath reduced it [i.e., led it back to], and daily strives to hold it. . . . [T]o keep the heart is carefully to preserve it from sin, which disorders it; and maintain that spiritual and gracious frame, which fits it for a life of communion with God.[6]

The idea here is that the "renewed man" (i.e., the regenerate or born-again believer) has been powerfully changed by the Holy Spirit in a basic, fundamental way—"If anyone is in Christ, he is a new creation" (2 Cor. 5:17)—and yet he must now, with God's help, actively press after a greater, more thorough realization of that new life that is already his—"Walk in a manner worthy of the calling to which you have been called" (Eph. 4:1).

This involves battling sin, of course, but beyond that, the idea of *keeping the heart* also suggests a positive cultivation, an active maintenance, and a daily "fight for joy."[7] To keep the heart is not just saying

---

5 John Owen, *Overcoming Sin and Temptation*, ed. Kelly M. Kapic and Justin Taylor (Wheaton, IL: Crossway, 2006), 201, 331.

6 Flavel, *Works*, 5:426.

7 This last phrase is a favorite of John Piper, who, in *When I Don't Desire God* and throughout his works, well articulates this important Puritan and biblical theme. See John Piper, *When I Don't Desire God: How to Fight for Joy*, 10th anniversary ed. (Wheaton, IL: Crossway, 2013).

no to sin but actively saying yes to God and the things of God. As a Christian strives to keep her heart "with all vigilance," she will be aware of a nagging tendency for her heart to drift toward false gods of every description, and her active attention will return again and again to how she might untangle herself from idols and instead, as Flavel put it, "maintain that spiritual and gracious frame, which fits it for a life of communion with God."[8] Thankfully, God gives us means or tools to use in this struggle, and the burden of this book's later chapters is to examine those as they were taken up by our Reformation-minded fathers and mothers in the faith.

One chief attraction of the phrase *keeping the heart* is the way it nicely captures the biblical sense that our Christian walk is holistic, encompassing all that we are and all that we do. This is primarily because in the conceptual world of the Bible, "the heart" is an all-encompassing term, and thus to "keep it" implies an all-around self-watch. When David says, "My heart is glad, and my whole being rejoices," the parallelism of the psalm suggests an equivalence between his "heart" and his "whole being" (Ps. 16:9)—as David's "heart" goes, so goes David. Likewise, when he laments, "My heart is in anguish within me" (Ps. 55:4), this clearly means that David himself is in anguish. Elsewhere, David's request to God "Unite my heart to fear your name" (Ps. 86:11–12) suggests a desire to see a comprehensive reordering of his entire person, an integration in which "the lines meet at a point beyond himself, the fear of the Lord."[9] When the Old Testament prophets celebrated the wholesale renewal of the human person that would accompany God's new covenant, they employed this same heart language, with God promising, "I will remove the heart of stone from your flesh and give you a heart of flesh" (Ezek. 36:26; cf. Jer. 31:33). Here these two hearts, one of stone and the other of flesh, suggest two completely different orientations toward life and

---

8 Flavel, *Works*, 5:426.
9 Derek Kidner, *Psalms 73–150*, Tyndale Old Testament Commentaries (Downers Grove, IL: Inter-Varsity Press, 2008), 344.

love and godliness. Later, Jesus drew on such Old Testament heart imagery when he wished to contrast superficial, external rule keeping with a deep and abiding commitment to God and the things of God. Quoting Isaiah's warning against a people who "honors me with their lips, / but their heart is far from me" (Matt. 15:8; cf. Isa. 29:13), Jesus went on to describe a wrongly oriented heart as the real source of a person's subsequent sinful thoughts and actions (Matt. 15:19).

Across Scripture, then, the heart is depicted as the vital center of a person's consciousness, feeling, and will, and thus the state of one's heart will dictate how one thinks, speaks, and acts. The heart, wrote Flavel, "is the source and fountain of all vital actions and operations."[10] Contemporary biblical scholars and theologians describe the Bible's use of "heart" in similar terms:

> The heart in Hebrew thought is not significant primarily for its role in organic existence, but as the hidden control-center of the whole human being. The entire range of conscious and perhaps even unconscious activities of the person is located in and emanates from the heart. It experiences emotions and moods, it has personality and character traits, it is the locus of thought and deliberation, choice and action, and it is above all the source of love or hate of God and neighbor. It may be hidden from other people and perhaps even from oneself. But God searches its depths and knows it altogether.[11]

Thus, across all life's varied circumstances, my sense of myself as an individual agent with emotions, ideas, desires, loves, and hatreds is captured with reference to the inner motions of my heart. And thus to keep my heart will involve all of me.

---

10 Flavel, *Works*, 5:424.

11 John W. Cooper, *Body, Soul, and Life Everlasting: Biblical Anthropology and the Monism-Dualism Debate* (Grand Rapids, MI: Eerdmans, 2000), 42; see also Anthony A. Hoekema, *Created in God's Image* (Grand Rapids, MI: Eerdmans, 1986), 171–72.

Moreover, this sense that heart keeping involves all of me is both comprehensive and intensive. It is *comprehensive* in the sense that all my activities, relationships, and roles are affected by it. Whether I am worshiping on Sunday morning at church, entering data into a spreadsheet at work, or sharing a meal with friends, I am obligated across various contexts to "keep my heart with all vigilance" (cf. Prov. 4:23). The actual work of heart keeping and the means employed to do it might differ across those varied contexts, but the concern for it never disappears.

But heart keeping is also *intensive* in the sense that the task touches on the deepest realities of the inner person, depths that are often invisible to others and sometimes invisible even to ourselves (e.g., Ps. 19:12). For this reason, Flavel insisted that "without this" genuine heart keeping, "we are but formalists in religion."[12] A person can externally participate in religious activity without any corresponding inner spiritual life, and thus the Christian life cannot be reduced to propositions learned or actions performed (though it certainly entails both). Rather, our spiritual walk is bound up ever and always with the inner motions of the heart—with desire, affection, and love. And for this reason, "keeping the heart" is "the most important business of a Christian's life."[13] The question of *how* we keep it is the subject of this book.

In this chapter, our goal will be first to trace some of the recent history of evangelical engagement with the concept of *spiritual formation*, then to advance a working definition of the term, and finally to disentangle the concept of *spiritual formation* from three related words that don't capture quite the same idea.

What Is *Spiritual Formation*?

We will return to the phrase *keeping the heart* in a moment, but first we need to think about another similar phrase that is far more frequently

---

12 Flavel, *Works*, 5:424.
13 Flavel, *Works*, 5:429.

heard in our day: *spiritual formation*. Popularized among evangelicals during the second half of the twentieth century by writers such as James Houston, Richard Foster, Dallas Willard (1935–2013), and Eugene Peterson (1932–2018), the term *spiritual formation* can now be found attached to a range of ministries, books, retreat centers, and theological degree programs. Indeed, in 2008 the Talbot School of Theology's Institute for Spiritual Formation launched the *Journal of Spiritual Formation and Soul Care*, a peer-reviewed academic journal dedicated exclusively to the subject.[14] Another telling measure of the degree to which spiritual formation looms large within contemporary American Protestantism is the fact that it must now be included within a master of divinity degree program in order for said program to be accredited by the Association of Theological Schools.[15] As Kirsten Birkett observes, " 'Spiritual formation' has come to be seen as the dominant mode of understanding Christian life."[16]

Clearly, spiritual formation is of great and growing interest, and it is equally clear that this interest has, at least among evangelicals, been largely directed toward remedying perceived weaknesses within the evangelical religious subculture. As referenced in the introduction to this book, Richard Lovelace helpfully identified a "sanctification gap" among evangelical Christians—that is, a blank space in our preaching and teaching where the rich "Protestant tradition of spiritual growth"

---

14 On the history and development of the spiritual formation movement, see Chris Armstrong, "The Rise, Frustration, and Revival of Evangelical Spiritual Ressourcement," *Journal of Spiritual Formation and Soul Care* 2, no. 1 (2009): 113–21; Evan B. Howard, *A Guide to Christian Spiritual Formation: How Scripture, Spirit, Community, and Mission Shape Our Souls* (Grand Rapids, MI: Baker Academic, 2018), 3–10; Nathan A. Finn, "Spiritualities in the Christian Tradition," in *Biblical Spirituality*, ed. Christopher W. Morgan, Theology in Community (Wheaton, IL: Crossway, 2019), 230–34.

15 An accredited program's "articulated learning outcomes" must address "personal and spiritual formation, including development in personal faith, professional ethics, emotional maturity, moral integrity, and spirituality." Commission on Accrediting of the Association of Theological Schools, "2020 Standards of Accreditation" (2020), 5, https://www.ats.edu/.

16 Kirsten Birkett, "Spiritual Formation: The Rise of a Tradition," *Churchman* 4, no. 133 (2019): 346.

ought to reside.[17] Those who have popularized the spiritual formation movement in evangelical circles have been motivated by this same problem and a desire to see it solved. In this vein, Chris Armstrong argues that the spiritual formation movement "was one of reaction" against some of the excesses and deficiencies of mid-twentieth-century Protestant fundamentalism. Such problematic aspects of conservative Protestantism, on Armstrong's reading, included a tendency to "identify the Christian life with cognitive belief" such that "discipleship, or growth in spiritual things, took a back seat," and an "unreflective pragmatism" focused on evangelism to the detriment of discipleship.[18] To the extent that twentieth-century evangelicals have neglected discipleship and formation—and it seems irrefutable that a great deal of neglect has occurred—then we are right to seek a better way.

And yet while few would take serious issue with this diagnosis, some evangelicals have nonetheless expressed concern that the remedies proposed by advocates of spiritual formation come with serious side effects that we neglect at our peril. As many have correctly observed, as a matter of historical development, the term *spiritual formation* seems to have originated from mid-twentieth-century Roman Catholic theological education, a potentially inconvenient fact that has prompted some to wonder, not unreasonably, whether *spiritual formation* is an appropriate term to use in Reformed-evangelical circles.[19]

Moreover, during the latter half of the twentieth century, as the so-called spiritual formation movement spread outside Catholic seminaries and began to gain momentum among Protestant evangelicals, its chief proponents demonstrated a willingness to cast their theological nets well beyond the usually consulted, Reformation-minded

---

17 Richard F. Lovelace, *Dynamics of Spiritual Life: An Evangelical Theology of Renewal*, expanded ed. (1979; repr., Downers Grove, IL: IVP Academic, 2020), 232.

18 Armstrong, "Rise, Frustration, and Revival," 114.

19 Birkett, "Spiritual Formation," 348–51.

evangelical sources. For example, in his bestselling *Celebration of Discipline* (1978)—a book that one historian describes as "the symbolic beginning of the spiritual formation movement among evangelicals"[20]—Richard Foster draws variously from Protestant authors such as Martin Luther (1483–1546) and John Calvin, Roman Catholic authors such as Ignatius of Loyola (1491–1556) and Thomas Merton (1915–1968), and various others such as the pre-Reformation mystic Meister Eckhart (ca. 1260–ca. 1328) and the twentieth-century Anglo-Catholic Evelyn Underhill (1875–1941). Throughout his book, Foster intermingles citations and recommendations of these and many other authors without caveat or explanation.[21]

In this aspect, *Celebration of Discipline* is characteristic of much that appears under the heading *spiritual formation*. The problem with this ecumenical sampling is that it seems to imply a far greater degree of coherence and overlap between the authors cited than is actually warranted by a careful study of their works. Even if we momentarily set to one side the not insignificant question whether John Calvin or Ignatius of Loyola represents a more sound and biblical guide to gospel growth, it would be very difficult to argue that they are consistently pointing readers in the same basic direction. Moreover, even if we grant that a person committed to the tradition of either Calvin or Ignatius could still profitably learn from aspects of the other's work without compromising his or her own overall position, far too much of the literature within the spiritual formation movement fails to acknowledge the deep theological differences between the spirituality of a Calvin and that of an Ignatius. According to historian Carlos Eire, Ignatius's most famous guide to the spiritual life, his *Spiritual Exercises* (1548), represents "a thorough repudiation of Protestant theology and a practical application of Catholic principles dismissed

---

20 Finn, "Spiritualities in the Christian Tradition," 231.

21 Richard J. Foster, *Celebration of Discipline: The Path to Spiritual Growth*, study guide ed. (London: Hodder, 2008).

by Protestants."[22] Yet one would never gain any inkling of this through an encounter with much of the spiritual formation literature marketed toward evangelical Protestants. Instead, authors with very different theological and biblical outlooks are presented on a more-or-less even footing as helpful guides to the Christian life for which all believers should give hearty thanks. Such an eclectic approach to identifying spiritual mentors, an approach that could be described as either generous and charitable or naive and dangerous depending on your perspective, has led many thoughtful evangelicals to shy away from anything bearing the *spiritual formation* label.

As I hope is clear, I would share many of these concerns, and yet I have used the term *spiritual formation* to describe what this book is all about. Why? Let me offer three reasons. First, some—though certainly not all—of the concern about spiritual formation inevitably leading Protestants astray seems overheated. As Tom Schwanda has argued, much of the loudest evangelical reaction against the idea of spiritual formation demonstrates "a general disdain for anything even remotely comparable to Roman Catholic spiritual practices" that lacks "any awareness of how Protestants from the sixteenth century onward adapted Roman Catholic practices that they inherited according to their own emerging Protestant sensibilities and theology."[23] I would be the first to object to the sort of naive ecumenical pastiche that sees no difficulty in uncritically mingling medieval mystics with Reformation stalwarts as though each represented an equally faithful guide to walking with God according to the Scriptures. And yet it is far too easy for a right reaction against something unhelpful to morph into an unmeasured overreaction that is almost as unhelpful as what it sought to repudiate.

22 Carlos M. N. Eire, *Reformations: The Early Modern World, 1450–1650* (New Haven, CT: Yale University Press, 2016), 445.

23 Tom Schwanda, " 'To Gaze on the Beauty of the Lord': The Evangelical Resistance and Retrieval of Contemplation," in *Embracing Contemplation: Reclaiming a Christian Spiritual Practice*, ed. John H. Coe and Kyle C. Strobel (Downers Grove, IL: IVP Academic, 2019), 98–99.

Second, as a way of concisely expressing a clear biblical reality, the term *spiritual formation* is undeniably attractive.[24] In the first place, it highlights that our deepest need is not physical, intellectual, or, strictly speaking, emotional, but spiritual. When Jesus asks, "What will it profit a man if he gains the whole world and forfeits his soul?" (Matt. 16:26), the implied answer is that it will not ultimately yield him anything at all. Scripture consistently portrays deep and lasting satisfaction and fullness as that which flows from spiritual rather than material flourishing. "You have put more joy in my heart," declares the psalmist, "than they have when their grain and wine abound" (Ps. 4:7). It's not that a biblical worldview forbids enjoying nonspiritual blessings; rather, in biblical perspective, the only reliable route to actually enjoying the real but relatively lesser joys of "grain and wine" is to prioritize spiritual realities, "seek[ing] first the kingdom of God," knowing that only then will "all these [other] things . . . be added to you" (Matt. 6:33). As God's image bearers, our longing for spiritual restoration and satisfaction thus both unites and transcends the host of other (lesser) longings we experience, and the term *spiritual formation* nicely underscores this point.

Furthermore, the term *spiritual formation* draws attention to the way our spiritual needs are most often to be met: slowly. The word *formation* does not call to mind an instantaneous, rapid, overnight sort of thing. Rather, to describe something as being *formed* naturally suggests something in process, something taking shape slowly over time. It invokes both organic images of flowers emerging from buds and babies strengthening their limbs to stand and walk, and also artisanal images of pots gradually taking shape with each spin of the wheel and finely rendered landscapes emerging more beautifully with each new application of paint. One can argue that the felicity of the phrase and its obvious biblical touchpoints—think of Paul's expression of the

---

24 For a fuller sense of how the term and its related linguistic permutations intersect with biblical realities and language, see Morgan, *Biblical Spirituality*.

Christian need to "set the mind on the Spirit" (Rom. 8:6) and his hope that "Christ is formed in you" (Gal. 4:19)—can be paired with its widespread usage within evangelical discourse as a way of capturing a biblical truth in short compass. And if so, it would be a shame to abandon this particular form of words simply because some have used it in a manner less helpful than we might have wished. Rather, my hope would be that we might reclaim and represent the phrase in a manner consistent with our Reformation heritage.

Third, the basic form of the project proposed by advocates of the spiritual formation movement is a timely and helpful one, even if people like myself would like to see the substance of said project more tightly tethered to our Reformation heritage. Describing that basic form, Armstrong notes that early leaders of the spiritual formation movement like Foster and Willard were dissatisfied with the same "sanctification gap" that bothered Lovelace, and in response, they "discovered what they were looking for in the historical spiritual traditions of the Christian faith." In so doing, they "began to teach that the spiritual resources of the past are a much-needed medicine, potent to heal us from a serious disease."[25] The instinct to seek wisdom from those who have gone before is a good one, but the past offers a multitude of counselors, and agreement on the need to look backward doesn't necessarily imply agreement on precisely where to look. Too often the old paths proposed by some spiritual formation advocates have led away from rather than back toward the Reformation heritage that has long nourished evangelical Protestantism. Armstrong describes a "new openness" toward "barrier-crossing within evangelicalism," in which advocates of spiritual formation began "using contemplative prayer techniques, attending retreats, sitting under spiritual directors, and reading Catholic and Orthodox books."[26] To my mind, such "openness" is unhelpful because it fails to appreciate the good theological reasons

25 Armstrong, "Rise, Frustration, and Revival," 114.
26 Armstrong, "Rise, Frustration, and Revival," 113.

that led the Reformers and their heirs to reject many of the things that the spiritual formation movement has rushed to embrace. This does not mean, however, that those early advocates for spiritual formation were wrong in either their diagnosis of evangelicalism's spiritual malaise or their basic desire to seek deeper and more satisfying remedies through an appeal to those who went before.

The burden of this book is to take up that same animating impulse that has propelled the broader spiritual formation movement but to argue that good, biblical solutions to evangelicalism's "sanctification gap" are readily found within the pages of historic Reformed authors. The Reformation heritage that gave birth to evangelicalism already has a rich and biblically faithful tradition of spiritual formation, such that we do not need to create a pastiche of spiritual practices drawn from medieval mystical, Roman Catholic, and Eastern Orthodox authors. If an evangelical thoughtfully concludes that those non-Reformed paths represent a more faithful way to walk with God, then he or she will not be the first to do so and is certainly free to make that choice. But what is unfortunate and frustrating is to see evangelical Christians depart from the Reformation's heritage of spiritual formation under the false assumption that no such thing actually exists. In other words, if you are going to reject your inheritance, you should first make sure you know what's in it. The hope is that this book will help readers make that (re)discovery and might persuade some along the way that the historic Reformed approach to spiritual formation is, in fact, the biblical one.

Spiritual Formation as Keeping the Heart

Throughout these pages I will use *spiritual formation* and *keeping the heart* more or less interchangeably as we explore the approach toward Christian growth that our Reformation-minded forebears exemplified and that we now may wish to emulate. *Keeping the heart* is an older form of words drawn directly from Scripture (Prov. 4:23), while *spiritual formation* is newer and attempts to pull some different biblical threads together. Both formulations capture and convey what we are trying to get at. But because these expressions are also open to misunderstanding, I will provide a definition before proceeding any further:

> **Spiritual formation** is the conscious process by which we seek to heighten and satisfy our Spirit-given thirst for God (Ps. 42:1–2) through divinely appointed means and with a view toward "work[ing] out [our] own salvation with fear and trembling" (Phil. 2:12) and becoming "mature in Christ" (Col. 1:28).

A Conscious Process

Several aspects of this definition are worth unpacking, beginning with the idea that spiritual formation as we are describing it is *a conscious process*. In other words, this isn't something that simply happens to us whether we are paying attention or not. Rather, it's something we actively pursue. The sort of heart keeping that this book has in view is not a mere background operation that every once in a while we pause to take note of. This is not to say that such background heart work isn't happening—of course it is, all the time! The Spirit of God is *always* working in and through *all* things—conscious, subconscious, planned, unplanned, noticed, unnoticed, and so on—to conform believers to the image of Christ (Rom. 8:28–29). This larger, all-encompassing process, however, is better termed *sanctification* and will be further distinguished below. When we talk about *spiritual formation* and *keeping the heart* in this volume, we are indicating that part of Christian growth in which we are active, aware, conscious participants working and striving toward growing in grace and in the knowledge of our Lord Jesus Christ (2 Pet. 3:18).

Concerned with Desire

Spiritual formation and keeping the heart are fundamentally concerned with our innermost desires and the orientation of our hearts. To say that we are concerned with inward realities like desire does not mean, of course, that we are not also interested in outward realities like concrete obedience to Christ's commandments and the pursuit of a holiness that is visible to our neighbors. Spiritually growing Christians will also be growing in their obedience to God's moral law. And yet a conceptual distinction can be drawn between our concern for external conformity to God's will (the kind of conformity that others might observe) and the internal, more difficult-to-track world of desire, motivation, and love—that is, the world of the heart.

The Bible teaches that these inner and outer realities can sometimes be at odds with one another—as they were in the case of the Pharisees and the wayward Israelites condemned by the prophets (Isa. 29:13; Matt. 15:7–9). But the wonder of regeneration and the Spirit's work in the hearts of believers is that said inner and outer realities can also be in sync, in harmony with one another, exhibiting a mutually reinforcing cycle in which growing desire *for* God leads to growing obedience *to* God. This is precisely the relationship between desire and obedience that Jesus says will characterize his followers: "If you love me, you will keep my commandments" (John 14:15). In that formulation, love *for* Jesus precedes and motivates obedience *to* Jesus. In this same way, our exploration of spiritual formation in this book takes as its starting point and primary locus of interest the ways Christians can kindle and stir up their desire for God and the things of God, with the expectation that such heart work will naturally lead to the fruit of greater conformity to God's revealed will. The pursuit of spiritual formation is a quest to lean into the psalmist's cry in Psalm 42:1–2:

> As a deer pants for flowing streams,
> so pants my soul for you, O God.

My soul thirsts for God,
    for the living God.
When shall I come and appear before God?

Keeping the heart means, as noted above, that "we seek to heighten and satisfy our Spirit-given thirst for God," both as an end in itself—indeed, "man's chief end"—and as the starting point for a Spirit-wrought overflow of obedience to God's law that is truly Christian in nature.[27]

Using Divinely Appointed Means

Another key component of our definition is the stipulation that biblical spiritual formation will employ "divinely appointed means"—that is, those means or methods that God plainly reveals to us in his word. God is the author of spiritual life, and in Scripture he has given clear and sufficient guidance for how we are to pursue it. To this end, the Bible repeatedly highlights some things rather than others as the tools that God has given his people for growing in their walk with him. Our job, then, is not to invent new "spiritual practices" that seem attractive or appealing to us but rather to take up with fresh vigor and appropriate creativity those practices already given.

This is important to underscore because one persistent feature within much of the literature on spiritual formation is the implicit (and sometimes explicit) suggestion that any imaginative practice we might come up with could properly be used to pursue communion with God. Sometimes these practices are obviously outside the scope of what the Bible commends to us—think of something like a prayer to Saint Joseph for protection.[28] But the drift away from a spirituality tied tightly to God's

---

27 The Westminster Shorter Catechism famously begins with the question "What is the chief end of man?" The answer: "Man's chief end is to glorify God, and to enjoy him forever." In *Creeds, Confessions, and Catechisms: A Reader's Edition*, ed. Chad Van Dixhoorn (Wheaton, IL: Crossway, 2022), 411 (q. 1).

28 One such prayer reads as follows: "Remember, O most chaste spouse of the Virgin Mary, that never has it been known that anyone who asked for your help and sought your intercession was

word can also be much more subtle. One book, for example, suggests "40 simple spiritual practices" that are meant to "help open the door to a deeper understanding of God and a more mindful way of faith." The practices described often seek to engage the senses and include things like deliberately enjoying "strongly scented flowers" or savoring a piece of chocolate while reflecting on the ingredients in the chocolate and "all of God's love that went into creating those ingredients."[29] There's nothing wrong, of course, with enjoying flowers or chocolate, and if these items prompt reflection on Christian truth, then so much the better. Indeed, in chapter 7, we investigate how the Reformed would regularly meditate on creation and the natural world. In their meditations, they would come very close to something like the aforementioned reflection on chocolate. So what's the problem?

The problem arises when such things become disconnected from the sort of word-based spirituality that the Bible constantly commends and are instead repackaged as stand-alone spiritual techniques and activities. In Psalm 104, after celebrating God's marvelous creativity and care as it is displayed in the natural world, the psalmist says,

> I will sing to the LORD as long as I live;
>> I will sing praise to my God while I have being. (Ps. 104:33)

If a person spends her morning meditating on the passion and logic of Psalm 104, then it seems good and right that her own enjoyment of God's creation later that afternoon—whether marveling at an oak tree or eating a piece of chocolate—would result in a spontaneous eruption of praise to the God who has made oak trees grand and chocolate deli-

---

left unaided. Full of confidence in your power, I hasten to you, and beg your protection. Listen, O foster-father of the Redeemer, to my humble prayer, and in your goodness hear and answer me. Amen." "The Memorare to St. Joseph," in Joseph Pronechen, "8 Powerful Prayers to St. Joseph You've Never Heard Of," National Catholic Register, May 1, 2021, https://www.ncregister.com/.

29 Sally Welch, *How to Be a Mindful Christian: 40 Simple Spiritual Practices* (Norwich: Canterbury, 2016), x, 48, 116.

cious. "I will sing to the LORD as long as I live" (Ps. 104:33). But an unhelpful shift has occurred when such things are isolated from their natural context within a word-based spirituality and prescribed on their own as "spiritual practices" that help us find "the fullness of life that Christ promises."[30] This conceptualization overloads these things with a religious weight they cannot comfortably bear. There is a subtle but ultimately profound difference between encouraging a Scripture-saturated mind to reflect on the beauty of God's creation (something the Bible expressly encourages) and teaching highly specific "spiritual" techniques and practices that are several steps removed from anything explicitly revealed to us.

Once this broader and more imaginative approach to "spiritual practices" takes hold, it then creates a context in which it becomes increasingly easy to drift further from Scripture's clear prescriptions and increasingly difficult to exclude anything that might be deemed "helpful" by its practitioners. And conversely, as the range of acceptable approaches to spiritual formation expands, it begins to feel more and more problematic to insist that those means of grace actually prescribed in Scripture are indeed nonnegotiable and mandatory for all believers. One book on this topic, for example, maintains that though

> the aims and task of Christian spiritual formation are definite and universal, the means of formation vary and are personal. . . . I repeat: the means of formation vary. Practices, possessions, relationships, attitudes, and more all can be employed as vehicles through which God's presence is welcomed.[31]

---

30 Welch, *Mindful Christian*, back cover.

31 In this section, Howard also states that "there is a defined set of distinctly Christian means that Christians employ to cultivate growth in their relationship with God." But he then broadens that "defined set" considerably through an appeal to Peter's charge to "make every effort" to grow in faith (2 Pet. 1:5): "The reasonable conclusion is that, in this effort, we would be making use of a wide range of means." As argued later in this chapter and touched on in chapter 6, sanctification and providence are the more appropriate concepts by which we can relate the breadth of

Later the author indicates that one of the "unhealthy ways of approaching our relationship with spiritual disciplines . . . is the way of legalism." In this context, "the way of legalism" is defined as that "in which one identifies a few 'required' practices that all 'good Christians' engage in regularly." The result of "this rigid standard" is that "we subtly impose some disciplines on others, effectively dividing the body of Christ."[32]

While one could certainly imagine a rigid and unhealthy approach to Christian growth that could fairly be described as "legalistic," it seems a mistake to apply this label to any who wish to see spiritual formation pursued exclusively according to those means of grace explicitly identified as such in Scripture. And though it is true that all life's varied circumstances are used by God to sanctify us, it is unhelpful to label anything and everything as a tool of spiritual formation. We have other words, categories, and concepts to talk about how God works across the entire breadth of history and human experience (e.g., providence, sanctification), and it muddies the waters considerably when we stretch the language of spiritual formation to include all that breadth. Our focus in this book, then, is on those "divinely appointed means" that God has clearly given in Scripture and that the Reformed tradition has consistently commended as unambiguously biblical and therefore consistently edifying.

Directed toward Conformity to Christ

Finally, our definition would be radically incomplete without underscoring the end toward which our spiritual formation must be directed: conformity to Christ. Only by upholding Christ as the end or telos of our spiritual formation can we ensure that the process is, in fact, authentically Christian. Within the wider popular culture, taking an interest in "spirituality" is typically presented as a means through which an individual can come to better understand not Christ but oneself.

---

human striving and experience to the concept of Christian growth. Howard, *Guide to Christian Spiritual Formation*, 102.

32 Howard, *Guide to Christian Spiritual Formation*, 108–10.

My "spiritual journey" becomes a process through which I come not to bow the knee before the Creator God who is my Judge and King but rather to realize that divine transcendence was actually inside me all along. This is what the columnist and cultural critic Ross Douthat has termed "God within" theology, a creed that he argues has become "the religious message with the most currency in American popular culture." In the following passage, Douthat identifies and analyzes a striking example of "God within" theology in the pages of Elizabeth Gilbert's bestselling book *Eat, Pray, Love*:

> Her final theological epiphany is the same as her first one. A journey that began with God speaking to her in "my own voice from within my own self"—albeit "as I had never heard it before"—ends with the realization that the Elizabeth Gilbert-ness of that Voice is the key to understanding the nature of divinity itself. The highest spiritual wisdom, she writes, isn't just that God waits for us inside our own hearts and minds and souls. It's that "God dwells within you as you yourself, exactly the way you are." The best way to remedy our "heartbreaking inability to sustain contentment," then, isn't to remake ourselves in imitation of Christ (or Buddha, or Krishna, or whomever), but rather to recognize that "somewhere within us all, there does exist a supreme self who is eternally at peace. That supreme Self is our true identity, universal and divine."[33]

It's difficult to imagine a description more antithetical to Christian spiritual formation than that. Christians are not called to go deeper into themselves for answers but are instead called out of themselves and into new life in Christ. "If anyone is in Christ, he is a new creation" (2 Cor. 5:17), and the Christian's unfolding hope as he marches toward glory is

---

33 Ross Douthat, *Bad Religion: How We Became a Nation of Heretics* (New York: Free Press, 2012), 214–15, quoting Elizabeth Gilbert, *Eat, Pray, Love: One Woman's Search for Everything across Italy, India, and Indonesia* (New York: Penguin, 2006), 192, 122.

that this new life will wax as the old life wanes. The converted person looks outside herself toward Christ and says with John the Baptist, "He must increase, but I must decrease" (John 3:30). Christian spiritual formation, then, is not about recognizing that we are actually just fine where and as we are but rather about "work[ing] out [our] own salvation with fear and trembling" (Phil. 2:12) and becoming "mature in Christ" (Col. 1:28). And this maturation involves not diving deeper into the self but denying the self and following the one in whom real fullness can be found (Matt. 16:24).

Three Related Words and Their Meanings

One prominent theme in this chapter has been the meaning of various words and phrases and why certain words and phrases might be helpful or unhelpful depending on their usage and context. To this end, we have considered why this book will use the phrases *keeping the heart* and *spiritual formation* to label the kind of deliberate cultivation of spiritual life that we explore in the pages that follow. But before we conclude the chapter, let's press a bit further into words and their meanings by briefly considering three words that are closely related to spiritual formation but do not mean quite the same thing.

Spirituality

New Testament scholar D. A. Carson has described *spirituality* as a potentially "frightening" word. It's not so scary in and of itself, but Carson suggests that it has become so through its increasing popularity and usage across an enormous range of disparate contexts. Through this frequent and varied deployment, spirituality "has become such an ill-defined, amorphous entity that it covers all kinds of phenomena an earlier generation of Christians, more given to robust thought than is the present generation, would have dismissed as error, or even as 'paganism' or 'heathenism.'"[34]

---

34 D. A. Carson, "When Is Spirituality Spiritual? Reflections on Some Problems of Definition," *Journal of the Evangelical Theological Society* 37, no. 3 (1994): 381.

It is not hard to see what he is talking about. Within the wider popular culture, interest in what might be deemed "spirituality" can be observed in everything from television shows with pagan and occult themes to the quasireligious descriptions used to market candles and herbal teas. These themes have gained such traction within the realm of consumer branding that one major marketing research firm has recently deemed "spirituality" to be " 'the next big thing' in millennial-focused marketing."[35] In an attempt to clarify just what people mean when they talk about "spirituality," the Canadian researcher Galen Watts interviewed millennials who self-identify as "spiritual but not religious." His conclusions are fascinating, if somewhat nebulous:

> When people call themselves spiritual they are basically signaling three things: first, that they believe there is more to the world than meets the eye, that is to say, more than the mere material. Second, that they try to attend to their inner life—to their mental and emotional states—in the hopes of gaining a certain kind of self-knowledge. Third, that they value the following virtues: being compassionate, empathetic and open-hearted.[36]

Clearly, the broader senses of *spirituality* and being *spiritual* are not entirely congruous with traditional Christianity, and yet despite all this recent pop-cultural baggage, the terms are not entirely foreign to the language of the Bible either. Long before millennial trendsetters were identifying as "spiritual but not religious," the nineteenth-century American theologian Charles Hodge explained that the Bible uses the term *spiritual* to indicate those things that come from the Holy Spirit: "Spiritual gifts and spiritual blessings are gifts and blessings of which the

---

35 Tara Isabella Burton, *Strange Rites: New Religions for a Godless World* (New York: PublicAffairs, 2020), 58.

36 Galen Watts, "What Does It Mean to Be Spiritual?," The Conversation, November 16, 2017; https://theconversation.com/.

Spirit is the author. Everything that God does in nature and in grace, he does by the Spirit."[37] If that last statement is correct—and it seems to be—then the theme of spirituality can be understood biblically as something that intersects with all redemptive history from creation to consummation.[38] And the spiritual life, in a biblical sense, would be a life that is given, sustained, and directed by the Holy Spirit. In the incarnation, Jesus offers the perfect example of such a life, as one whom "God anointed . . . with the Holy Spirit and with power" (Acts 10:38) and who, in his humanity, depended on the Spirit in all circumstances (e.g., Luke 4:1, 14).

As those who are in Christ, Christians are likewise called to pursue the spiritual life in this sense, and the word *spirituality* could be used in connection with exploring the quality, purpose, and character of such a life. This way of thinking about spirituality would dovetail nicely with the definitions of Christian spirituality offered elsewhere: "Christian spirituality is the domain of lived Christian experience. It is about all of life—not just some esoteric portion of it—before God, through Christ, in the transforming and empowering presence of the Holy Spirit."[39] Such definitions of *spirituality*, with their strong emphasis on a holistic experience of life lived in the Spirit, seem to be getting close to what we mean when we talk about spiritual formation and keeping the heart. And yet these terms don't quite align perfectly.

Clearly, they are closely related, but *spirituality* and *spiritual* seem to have a wider scope than what we are interested in here. If, as Hodge

---

37 Charles Hodge, *1 Corinthians*, Crossway Classic Commentaries (Wheaton, IL: Crossway, 1995), 164.

38 See Christopher W. Morgan and Justin L. McLendon, "A Trajectory of Spirituality," in Morgan, *Biblical Spirituality*, 19–53.

39 Glen G. Scorgie, "Overview of Christian Spirituality," in *Zondervan Dictionary of Christian Spirituality*, ed. Glen G. Scorgie (Grand Rapids, MI: Zondervan, 2011), 27. For examples of other definitions, see Alister E. McGrath, *Christian Spirituality: An Introduction* (Oxford: Blackwell, 1999), 2; Philip Sheldrake, "What Is Spirituality?," in *Exploring Christian Spirituality: An Ecumenical Reader*, ed. Kenneth J. Collins (Grand Rapids, MI: Baker, 2000), 25; Sandra M. Schneiders, "Approaches to the Study of Christian Spirituality," in *The Blackwell Companion to Christian Spirituality*, ed. Arthur Holder (Oxford: Blackwell, 2005), 16.

said, the term *spiritual* is used "to indicate those things that come from the Holy Spirit," and if all God's works and ways in creation, redemption, and consummation are done by the Spirit, then these words paint with a far broader brush than we intend when we use the term *spiritual formation*. Our interest is in that narrower slice of Christian life in which redeemed men and women actively use God-given means to pursue richer fellowship with the triune God and better cultivate what theologian John Murray (1898–1975) called "God-consciousness" or "an all-pervasive sense of God's presence."[40] A person doing that could certainly be described as taking an active interest in biblical spirituality or spiritual things, but spiritual formation would still be just one aspect of those much larger categories.

Sanctification

Another term closely related to *spiritual formation* but not entailing quite the same thing is *sanctification*. The Westminster Shorter Catechism (1647) defines sanctification as "the work of God's free grace, whereby we are renewed in the whole man after the image of God, and are enabled more and more to die unto sin, and live unto righteousness."[41] Upon reading such a definition, one might imagine that what the catechism describes is precisely what we are after when we seek to define spiritual formation. After all, what sort of "formation" are we looking for if not the sort by which we are "enabled more and more to die unto sin, and live unto righteousness"?

There is an obvious logic to this thinking, and indeed, one often finds people using the terms *spiritual formation* and *sanctification* more or less synonymously. For instance, when the twentieth-century Reformed apologist Francis Schaeffer (1912–1984) wrote *True Spirituality*, he explained that his "study of the Christian life and true spirituality"

---

40 John Murray, *Collected Writings of John Murray* (Edinburgh: Banner of Truth, 1982), 1:183.

41 "Westminster Shorter Catechism," in Van Dixhoorn, *Creeds, Confessions, and Catechisms*, 418 (q. 35).

was "in reality a study of the biblical teaching of sanctification."[42] One popular book canvasing different perspectives on this subject is titled *Christian Spirituality: Five Views of Sanctification.*[43] The relationship between the title and the subtitle expresses this same common perception that reflection on spirituality and spiritual formation is essentially reflection on the doctrine of sanctification.

I would argue, however, that spiritual formation can helpfully be distinguished from sanctification by identifying the former as a subset of the latter. Sanctification is a much broader concept than spiritual formation. Sanctification includes spiritual formation, but it also includes a whole lot more within its conceptual scope. Scripture teaches that God uses *all* our circumstances to sanctify us and conform us to the image of Christ (Rom. 8:28–29). Whether we experience trial and suffering (e.g., Rom. 5:3–5; 2 Cor. 4:17) or blessing and victory (e.g., Ps. 128; Acts 3:8–10), the Spirit of God is at work in the people of God to build them up in faith and Christian virtue (Phil. 4:12–13)—that is, to sanctify them. Spiritual formation, by contrast, refers more narrowly to those God-appointed means that we actively and consciously employ in the pursuit of spiritual growth.

To see the distinction and its significance more clearly, consider something like the sudden death of a loved one. Under such circumstances, a Christian should be encouraged by the biblical promise that "for those who love God all things work together for good" (Rom. 8:28). This promise means, among other things, that God will use even this tragic loss to bring blessing, blessing that, in the context of the passage, is explained in terms of God's good purpose to conform his people to the image of Christ—that is, to sanctify them (Rom. 8:28–29). The Spirit's work of sanctification thus continues not in spite of difficult

---

42 Francis A. Schaeffer, *The Complete Works of Francis A. Schaeffer: A Christian Worldview* (Wheaton, IL: Crossway, 1994), 3:269.

43 Donald L. Alexander, ed., *Christian Spirituality: Five Views of Sanctification* (Downers Grove, IL: InterVarsity Press, 1988).

circumstances but actually in and through them. But does it make sense to describe the loss of a loved one in terms of spiritual formation? This seems a very unhelpful way to speak, as it blurs the distinction between tools and means that we are encouraged to seek out and tragic events that we rightly hope to avoid. Because sanctification is ultimately God's gracious work in us, we trust that it continues through all life's ups and downs, but insofar as our spiritual formation is something we are called to consciously choose and actively pursue, it makes sense to think of it as a subset of God's larger work of renewal in our lives.

Piety

Finally, we must say something about the word *piety*. Defined in a modern dictionary as "reverence and obedience to God," *piety* was the preferred term among early modern Protestants when they sought to capture what a Christian was trying to cultivate through his or her religious exercises.[44] For the Swiss Reformer John Calvin, piety (Lat. *pietas*) was "the shorthand symbol for his whole understanding and practice of Christian faith and life."[45] Calvin introduced the concept quite early on in his *Institutes of the Christian Religion* (1559), defining piety as "that reverence joined with love of God which the knowledge of his benefits induces."[46] Similarly, across the channel, the most popular English devotional manual during the seventeenth century was titled *The Practice of Piety* (1611). In the book, author Lewis Bayly (1575–1631) invoked Jesus's parable of the ten virgins (Matt. 25:1–12) and urged his readers to "get forthwith, like a wise virgin, the oil of piety in the lamp

---

44 *Oxford English Dictionary*, s.v. "piety (*n.*)," accessed July 17, 2024, https://doi.org/10.1093/OED /1007268312.

45 Ford Lewis Battles, ed., *The Piety of John Calvin: A Collection of His Spiritual Prose, Poems, and Hymns* (Phillipsburg, NJ: Presbyterian & Reformed, 1978), 27.

46 John Calvin, *Institutes of the Christian Religion*, ed. John T. McNeill, trans. Ford Lewis Battles, Library of Christian Classics (Philadelphia: Westminster, 1960), 1:41 (1.2.1). See also Joel R. Beeke, "Calvin on Piety," in *The Cambridge Companion to John Calvin*, ed. Donald K. McKim (Cambridge: Cambridge University Press, 2004), 125–52; John Calvin, *John Calvin: Writings on Pastoral Piety*, ed. Elsie Anne McKee, Classics of Western Spirituality (New York: Paulist, 2001), 2–6.

of thy conversation, that thou mayest be in a continual readiness to meet the bridegroom, whether he cometh by death or by judgment."[47] That passage captures something of both Bayly's use of the word *piety* and also the emphasis we've established already on *keeping the heart* as the Christian's perpetual and joyful duty.

Clearly, when an earlier generation of Protestant authors spoke of piety, they were coming very close to what we are interested in here when we speak of spiritual formation and keeping the heart. And if this book were strictly a historical study, *piety* would probably be our preferred term. In the present volume, however, we are more interested in historical retrieval than historical study strictly for its own sake, and in a modern context, spiritual formation is a more widely recognized term, one that doesn't carry some of the old-fashioned connotations that the word *piety* can sometimes carry. Moreover, the term *piety* focuses our attention on the desired result rather than the means to get there, piety being the quality we want to cultivate or stir up. By contrast, *spiritual formation* and *keeping the heart* carry a dynamic sense that nicely draws attention to the active, ongoing nature of the endeavor we have in view.

———

Our goal in this chapter has been to unpack what we mean when we talk about spiritual formation and keeping the heart. Our goal in subsequent chapters is to explore how that formation takes place by listening carefully to those who went before us.

Spiritual formation is not an easy task. For John Flavel, earnest heart work is "the hardest work" in which a Christian can engage: "to shuffle over religious duties with a loose and heedless spirit, will cost no great pains; but to set thyself before the Lord, and tie up thy loose and vain thoughts to a constant and serious attendance upon him: this will cost

---

47 Lewis Bayly, *The Practice of Piety: Directing a Christian to Walk, That He May Please God* (Grand Rapids, MI: Soli Deo Gloria, 2019), 101.

thee something."[48] It will cost us because it requires us to put aside the quick and easy attractions of our entertainment-entranced world. It will cost us because it requires us to engage in a spiritual battle "against the spiritual forces of evil in the heavenly places" (Eph. 6:12). And it will cost us above all because real heart work requires that we say no to our own sinful impulses and desires, denying ourselves and attuning our hearts to the God who made us in his image and now calls us back to himself. It is a work that will not cease this side of glory: "The keeping of the heart is such a work as is never done till life be done: this labour and our life end together."[49] But if we pursue it, the rewards are great, both in this life and the next.

Keep your heart with all vigilance,
    for from it flow the springs of life. (Prov. 4:23)

---

[48] Flavel, *Works*, 5:428.
[49] Flavel, *Works*, 5:428–29.

2

Spiritual Formation in a Reformation Key

Five Solas *for Head and Heart*

WE LIVE IN AN AGE of personal choice. Rooted in an Enlightenment-era distaste for inherited authorities and propelled forward by digital technologies that empower an on-demand approach to just about everything, twenty-first-century Westerners are committed to the idea that I should self-determine my reality, mixing and matching particulars until I get the combination I prefer.

Sometimes this urge to customize, to choose, and to create a tailor-made experience is harmless and appealing. Just the other day I received an email from my favorite music streaming app featuring the following subject line: "Personalized playlist recommendations, curated just for your taste." Though some musical purists might disagree, I think that sort of choice is exciting and fun. And who doesn't appreciate the amazing range of news stories, essays, and articles available on call to engage every interest? Or the incredible ability to instantly hear sermons preached and recorded across several decades and thousands of different churches?

This is all well and good, but our twenty-first-century cultural landscape also affords plenty of less benign examples of where a pick-and-choose mindset can lead. Carl Trueman, for instance, argues persuasively that this prioritization of individual tastes, preferences, and feelings has been the key factor driving the sea change in sexual ethics that began in earnest during the 1960s and has rapidly accelerated during the twenty-first century.[1] And just as this spirit of extreme individualism has eroded a sense of coherence regarding sexual ethics, the modern age has also promoted an individual approach to spirituality in which my right to pick and choose trumps all other considerations.

In his book *Man Seeks God: My Flirtations with the Divine*, journalist Eric Weiner narrates how a personal health scare sent him on "a worldwide exploration of religions" through which he hoped to reach "a personal understanding of the divine." As his journeys took him to places like Nepal, Israel, Turkey, and Las Vegas, he accumulated a cornucopia of religious ideas and spiritual practices before eventually concluding that "instead of looking for my God, I must invent Him." By this Weiner meant that he must "not exactly invent" but rather "construct" or "assemble" his god: a god whose "foundation is Jewish, but His support beams Buddhist. He has the heart of Sufism, the simplicity of Taoism, the generosity of the Franciscans, the hedonistic streak of the Raëlians." For Weiner, this "composite God" isn't necessarily "true" in the ordinary sense, but ultimately, that apparent deficiency seems to actually be the main point: "Together . . . these parts add up to *something*. Is it true? Yes. No. *Truth is what works.* And this composite God works for me."[2]

---

1   Carl R. Trueman, *The Rise and Triumph of the Modern Self: Cultural Amnesia, Expressive Individualism, and the Road to Sexual Revolution* (Wheaton, IL: Crossway, 2020); Trueman, *Strange New World: How Thinkers and Activists Redefined Identity and Sparked the Sexual Revolution* (Wheaton, IL: Crossway, 2022). On the significance of the 1960s, see Hugh McLeod, *The Religious Crisis of the 1960s* (Oxford: Oxford University Press, 2010).

2   Eric Weiner, *Man Seeks God: My Flirtations with the Divine* (New York: Twelve, 2011), dust jacket, 339–40 (emphasis original).

Weiner's conclusion nicely distills the conventional wisdom of our age regarding spirituality: what's right for you is what works for you, wherever you might find it. Now of course, all truth is God's truth, and we shouldn't dismiss it even when it comes from an unexpected source. But that is *not* what Weiner is saying. Rather, he is suggesting that the primary if not exclusive criterion for accepting or rejecting a spiritual practice is how it makes me feel. Do I respond well to it? Does it "work" for me? If so, we'll call it "true" and move on.

As contemporary evangelicals looking to walk faithfully in the twenty-first century, we are not immune to these cultural crosscurrents. All of us are affected by the culture's elevation of individual preferences, and all of us are, to some extent, conditioned by our culture to look for and expect a customized experience. And if we are not careful, we will carry that expectation beyond our quest for the latest and greatest on-demand streaming service and into our Christian life.

An overarching burden of this book, and the primary aim of this chapter, is to retrieve, explore, and commend an approach to spiritual formation that is based on and congruent with the Reformation heritage out of which evangelicalism arose. And one of the key motivations behind that aim is a desire to counter a creeping sense among many evangelicals that our spiritual life can be a custom-made affair. For example, in his book *The Sacred Way*, Tony Jones warns readers to "leave at the front cover . . . any denominational bigotry you have." Dismissing concerns that some of the practices he recommends should be avoided simply because they "will seem very 'Catholic' or very 'Eastern Orthodox,'" Jones ultimately grounds his approach to spiritual formation on a personal pragmatism that sounds eerily familiar to that described by Weiner. Jones writes, "To be honest, I don't really know how you're best going to achieve intimacy with God. *I know what's worked for me,* and I'll try to indicate that along the way."[3]

---

3   Tony Jones, *The Sacred Way: Spiritual Practices for Everyday Life* (Grand Rapids, MI: Zondervan, 2004), 20 (emphasis added).

Such statements have an apparent air of open-minded generosity that is undeniably attractive in our cultural moment. But ultimately, your spiritual life is not a Spotify playlist, and we must be on guard against the naive notion that the best way to judge a spiritual tool is to ask whether it works for us. John Coe and Kyle Strobel offer wise counsel on this point:

> There is a theoretical and experiential package deal that we have to take seriously when it comes to Christian practice. In other words, it is not helpful to break off spiritual practices from their theological framework, because theory and practice are necessarily intertwined. This means that evangelicals must not simply adopt practices naively without considering what sort of theological axioms a given practice assumes.[4]

Our evaluation of a spiritual practice must be rooted not in pragmatism but in Scripture, and it has long been the conviction of evangelical Christians that, in the main, the Reformers and their theological heirs saw deeply into what the Bible had to teach us, not just about theology and doctrine but also about spiritual formation. Commenting on John Calvin's reforming agenda, Joel Beeke observes that "for Calvin, the Reformation includes the reform of piety (*pietas*), or spirituality, as much as a reform of theology."[5]

In this chapter, our goal is to recover and explore something of that "reform of piety" the Reformers pursued so vigorously. If we believe that the Reformation got the gospel right, then we should be equally attentive to the way a Reformation vision of spiritual formation follows from that same understanding of the gospel. Theology and practice

---

4 John H. Coe and Kyle C. Strobel, "Conclusion," in *Embracing Contemplation: Reclaiming a Christian Spiritual Practice*, ed. John H. Coe and Kyle C. Strobel (Downers Grove, IL: IVP Academic, 2019), 284.

5 Joel R. Beeke, "Calvin on Piety," in *The Cambridge Companion to John Calvin*, ed. Donald K. McKim (Cambridge: Cambridge University Press, 2004), 145.

are interconnected, and in this chapter, we want to sketch the contours of those interconnections in order to set the stage for examining specific spiritual practices throughout the rest of the book. Here we consider spiritual formation in relation to the Reformation *solas*, to the connection between justification and sanctification, and to the doctrine of union with Christ, concluding with a discussion of three emphases in a Reformed approach to spiritual formation.

Spiritual Formation and the Reformation *Solas*

The Reformers' vision was headlined by the doctrine of justification by faith alone and the so-called five *solas*, which collectively capture the movement's theological heartbeat.[6] In this chapter, we consider some of the specific qualities that mark out an approach to spiritual formation that is shaped by these doctrines. But before proceeding any further, we need to address an elephant-in-the-room question that looms over our entire project: How well exactly do spiritual formation and Reformation theology fit together? Is it possible that the reason Tony Jones's book on spiritual formation recommends so many practices that, by his own description, "seem very 'Catholic' or very 'Eastern Orthodox'" is that Reformation theology just doesn't really lend itself well to the pursuit of spiritual growth? Is it possible that the five *solas* somehow militate against spiritual formation by their own internal logic? Does a Reformation gospel in which grace alone through faith alone in Christ alone are consistently emphasized really allow for the sort of hard work and intentional effort that much spiritual formation literature seems to commend?

Many have concluded that the two are indeed simply at odds with one another. The scholar, organist, and physician Albert Schweitzer (1875–1965) famously declared that the Reformation doctrine of

6   For a clear, concise, and useful restatement of the five Reformation *solas* and their significance for the contemporary church, see "Cambridge Declaration Heritage and Resources," Alliance of Confessing Evangelicals, April 20, 1996, https://www.alliancenet.org/.

justification by faith alone was "a conception of redemption, from which no ethic could logically be derived."[7] In his book *Spiritual Theology*, Simon Chan has criticized "modern evangelicalism's inability to develop a consistent doctrine of the Christian life," suggesting that "evangelicalism's strict adherence to the Reformation doctrine of justification by faith has not been brought into a meaningful relationship with the means of grace."[8] To the extent that such analysis is correct, it might seem to reveal some sort of inescapable contradiction between Protestant doctrine and robust Christian living. And if that were in fact the case, then any attempt to sketch spiritual formation in a Reformation key would be doomed from the outset.

As mentioned in the previous chapter, some conservative evangelicals are highly critical of the so-called spiritual formation movement, arguing that the concept invariably tilts toward Roman Catholic and Eastern Orthodox understandings of spiritual growth. And while I don't ultimately agree with their underlying antipathy toward the term itself, these critics are not wrong to observe that some of the wider literature associated with "spiritual formation" displays a reliance on non-Protestant source material that ought to worry Reformation-minded evangelicals. Why, for example, does the all-time bestselling book on spiritual formation, Richard Foster's *Celebration of Discipline* (1978), a book marketed to and much beloved by evangelicals, seem to privilege voices from *without* rather than *within* the Reformation heritage out of which evangelicalism arose? Does Protestantism lack the inner resources to develop its own internally coherent account of what spiritual formation ought to look like?

Some of this may well result from a historical accident: perhaps, as it happened, early and influential writers on spiritual formation

---

7   Albert Schweitzer, *The Mysticism of Paul the Apostle*, trans. William Montgomery (New York: Henry Holt, 1931), 225.

8   Simon Chan, *Spiritual Theology: A Systematic Study of the Christian Life* (Downers Grove, IL: InterVarsity Press, 1998), 24.

were, for their own reasons, drawn to an eclectic theological source base, which in turn inspired subsequent authors to follow their lead. Describing her own context within the Church of England, Kirsten Birkett has documented just such a "historical process," one through which "Roman Catholic ideas have shaped Anglican spirituality and Anglican theological education philosophy, to a large extent without critical examination."[9] Surely there is some truth to the idea that the perceived connection between spiritual formation and non-Protestant theology simply represents the way it all happened to play out and that it could well have been otherwise.

At the same time, I can't help but wonder if a larger part of the disconnect stems from the deeply rooted (mis)perception that Reformation theology cannot actually account for Christian growth in godliness. This charge goes all the way back to the Reformation itself. For defenders of the Roman Catholic position, the Reformers' doctrine of justification by faith alone amounted to a lie about our status before God. Catholics rejected the Protestant claim that a sinner could be justified before God on account of Christ's righteousness and without a corresponding inner righteousness of her own, dismissing such an idea as a "legal fiction" that would inevitably lead to a lack of real moral and spiritual seriousness. To appreciate the logic of this charge, consider how the doctrine of justification by faith alone is expressed by one of the great statements of Reformation theology, the Heidelberg Catechism:

> Even though my conscience accuses me of having grievously sinned against all God's commandments, of never having kept any of them, and of still being inclined toward all evil, nevertheless, without any merit of my own, out of sheer grace, God grants and credits to me the perfect satisfaction, righteousness, and holiness of Christ, as if I had never sinned nor been a sinner, and as if I had been as perfectly

9   Kirsten Birkett, "Spiritual Formation: The Rise of a Tradition," *Churchman* 4, no. 133 (2019): 358.

obedient as Christ was obedient for me—if only I accept this gift with a believing heart.[10]

The catechism forcefully draws out the notion that our justification before God is wholly based on Christ's righteousness imputed or credited to us. God pronounces us righteous in his sight not because of anything we've done but only because of what Christ has done for us. Well before the Heidelberg Catechism was published in 1563, this had already become the consensus view among the Reformers, and it is accordingly reflected in all the major Reformed confessions.[11] To Reformation-minded Protestants, this understanding of justification represents the heart of the gospel itself.

But to Catholic ears, such formulations sound drastically off the mark. Catholic critics declared the Protestant position on justification to be a "legal fiction." Why? They thought that when the Reformers pronounced sinners to be righteous when they are in fact, as the Heidelberg Catechism emphatically states, very much not righteous in themselves (e.g., "My conscience accuses me . . . of still being inclined toward all evil"), the Reformers appeared to be declaring as true what was patently false. The Bible teaches that "a false balance is an abomination to the LORD" (Prov. 11:1), and yet it appeared to Catholic critics that here, on the most crucial soteriological point, Protestants were suggesting that God will weigh a person's sins using just such a faulty measure. Thus, from a Catholic perspective, the famous Reformation formulation that Christians are simultaneously justified in Christ and sinners in themselves (*simul justus et peccator*) makes no sense: to be *justus* is, by definition, not to be *peccator*! If one is following this logic,

---

10 "Heidelberg Catechism," in *Creeds, Confessions, and Catechisms: A Reader's Edition*, ed. Chad Van Dixhoorn (Wheaton, IL: Crossway, 2022), 308 (q. 60).

11 Alister E. McGrath, *Iustitia Dei: A History of the Christian Doctrine of Justification*, 4th ed. (Cambridge: Cambridge University Press, 2020), 188; Korey D. Maas, "Justification by Faith Alone," in *Reformation Theology: A Systematic Summary*, ed. Matthew Barrett (Wheaton, IL: Crossway, 2017), 511–47.

the incongruity between what a person is in himself and what he is in Christ appears both offensive and absurd, a reaction evident in the Roman Catholic theologian Karl Adam's uncomprehending dismissal of the Protestant gospel as "like some brilliant cloak of gold thrown over the human corpse."[12]

For this reason, Roman Catholic soteriology insists that when people are justified, they are internally renewed and actually made to be just in and of themselves, not "merely" credited with the external-to-themselves righteousness of Christ. Once so transformed inwardly, one must then, with the Spirit's help and in communion with the church, strive to maintain this state of grace, preserving and growing the grace received so that one might ultimately be pronounced just or righteous on the last day, a judgment rendered on the basis of a person's entire Spirit-empowered life lived. The Catechism of the Catholic Church puts it this way:

> No one can merit the initial grace of forgiveness and justification, at the beginning of conversion. Moved by the Holy Spirit and by charity, we can then merit for ourselves and for others the graces needed for our sanctification, for the increase of grace and charity, and for the attainment of eternal life.[13]

Note the contrast between this statement and what we saw from the Heidelberg Catechism. For Heidelberg, the ground on which a Christian will stand before God's bar of justice on the last day is "the perfect satisfaction, righteousness, and holiness of Christ." This is a righteousness to which the sinner cannot and does not contribute. It's all of grace, all a free gift. In no sense does an individual Christian merit or earn any part of his or her eternal life. By contrast, the Catholic

---

12 Karl Adam, *The Spirit of Catholicism*, trans. Justin McCann (London: Sheed & Ward, 1938), 214.

13 *Catechism of the Catholic Church: Revised in Accordance with the Official Latin Text Promulgated by Pope John Paul II*, 2nd ed. (Vatican City: Libreria Editrice Vaticana, 1997), sec. 2010.

Catechism teaches that after an initial, unmerited infusion of grace through the sacrament of baptism leading to justification, we "can then merit for ourselves . . . the graces needed . . . for the attainment of eternal life."[14] Karl Adam expresses the same idea when he writes that "the creative and quickening power of justification is manifested exactly in the fact that it . . . makes us bear fruit worthy of eternal life. So that eternal life becomes, as St. Paul expresses it, a wage and a reward."[15] While Adam would be quick to describe that fruit worthy of eternal life as wholly enabled by the gracious work of the Spirit, he still insists strenuously that a person is ultimately justified on the last day by his or her own meritorious good works and not by the imputed righteousness of Christ.

Though the language can be nuanced and slippery, this represents a very wide gulf between the two positions, a reality that has been acknowledged by both Protestants and Catholics from the sixteenth century onward. In Rome's estimate, the doctrine of justification by faith alone would sever the necessary connection between salvation and subsequent moral striving, potentially sapping the zeal for godliness that ought to define the people of God. After all, the logic goes, if one can be reckoned righteous by God without the need to *actually be* righteous in oneself, what possible motivation remains for the pursuit of spiritual growth?

This repudiation of the Reformation doctrine of justification by faith alone (*sola fide*) was dogmatically defined by the Roman Catholic Church at the Council of Trent (1545–1563). Trent represented something of an official Catholic response to the dramatic events of

---

14   For an evangelical analysis of justification in Reformed and Catholic perspective, see Cornelis P. Venema, "Justification: The Ecumenical, Biblical and Theological Dimensions of Current Debates," in *Always Reforming: Explorations in Systematic Theology*, ed. A. T. B. McGowan (Downers Grove, IL: InterVarsity Press, 2006), 289–327; for a more comprehensive evangelical treatment of Roman Catholicism, see Gregg R. Allison, *Roman Catholic Theology and Practice: An Evangelical Assessment* (Wheaton, IL: Crossway, 2014).

15   Adam, *Spirit of Catholicism*, 217–18.

the Reformation, and though justification was not the only aspect of Protestant theology to be critiqued and rejected, the Council's statements on it were extensive and strongly worded: "If any one saith, that by faith alone the impious is justified, . . . let him be anathema."[16] This unequivocal conclusion stands today as a statement of the Catholic position, and insofar as it rejects the idea that in justification God pardons all our sins and accepts us as righteous only because of Christ's righteousness imputed to us and received by faith alone, Trent's rejection of Protestant orthodoxy has attracted a large number of adherents, even among some ostensibly Protestant theologians.[17]

Justification and Sanctification

As we seek to understand why spiritual formation is sometimes felt to be at odds with our Reformation heritage, it seems that this history of Catholic critique has played no small role. And yet as Alister McGrath has observed in his analysis of Trent's decrees, "It appears that it is certain caricatures of Protestantism which are actually condemned, rather than Protestantism itself."[18] Similarly, those today who maintain that the historic Protestant gospel is somehow ill-equipped to facilitate spiritual formation and Christian growth have not fully grasped the Reformers' vision. In fact, as the Dutch theologian G. C. Berkouwer (1903–1996) maintains, the reality is precisely the opposite:

To understand the *Sola-fide* of the Reformation as the only proper response to the biblical message of sovereign grace is to know that

---

16 Council of Trent, session 6, "Decree on Justification, January 13, 1547," canon 9, in *The Canons and Decrees of the Sacred and Oecumenical Council of Trent*, trans. J. Waterworth (London: Dolman, 1848), 30–53, available at Hanover Historical Texts Project, https://history.hanover.edu/texts/.

17 For example, Clark Pinnock states that the historic Protestant position on imputation would amount to God "engaging in fantasies." Clark H. Pinnock, *Flame of Love: A Theology of the Holy Spirit* (Downers Grove, IL: InterVarsity Press, 1996), 156. See also N. T. Wright, "New Perspectives on Paul," in *Justification in Perspective: Historical Developments and Contemporary Challenges*, ed. Bruce L. McCormack (Grand Rapids, MI: Baker Academic, 2006), 243–64.

18 McGrath, *Iustitia Dei*, 330.

this *Sola-fide* can never be a threat to real sanctification. Such a threat can emerge only from a denial or devaluation of this doctrine. The ancient feud of Rome with the *Sola-fide* doctrine, based as it is on the view that *Sola-fide* is subversive of sanctification, must be called Rome's most fundamental error. It was no other than *Sola-fide* which made clear the true significance of sanctification, and distinguished it from all moralistic effort at self-improvement, in short, from all practices and beliefs which do violence to *Sola-fide* and, therefore, to *Sola-gratia*.[19]

Rome rejects the Reformers' doctrine of justification *sola fide* as "subversive of sanctification," but Berkouwer insists that the opposite is true, that only *sola fide* "made clear the true significance of sanctification, and distinguished it from all moralistic effort at self-improvement." Why would this be so?

Among the most fundamental Reformation insights was the recognition that biblical salvation contains two related yet distinct elements, both of which must always be held together but never comingled or confused: justification and sanctification. Justification, as we have established, refers to God's work on our behalf to pardon believers on the basis of our sin having been imputed to Christ and borne away on the cross and of Christ's own righteous life freely imputed or credited to us as though we had lived his perfect life of obedience to God's law. Sanctification, by contrast, refers to God's work of inner renewal in the life of the Christian, an ongoing process stretching from new birth to glory, wherein the Holy Spirit steadily brings believers into greater and greater conformity with the image of Christ.

This conceptual distinction between justification and sanctification is denied by Roman Catholicism, which teaches instead that "justification . . . is not remission of sins merely, but also the sanctification and

---

19 G. C. Berkouwer, *Faith and Sanctification* (Grand Rapids, MI: Eerdmans, 1952), 14.

renewal of the inward man."[20] Compare that merger with the following statement from the Westminster Larger Catechism, in which the two concepts are clearly differentiated:

> Although sanctification be inseparably joined with justification, yet they differ, in that God in justification imputeth the righteousness of Christ; in sanctification his Spirit infuseth grace, and enableth to the exercise thereof; in the former, sin is pardoned; in the other, it is subdued: the one doth equally free all believers from the revenging wrath of God, and that perfectly in this life, that they never fall into condemnation; the other is neither equal in all, nor in this life perfect in any, but growing up to perfection.[21]

A biblical understanding of salvation must contain both elements, both the free forgiveness of sins and imputed righteousness given through justification *and* the reality of ongoing inward renewal through sanctification. Both concepts must be maintained, but a biblical doctrine of salvation must also uphold the conceptual distinction between them. They are both real and inextricably linked, but they are two different things.

Here is where the Reformers saw more deeply into the revealed reality of the gospel than did their Roman Catholic counterparts. It's not that Rome has no place in its soteriology for both free forgiveness and inward renewal—it very much insists on both. The problem is that the Catholic doctrine mingles and confuses them, ultimately leading to a scenario in which a believer's final justification is based on his or her sanctification, a sanctification that, though graciously Spirit enabled and church assisted at every point, still amounts to the meritorious good work of the believer. From a Protestant perspective, that mingling

---

20 Council of Trent, session 6, "Decree on Justification," chap. 6, in Waterworth, *Council of Trent,* 30–53; https://history.hanover.edu/texts/.

21 "Westminster Larger Catechism," in Van Dixhoorn, *Creeds, Confessions, and Catechisms,* 359 (q. 77).

of my work with God's work as the ground for my final justification represents a fundamental overthrow of the gospel itself.

By clearly and consistently distinguishing between God's work *for us* in justification—a work to which we contribute nothing but our need—and God's work *in us* through sanctification—a work in which we play an active and ongoing part—the Reformers reflected the Bible's own teaching on the structure of salvation and created a theological framework within which to understand how, returning to Berkouwer's wording, a "real sanctification" can be "distinguished . . . from all moralistic effort at self-improvement."[22] When we insist that God justifies by faith alone, we effectively establish a playing field for a Spirit-wrought striving that necessarily follows our justification and yet will itself play no role in justifying the one who performs it.

This free pursuit of God and the things of God is the heart of our spiritual formation, and it is born out of joy and gratitude for a justification that those in Christ have already received and been eternally assured of. This represents the "real sanctification" that Berkouwer contrasts with "all moralistic effort at self-improvement." Drawing such a distinction unlocks the logic of Paul's pivot from gracious indicatives to moral imperatives in places like Romans 12:1 and Ephesians 4:1, allowing the Christian "to strive with a free conscience against sin and the devil in this life, and afterward to reign with Christ over all creation for eternity."[23]

If one fails to distinguish between God's perfect work in justification and our still very imperfect work in sanctification, the result is a continual temptation to either collapse justification into sanctification or collapse sanctification into justification. With the former temptation, the biblical reality of a full and complete justification based solely on the righteousness of Christ is lost—and with it any real sense of Christian hope and assurance. Instead, one's own works become the

---

22 Berkouwer, *Faith and Sanctification*, 14.
23 "Heidelberg Catechism," in Van Dixhoorn, *Creeds, Confessions, and Catechisms*, 300 (q. 32).

basis for vindication before God, an error that leads to either pharisaical pride or hopeless despair, depending on one's self-evaluation in the moment. With the latter temptation, the biblical reality of ongoing Spirit-wrought change is lost—and with it any sense that the authentic Christian life is marked by growing faithfulness and fruitfulness before the Lord. Those caught in this error are liable to fall into the trap of a lazy antinomianism, imagining that their one-time profession of faith exempts them from the Bible's many moral imperatives and forgetting that there is a "holiness without which no one will see the Lord" (Heb. 12:14).[24]

Both temptations are real, both regularly surface within contemporary evangelicalism, and both result from a failure to properly distinguish between justification and sanctification. It is also the case that unless we get these two aspects of salvation into proper Reformation alignment, our attempts to pursue spiritual formation will be ineffective at best and deforming at worst. We must be free to give ourselves to the real work of keeping the heart for God without worrying that our imperfect efforts to that end will result in eternal damnation. The boldness to "work out your own salvation with fear and trembling" today is grounded on the gospel confidence that on the last day I will be "found in [Christ], not having a righteousness of my own that comes from the law, but that which comes through faith in Christ, the righteousness from God that depends on faith" (Phil. 2:12; 3:9). But in order to properly align justification and sanctification and to correlate them with the task of spiritual formation, we must now consider both in light of the theological category that Reformed theologians have always upheld as central to any authentically Christian spiritual life: union with Christ.

---

24 The term *antinomianism* refers broadly to any tendencies that downplay, disregard, or even deny altogether the proper role for God's law in the life of a Christian. Such a posture has repeatedly surfaced within church history. See Mark Jones, *Antinomianism: Reformed Theology's Unwelcome Guest?* (Phillipsburg, NJ: P&R, 2013).

Union with Christ

When the Puritan allegorist John Bunyan (1628–1688) finally discovered spiritual peace, he described the awakening as a dramatic release from bondage: "Now did my chains fall off my legs indeed; I was loosened from my afflictions and irons. . . . [N]ow went I also home rejoicing, for the grace and love of God." But even more significant than his striking imagery was the theological breakthrough that produced it:

> I saw, with the eyes of my soul, Jesus Christ at God's right hand; there, I say, was my righteousness. . . . I also saw, moreover, that it was not my good frame of heart that made my righteousness better, nor yet my bad frame that made my righteousness worse; for my righteousness was Jesus Christ himself, "the same yesterday, and to-day, and for ever," Heb. xiii 8. . . . Now Christ was all; all my righteousness, all my sanctification, and all my redemption. Further, the Lord did also lead me into the mystery of union with the Son of God; that I was joined to him, that I was flesh of his flesh, and bone of his bone. . . . If he and I were one, then his righteousness was mine, his merits mine, his victory also mine.[25]

In this passage, Bunyan's joy in God flows directly from recognizing that justification and sanctification are united but distinct salvific realities. His justification is secure because it is based on a righteousness that comes from outside himself, from Christ, and his "not guilty" verdict before God thus depends not on whether he has "a good frame of heart" or "a bad frame" from moment to moment. But rather than eliminating the need for inward moral renewal, such an insight carves out space for it: he goes "home rejoicing" in God and glorifying him from the secure position of freedom in Christ. This is the Reformation alignment

---

25 John Bunyan, *Grace Abounding to the Chief of Sinners* (Glasgow: Porteous and Hislop, 1863), 90–92.

of justification and sanctification. But notice also how, for Bunyan, these two aspects of salvation are held together by a common center point: union with Christ. The entire passage celebrates how union with Christ by his Spirit is the source of all spiritual good: "Christ was all; all my righteousness, all my sanctification, and all my redemption." For Bunyan, union with Christ was the key to understanding salvation in all its facets, the sum and substance of our spiritual life—justification and sanctification each originating together from the one same union.

And Bunyan was not alone in this thinking. Whether we examine pioneering sixteenth-century Reformed theologians such as John Calvin and Peter Martyr Vermigli (1499–1562), post-Reformation thinkers such as Jerome Zanchi (1516–1590) and Theodore Beza (1519–1605), or English divines such as William Perkins (1558–1602) and William Ames, the conclusion is the same: union with Christ is the controlling idea from which flows the entirety of our redemption.[26] Union played a central role in the theology of the English Puritans, for whom it has been described by one historian as "the existential nerve" of their piety.[27] Likewise, among twentieth-century and contemporary Reformed theologians, union with Christ continues to function as the key to rightly aligning justification, sanctification, and the very idea of an authentically Christian spiritual life: "Union with Christ is really the central truth of the whole doctrine of salvation not only in its application but also in its once-for-all accomplishment in the finished work of Christ."[28]

Why has this doctrine been so important for Reformed theologians? Surely in large part it emerged organically, for as the Reformers pursued

---

26 Richard A. Muller, *Calvin and the Reformed Tradition: On the Work of Christ and the Order of Salvation* (Grand Rapids, MI: Baker Academic, 2012), 202–43.

27 R. Tudur Jones, "Union with Christ: The Existential Nerve of Puritan Piety," *Tyndale Bulletin* 41, no. 2 (1990): 186–208, https://doi.org/10.53751/001c.30522.

28 John Murray, *Redemption Accomplished and Applied* (Grand Rapids, MI: Eerdmans, 1955), 161. See also Michael S. Horton, *Covenant and Salvation: Union with Christ* (Louisville: Westminster John Knox, 2007); Richard Gaffin, "The Work of Christ Applied," in *Christian Dogmatics: Reformed Theology for the Church Catholic*, ed. Michael Allen and Scott R. Swain (Grand Rapids, MI: Baker Academic, 2016).

a theology driven by the principle of *sola Scriptura*, they couldn't have helped but notice the centrality of union in the biblical texts themselves: "Once you have had your eyes opened to this concept of union with Christ, you will find it almost everywhere in the New Testament."[29]

And of course, the Reformation more generally was a *solus Christus* (Christ alone) movement, an effort to reclaim and recenter the person and work of Christ from a medieval Catholic religious culture that often allowed him to be functionally obscured. As historian Elsie McKee has noted, medieval theology often, at least in practice, "seemed to make the church with its sacraments, saints, and good works the source of salvation, rather than God," and the lavish attention paid to various saints and the Virgin Mary "seemed to make Christ one among many intercessors."[30] Indeed, early on in his road to reform, Huldrych Zwingli was deeply moved by a poem titled "The Complaint of Jesus." A satirical piece written by the Renaissance humanist Desiderius Erasmus (ca. 1466–1536), the poem imagined Jesus in heaven lamenting that he no longer receives many prayers since they all go toward the company of saints and his mother Mary. Upon reading it, Zwingli "arrived at the opinion and the firm belief that we need no mediator other than Christ."[31] Surely these dissatisfactions with medieval piety and a return to the New Testament emphasis on Christ alone would have left the Reformers primed and ready for a renewed emphasis on the doctrine of union with Christ.

But perhaps above all, union takes a central place in Reformed theology because of the way it effectively solves the puzzle of precisely how justification and sanctification relate to each other. Both blessings are necessarily present in the life of every believer because both blessings

---

29 Anthony A. Hoekema, *Saved by Grace* (Grand Rapids, MI: Eerdmans, 1989), 64.

30 Elsie Anne McKee, "Reformed Worship in the Sixteenth Century," in *Christian Worship in Reformed Churches Past and Present*, ed. Lukas Vischer (Grand Rapids, MI: Eerdmans, 2003), 7.

31 Ulrich Zwingli, *Selected Works*, ed. Samuel Macauley Jackson (Philadelphia: University of Pennsylvania Press, 1972), 2:217. For the historical background, see Carlos M. N. Eire, *Reformations: The Early Modern World, 1450–1650* (New Haven, CT: Yale University Press, 2016), 224.

flow from the same source: Christ himself and our Spirit-wrought union with him. In a classic passage from his *Institutes*, John Calvin explains this as the believer's "double grace" (*duplex gratia*):

> Christ was given to us by God's generosity, to be grasped and possessed by us in faith. By partaking of him, we principally receive a double grace: namely, that being reconciled to God through Christ's blamelessness, we may have in heaven instead of a Judge a gracious Father; and secondly, that sanctified by Christ's spirit we may cultivate blamelessness and purity of life.[32]

This description emphasizes the simultaneous and inseparable nature of justification and sanctification, both of which you receive when you receive Christ. Indeed, what it means to be joined to Christ *is* to have both:

> As Christ cannot be torn into parts, so these two which we perceive in him together and conjointly are inseparable—namely, righteousness [i.e., justification] and sanctification. Whomever, therefore, God receives into grace, on them he at the same time bestows the spirit of adoption [Rom. 8:15], by whose power he remakes them to his own image.[33]

Notice that the reason why justification and sanctification cohere is because Christ himself coheres, and to suggest that a justified person might not also be sanctified (the Catholic charge against Protestants) is to suggest that Christ could be "torn into parts."

When we think about spiritual formation in Reformation perspective, it is vital to grasp that any real growth we achieve flows out of this Spirit-wrought union. This is what distinguishes a biblical *keeping*

---

32 John Calvin, *Institutes of the Christian Religion*, ed. John T. McNeill, trans. Ford Lewis Battles, Library of Christian Classics (Philadelphia: Westminster, 1960), 1:725 (3.11.1).

33 Calvin, *Institutes*, 1:732 (3.11.6).

the heart from a moralistic self-striving. Anyone can engage in spiritual disciplines—indeed, one finds dedicated practitioners of rigorous spiritual techniques across all major religions—but real heart change is the work of God's Spirit alone. Yes, the Spirit uses means, and in the chapters that follow, we examine the means that Reformation-minded Protestants have historically used. But by following the Reformers in recognizing that justification and sanctification exist as distinct but inseparable realities, both flowing from union with Christ, we can rest in the knowledge that our justification is secure and finished while vigorously pursuing Spirit-empowered sanctification. Knowing that our justification is final, finished, and perfect, we can joyfully give ourselves to the work of spiritual formation.[34]

A Reformed Approach to Spiritual Formation

Having considered how Reformed theology's emphasis on union with Christ reconciles the apparent tension between the call to rest in justification and the call to work in sanctification, we can now give some further thought to how this theological foundation shapes a distinctive approach to spiritual formation. In chapter 1, we defined spiritual formation as the conscious process by which we seek to heighten and satisfy our Spirit-given thirst for God (Ps. 42:1–2) through divinely appointed means and with a view toward "work[ing] out [our] own salvation with fear and trembling" (Phil. 2:12) and becoming "mature in Christ" (Col. 1:28). This pursuit would presumably be attractive to Christians across a range of traditions, and yet we know that not all traditions within historic Christianity pursue spiritual formation in quite the same way.[35]

There are emphases and nuances that distinguish a Reformed approach to growing in the Christian life from other approaches to the

---

34 Although there have been many wonderful expositions of how justification and sanctification relate to each other, if I had to recommend just one, it would probably be John Murray's treatment in *Redemption Accomplished and Applied*, 117–50.

35 See, e.g., Bruce A. Demarest, ed., *Four Views on Christian Spirituality*, Counterpoints (Grand Rapids, MI: Zondervan, 2012).

same. And as we mentioned in the previous chapter, one legitimate criticism of some manifestations of the spiritual formation movement within evangelicalism is that it has tended to inappropriately flatten those distinctions, suggesting that the spiritual insights of a Martin Luther might be happily blended with those of a Roman Catholic like Thomas Merton without fully appreciating how Christian thinkers' approaches to spiritual formation cannot be so easily extricated from the theological assumptions that underlie them. As historian Steven Ozment observes, "At the base of all the religious changes brought about by the Reformation lay the new theology of justification by faith."[36] In other words, the Reformation's theology of salvation profoundly shaped its approach to spiritual formation, and one cannot abandon the latter without losing something of the former along the way.

With that in mind, let us now identify three interrelated emphases that characterize a distinctively Reformed approach to spiritual formation. In putting these forward, I don't intend to imply that they are found exclusively within the Reformed tradition. All three of the emphases can find points of contact and congruity across a range of Christian expressions. That said, it is also true that their particular arrangement, proportion, and conjunction within the Reformed tradition constitute a distinctive constellation, even if the constituent parts are not the sole possession of Reformed Christianity. Here we set down the three emphases in summary form, but listen for them to recur again and again in the pages that follow. Each one represents a leitmotif marking an important, repeated aspect of spiritual formation in a Reformation key.

Word Centered

A foundational conviction sits at the heart of Reformed spirituality and, consequently, at the heart of everything else we say in this book: God's people are most profoundly shaped and formed by God's word. "Those

---

36 Steven E. Ozment, *The Age of Reform, 1250–1550: An Intellectual and Religious History of Late Medieval and Reformation Europe* (New Haven, CT: Yale University Press, 1980), 231.

Christians, therefore, who are most diligent in attending upon the Word in public and private," explained nineteenth-century Princeton theologian Archibald Alexander, "will be most likely to make progress in piety."[37] Or as another Princeton theologian, B. B. Warfield, would memorably put it, "Life close to God's Word is life close to God."[38] In chapter 3, we examine the role of Scripture in the Christian life and return to this idea at some length, but for now it is important to underscore that a Reformed approach to spiritual formation is always profoundly word centered and that this relentless return to Scripture as the basis of authentic spirituality is something that has historically distinguished Reformation-minded Protestants from their Roman Catholic and Eastern Orthodox counterparts.

This should not surprise us since the centering—or rather, recentering—of God's word sat atop the agenda for the Protestant Reformers. "Though they differed in many respects," observes historian Helmut Puff, "all Protestant confessions shared a concern with getting the Word out to believers."[39] Such a concern for the primacy of Scripture had both a positive and a negative element. Positively, the Reformers saw clearly that the Bible itself commends God's word as that through which God shapes his people. In the beginning, God created all that is through his powerful, world-making word (Gen. 1:1). Abraham was set apart through God's word of promise (Gen. 12:1). And as the Israelites gathered at Sinai, they waited together to *hear* what God would *say*: "So Moses came and called the elders of the people and set before them all these words that the LORD had commanded him" (Ex. 19:7).

Again and again, the Old Testament portrays God's people as a people of the word, holding fast to God's promise until the fullness of time, when the eternal Word, who "was with God" and "was God," would

---

37 Archibald Alexander, *Thoughts on Religious Experience* (Edinburgh: Banner of Truth, 2020), 176.

38 Benjamin B. Warfield, *Selected Shorter Writings of Benjamin B. Warfield*, ed. John E. Meeter (Nutley, NJ: Presbyterian and Reformed, 1970), 2:485.

39 Helmut Puff, "The Word," in *The Oxford Handbook of the Protestant Reformations*, ed. Ulinka Rublack (Oxford: Oxford University Press, 2017), 399.

become flesh, dwelling among his people, "full of grace and truth" (John 1:1, 14). When one combines the Bible's basic, overriding redemptive-historical orientation toward the Word and the words of God with the New Testament's consistent assumption that a Christian pastor's first priority is to "present [himself] to God as one approved, a worker . . . rightly handling the word of truth" (2 Tim. 2:15), one can clearly see how the Reformers' positive agenda began with the need to prioritize the word of God for the people of God.

Alongside this positive move *toward* Scripture, the Reformers also wanted to move *away* from the tendencies within medieval Catholicism to minimize the role of the word in the lives of God's people. Whether through claiming that extrabiblical tradition was equal to (or, in practice, functionally superior to) Scripture[40] or through identifying the ever more elaborate sacramental system (rather than the ministry of the word) as the primary locus of God's salvation and grace, medieval Catholicism consistently subordinated Scripture in ways that the Reformers found offensive and unbiblical. Regarding the sacraments, it is certainly not that the Reformers rejected them or had little interest in them—far from it. Rather, they believed that medieval Catholicism had become unduly tilted toward an overemphasis on the sacraments and their role in shaping the Christian community, and the Reformers sought to redress the balance.

By prioritizing the word, the Reformers created a stark contrast with the medieval context out of which they arose, and this contrast continues to differentiate a Reformation-minded approach to spiritual formation in the present day. To see the difference, consider the following passage from the Eastern Orthodox bishop Kallistos Ware (1934–2022):

---

40 For example, here is Sylvester Prierias (1456–1527) writing in 1518 in response to Martin Luther and his recently published Ninety-Five Theses: "Whoever does not hold fast to the teachings of the Roman Church and of the Pope as the infallible rule of faith, from which even Holy Scripture draws its strength and authority, is a heretic." Quoted in Kevin Vanhoozer, *Biblical Authority after Babel: Retrieving the Solas in the Spirit of Mere Protestant Christianity* (Grand Rapids, MI: Brazos, 2016), 112.

The spiritual Way presupposes not only life in the Church but life in the sacraments. As Nicolas Cabasilas affirms with great emphasis, it is the sacraments that constitute our life in Christ. . . . [T]he whole of the ascetic and mystical life is a deepening and realization of our Eucharistic union with Christ the Saviour. In the Orthodox Church Communion is given to infants from the moment of their Baptism onwards. . . . So [an Eastern Orthodox Christian's] experience of Holy Communion extends over the whole range of his conscious life. It is above all through Communion that the Christian is made one with and in Christ, "christified," "ingodded" or "deified"; it is above all through Communion that he receives the firstfruits of eternity.[41]

Ware communicates with some vigor a sense that growth in the Christian life centers on the sacraments generally and on the bread and wine given in Communion especially.

Again, it's not as if an evangelical Protestant can't sympathize with any of these sentiments if rightly qualified. But contrast Ware's approach to spiritual formation with the following passage from D. A. Carson, who, though writing in the late twentieth century, speaks well for Reformation-minded Protestants in any age as he explains the relationship between evangelical spirituality and the word:

On the night he was betrayed, Jesus prayed, "Sanctify them by the truth; your word is truth" (John 17:17)—and there will never be much sanctification apart from the word of truth. It is the entrance of God's Word that brings light. It is constant meditation on God's law that distinguishes the wise from the unwise, the just from the unjust (Psalm 1). . . . [T]he heavy stress in Scripture on understanding, absorbing, meditating upon, proclaiming, memorizing ("hiding

41 Kallistos Ware, *The Orthodox Way*, rev. ed. (Crestwood, NY: St. Vladimir's Seminary Press, 1995), 108–9.

it in one's heart"), reading, and hearing the word of God is so striking that it will be ignored at our peril. That is why the best of the evangelical heritage has always emphasized what might be called the spirituality of the Word.[42]

Carson's comments are both descriptive and prescriptive, accurately describing the stance that Protestant evangelicals have historically adopted and pointing forward toward the path we must continue to tread. And while evangelicalism's word-centered approach is often criticized by Orthodox and Catholic observers, note the following from Eastern Orthodox theologian Bradley Nassif:

> But what have we to say about average laypeople in our parishes? Can we honestly say they know the Bible well? Or even as proficiently as evangelical Protestants do today? I don't think so. Fortunately, this is beginning to change. Orthodox Christians in America probably know the Bible better than their counterparts outside the continent due to the positive influence of evangelicalism on Orthodox parishioners. Likewise, Catholic laypeople in North America probably know the Bible better than their counterparts outside America for the same reason.[43]

Nassif's observations highlight both the distinctively word-centered nature of evangelicalism and the appeal that such an emphasis can hold for those outside the tradition. Reformed spirituality is word-centered spirituality, a conviction to which we return many times throughout this book and that leads neatly to our second distinctively Reformed emphasis.

---

42 D. A. Carson, "When Is Spirituality Spiritual? Reflections on Some Problems of Definition," *Journal of the Evangelical Theological Society* 37, no. 3 (1994): 393.

43 Bradley Nassif, "Response" to Scott Hahn, "'Come to the Father': The Fact at the Foundation of Catholic Spirituality," in Demarest, *Four Views on Christian Spirituality*, 99.

Marked by a Biblical Simplicity

A Reformed approach to spiritual formation is marked by a biblical simplicity. It is not "simplistic" in the pejorative sense; rather, it is simple insofar as it is a spirituality shorn of all extrabiblical accretions. The appeal of such biblically bounded simplicity flows directly out of the previous emphasis on the centrality of God's word. For the Reformers, the centrality of Scripture entailed both the word-centered approach just described and the requirement that our spiritual formation should be directed by what we read there. According to John Owen, holiness among God's people "consists in their conformity to the revealed will of God." For Owen, when considering any "outward actions and duties, private and public, of piety, of righteousness, towards ourselves or others," God's word "is the rule of our holiness." To the extent that "what we are and what we do" conform to what God has revealed, "so far are we holy, and no farther."[44]

We touched on this point already in the previous chapter when we maintained that spiritual formation ought to employ only God-appointed means, and now it is important to recognize that this emphasis is distinctively Reformed, one that flows out of both the tradition's commitment to *sola Scriptura* and its pervasive critique of idolatry in life and worship. As Leland Ryken concludes, "If we are looking for a principle that will unify the various facets of the public worship services of the Puritans, the idea of simplicity will suffice."[45] In this spirit, the Reformed pressed for things like a simplified ecclesiology characterized by fewer church offices and the elimination of rank and hierarchy among ordained ministers. They sought a simplified approach to the sacraments, reducing the number of sacraments from seven to two and significantly simplifying the ceremonial that attached to those they retained. They

44 John Owen, *A Discourse concerning the Holy Spirit*, in *The Works of John Owen*, ed. William H. Goold (Philadelphia, 1869), 3:470–71.

45 Leland Ryken, *Worldly Saints: The Puritans as They Really Were* (Grand Rapids, MI: Zondervan, 1990), 119.

radically simplified their soteriology by eliminating, among other things, unbiblical Marian devotion, the cult of the saints and their "treasury of merit," and the elaborate system of mortal and venial sins along with the sacrament of penance that remedied them. And of course, the Reformed radically simplified worship and liturgy, removing images and statuary altogether and greatly reducing the complexity of things like the liturgical year, the use of music, and ministerial dress.[46]

This commitment to biblical simplicity profoundly shapes a Reformed approach to spiritual formation, a fact that becomes immediately evident when one considers non-Reformed alternatives. Such alternatives often draw on the mystical theology of ancient and medieval authors and can be very complex indeed, typically dividing progress in the spiritual life into multiple formal stages through which one may pass. For example, Eastern Orthodox theologian Kallistos Ware explains that "it is customary likewise to divide the spiritual Way into three stages." The different theologians he then draws on—a group including Gregory of Nyssa (ca. 335–ca. 394), Pseudo-Dionysius (fl. 500), and Maximus the Confessor (ca. 580–662)—exhibit some variation in precisely how they characterize the three stages, but the tripartite division itself seems to remain a constant. Ware ultimately settles on a sequence of "the practice of the virtues," "the contemplation of nature," and "*theologia* or 'theology' in the strict sense of the word, that is, the contemplation of God himself."[47]

While Reformed theologians are happy to talk about progress and growth in the Christian life, this tendency to conceptualize the spiritual life in terms of formal, discrete, normative stages is foreign to the tradition because, in the Reformers' view, such distinctions are foreign to the Bible itself. The example given above is from an Eastern Orthodox theologian, but similar patterns can be found among Roman Catholic

46 Philip Benedict, *Christ's Churches Purely Reformed: A Social History of Calvinism* (New Haven, CT: Yale University Press, 2002), 491–509.

47 Ware, *Orthodox Way*, 105–6.

writers as well. Indeed, the spiritual resources and consequent obligations for those pursuing spiritual formation within the Roman Catholic tradition are, if anything, even more elaborate and multifaceted than those available within Orthodoxy.

To illustrate the complexity of Roman Catholic spirituality, consider their sacramental system. In addition to the seven sacraments themselves, Rome also endorses a whole range of so-called sacramentals. Though not as significant as the seven sacraments, sacramentals are nonetheless spiritually significant items through which the faithful may obtain a blessing.[48] They are "sacred signs instituted by the Church" that "prepare men to receive the fruit of the sacraments and sanctify different circumstances of life."[49] Common examples would include things like holy water, crucifixes, incense, and rosaries, but the list of possible sacramentals is, by its very nature, unbounded, as Roman Catholic priest Richard Whinder explains:

> The Church has the power to institute new sacramentals as the needs of the faithful require. This means that, in theory, there could be an almost infinite number of sacramentals. In practice, there are indeed a great number—too many for us to do justice to them fully here. We can only offer an introduction which we hope will be useful.[50]

Whinder goes on to detail a wide array of Roman Catholic sacramentals, a list that includes things like blessed palm branches, medals bearing the images of saints, and relics divided into three "classes" based on their proximity to the saint from whom they derive their significance. Also included is an assortment of scapulars (rectangular pieces of cloth draped over the front and back of the body), including the "Brown Scapular of

---

48 Euan Cameron, *Enchanted Europe: Superstition, Reason, and Religion, 1250–1750* (Oxford: Oxford University Press, 2010), 58–62.

49 *Catechism of the Catholic Church*, sec. 1677.

50 Richard Whinder, *Sacramentals: Explaining Actions, Signs and Objects That Catholics Use* (London: Catholic Truth Society, 2009), 6.

Our Lady of Mount Carmel," to which is attached "a promise of Our Lady" that she "will personally intervene to release from purgatory, on the first Saturday following their death, anyone who has worn the brown scapular, observed chastity and recited the Little Office of Our Lady." Whinder also points to various kinds of sacred oil, "a notable example" being "the oil of St. Walburga," which is "collected by the nuns of the convent in which [Walburga's] tomb is situated" and "can be used in private devotion or kept as a memento of pilgrimage."[51]

Why include such a lengthy description of Roman Catholic sacramentals? When we describe a Reformed approach to spiritual formation as being marked out by a biblical simplicity, it is difficult to feel the force of that distinctive emphasis unless one first grasps the highly elaborate array of extrabiblical practices against which the Reformers were reacting and that continue to characterize many non-Reformed approaches to piety up to the present day. Such is the contrast on this point that many evangelical converts to Roman Catholicism describe the experience coming to Rome as one in which their spiritual world was enlarged or expanded. One such convert writes,

> Protestantism has (rightly or wrongly) been described as a "religion of the book"; that is to say, the Bible is considered the nucleus of Protestantism, and very little else is considered relevant or part and parcel of Christianity. . . . Protestantism is paltry, and this paltriness just kept me searching for something more.[52]

Such statements are common among those raised in evangelical churches who end up leaving them for what they regard as "richer" and "fuller" religious traditions. And when they are well framed and set against the

---

51 Whinder, *Sacramentals*, 23, 34, 36–37, 26.

52 Jeremiah Cowart, "Crawl, Walk, Run: My Progression toward Mother Church," in *Evangelical Exodus: Evangelical Seminarians and Their Paths to Rome*, ed. Douglas M. Beaumont and Francis Beckwith (San Francisco: Ignatius, 2016), 79–80.

backdrop of an evangelical pop culture that at times can feel "paltry" and lacking weight, it's not hard to feel the allure of such claims.

And yet when one puts aside the high-handed rhetoric and examines what the "something more" on offer within Roman Catholic piety actually entails, one finds a host of items and practices that are nowhere mentioned in the Bible, things like scapulars, relics, and the oil of Saint Walburga. But if this is the "more" one requires to avoid "paltriness," how does such a charge avoid making an indictment against the Bible itself? For whatever "paltriness" one might find in the shallow end of the pop-evangelical pool, the Bible is decidedly *not* "paltry." For the psalmist, spiritual plenitude and fullness is found in God's word, and one need not look beyond it for an imagined spiritual "more":

> How sweet are your words to my taste,
> > sweeter than honey to my mouth!
> Through your precepts I get understanding;
> > therefore I hate every false way. (Ps. 119:103–104)

This is the biblical simplicity championed by the Reformers, and insofar as they are following Psalm 119 in delighting in the "honey" of God's word alone, then we would be wise to follow their lead.

Committed to Engaging the Heart via the Mind

Third and finally, the Reformed authors on whom we draw in this book consistently affirm that the ordinary God-ordained means for keeping the heart and cultivating God-honoring affections involve setting one's mind on God's truth. This emphasis flows from the more general Reformation orientation toward a word-centered piety, for one encounters God's truth within and through God's word. Here we return to the interplay of head and heart, a theme that recurs again and again in what follows. In setting forth a distinctively Reformed approach to spiritual formation, we must recognize both the tradition's great emphasis on the heart and the affections and the way it views the mind as the vehicle through which such affections are formed.

The Reformed emphasis on the heart and the affections emerged quite naturally from the context out of which the tradition arose. Reacting as they did against a medieval Christendom in which nominal Christian affiliation was required by the state, the Reformers were highly attuned to the reality that participating outwardly in religious ceremony cannot guarantee that a person's heart is in the right place. As we touched on in the previous chapter, this is a very biblical insight:

This people honors me with their lips,
   but their heart is far from me. (Matt. 15:8)

Medieval Catholicism stressed (as Roman Catholicism does today) the objective, outward reality and efficacy of the church and its sacramental life: attending Mass, visiting the priest for confession, doing penances as prescribed, contacting holy items like relics and other sacramentals, visiting sacred sites on pilgrimage, and so forth. It's not that such thinking entirely ignores the inner person, but it's a question of emphasis. Similarly, for the Reformers, it's not that they completely disregarded the significance of the external and objective—the Reformers did not eliminate things like baptism, the Lord's Supper, or the requirement to be physically present for worship—but they did seek to reestablish a biblical balance by paying more attention to the intent of the worshiper and the keeping of the heart.

And in this connection, Reformed authors often stress the affections emerging from the heart as the most reliable guide to its inner disposition and intent. Such godly longings and desires are, according to the Puritan Richard Sibbes, "the breathings of the Spirit" that, more plainly than anything else, "shew the temper and frame of the soul."[53] In his

---

53 Richard Sibbes, quoted in Alec Ryrie, *Being Protestant in Reformation Britain* (Oxford: Oxford University Press, 2013), 67.

book *The Distinguishing Marks of a Work of the Spirit of God*, Jonathan Edwards surveyed a range of external marks or signs to which people often look but then concluded that none of them are as significant as the desires of the heart:

> The influence of the Spirit of God is yet more abundantly manifest, if persons have their hearts drawn off from the world, and weaned from the objects of their worldly lusts, and taken off from worldly pursuits, by the sense they have of the excellency of divine things, and the affection they have to those spiritual enjoyments of another world, that are promised in the gospel.[54]

Such an emphasis, of course, like anything else, can itself become imbalanced, and at its worst, this aspect of Reformed piety can devolve into a sort of neurotic, unhealthy introspection—as seen at times among the Puritans. But when this happens, it indicates a failure to take the gospel seriously rather than providing a reason to deprioritize the heart. For throughout Scripture one finds a tight and necessary connection between God-glorifying outward worship and real, inward, Holy Spirit–wrought heart change, and it is precisely this connection that the Puritans sought to honor and protect through their emphasis on right affections as a marker of authentically Christian spirituality.

But how ought one to go about stirring and cultivating such affections? How does one best *keep the heart*? Different answers have been given. Many, as we've already noted, have concluded that regular religious ritual is the most appropriate tool for the task, trusting that the rhythms of the church's sacramental life will tune the heart with an *ex opere operato* inevitability.[55] Others have looked to beauty, art, or

---

54 Jonathan Edwards, *The Works of Jonathan Edwards* (Peabody, MA: Hendrickson, 2006), 2:267.

55 This Latin term means "by the work performed" and communicates the "assumption of medieval scholasticism and Roman Catholicism that the correct and churchly performance of the rite

music as the primary vehicles of spiritual delight. By contrast, during the third and fourth centuries, some Christians ventured out alone into wild places to search for a spiritual satisfaction they believed would come from extreme self-denial. Thus they embarked, not as those pursuing aesthetics but as practicing ascetics: "The desert sages warred against the addictive, anxious, craving tendencies within and set out to lead a hard life of grinding down their passions through solitude, simplicity, and fasting."[56] Few contemporary evangelicals seem inclined toward that particular path, but a growing number are drawn toward the idea that the "way to the heart is through the body" and that real spiritual formation occurs through the deliberate practice of embodied rituals.[57]

These various answers have lessons to teach us, and I do not want to imply otherwise. Who would deny that music is a wonderful blessing to the people of God and has the power to stir the heart deeply? Who could possibly quarrel with the assertion that a biblically defined self-denial is at the heart of discipleship (Matt. 16:24)? The question here, as elsewhere, is about arriving at a biblical balance, placing our accents in the right places, and keeping primary what Scripture makes primary. And when asked about the primary means through which one engages the heart, the Reformed tradition, following Scripture, answers that the affections of regenerate Christians are primarily stirred through reflecting on God's truth as revealed in his word:

Oh how I love your law!
　　It is my meditation all the day. (Ps. 119:97)

---

conveys grace to the recipient," a view of the sacraments that "is denied by both Lutherans and Reformed." Richard Muller, *Dictionary of Latin and Greek Theological Terms: Drawn Principally from Protestant Scholastic Theology*, 2nd ed. (Grand Rapids, MI: Baker Academic, 2017), 113.

56　Jason M. Baxter, *An Introduction to Christian Mysticism: Recovering the Wildness of Spiritual Life* (Grand Rapids, MI: Baker Academic, 2021), 105.

57　James K. A. Smith, *You Are What You Love: The Spiritual Power of Habit* (Grand Rapids, MI: Brazos, 2016), 46. We will return to the role of the body in spiritual formation in chap. 9.

As a result of this conviction, Reformed Christians have historically been skeptical of any proposal that seems to bypass the rational faculties in an attempt to more directly influence the heart.

In this connection, historian Alec Ryrie argues that "the intellectualism of early Protestantism is hard to overestimate." He continues,

> Protestantism was a movement born and bred in universities, and it aspired to turn Christendom into a giant university, in which Christians would spend their time in private study or in attending the lectures and seminars which they called sermons, prophesyings, and conferences. . . . Protestants stressed learning because they believed that salvation came, not merely through faith, but through well-informed faith.[58]

Upon reading that assessment, some might get a bit nervous. Won't this sort of intellectual approach to Christianity lead to an emotionally barren faith, a religion full of propositions asserted and arguments made yet devoid of the joy, love, and overflowing life that Scripture so heartily endorses? One can certainly find individual and perhaps even institutional examples of nominally Reformed Christians who seem to fit that stereotype. But while a lack of spiritual heat might be evident in such cases, it is not at all evident that a Reformation approach to piety is what lowered the temperature. Listen to how Ashbel Green (1762–1848) explained it in an 1831 address to Princeton Seminary students:

> I am ready to admit, and do freely admit, that it is very possible a man may be frozen to the core in the ice of biblical criticism, even of orthodox doctrine. But I deny that the truths and study of the Bible, and the orthodox faith, ever did, by their direct and proper influence, freeze any man. It was something else, or the want of something else, that froze him, if he was frozen; and if he was ever thawed out into spiritual life and

---

58 Ryrie, *Reformation Britain*, 261–62.

vigor, the truths of the Bible and the orthodox faith, in the hand of the Spirit of God, were the instrument of producing this desirable change.[59]

Or in the rather more pithy formulation of one Puritan writer, "As the head acts, the heart glows."[60] The Puritan Richard Baxter (1615–1691) sounded a similar note when he urged his people to pursue "knowledge and sound understandings." Why was this so important? As Baxter argued, "Your understandings are the inlet or entrance to the whole soul, . . . and if the enemy be once let in there, the whole city will quickly be his own." Thus, he concluded that "a sound judgment" leads to "soundness of heart and life" and that Christians must "let the Bible be much in [their] hands and hearts."[61] Not only did these authors see no contradiction between a mind focused on God's truth and a heart alive for God's service, they actually believed that the former was the God-ordained means through which the latter is achieved.

It is here that we desperately need to keep steady and retrieve the sorts of lessons in godliness that people like Green and Baxter would be quick to teach us. Is it possible to engage in a sort of arid philosophizing that is unappealing, unedifying, and unbiblical? Yes, it is, and if we are guilty on that score, we should repent. But we need to recognize that in recent years, this has not been the primary danger for evangelicalism. Rather, for some time now, evangelicalism has been tempted to embrace an anti-intellectual aversion to thinking and reading and meditating deeply on God's truth, a trend that is also unappealing, unedifying, and unbiblical. What's more, this "juvenilization of American Christianity," as one author termed it, represents a dramatic departure from our Reformation heritage.[62]

---

59 Ashbel Green, "Address to the Students," in *Princeton and the Work of the Christian Ministry*, ed. James M. Garretson (Edinburgh: Banner of Truth, 2012), 2:9–11.

60 Nathanael Ranew, *Solitude Improved by Divine Meditation* (Grand Rapids, MI: Soli Deo Gloria, 2019), 45.

61 Richard Baxter, *The Practical Works of Richard Baxter* (London: James Duncan, 1830), 12:4–5.

62 Thomas E. Bergler, *The Juvenilization of American Christianity* (Grand Rapids, MI: Eerdmans, 2012).

Even as he famously documented "the scandal of the evangelical mind," Mark Noll was quick to note that "the twentieth-century evangelical neglect of the mind is an aberration in a long history of Protestant efforts to give the intellect its due." The Reformers, Noll continues, "saw quickly that the cultivation of a more biblical spirituality required a more thorough attention to the mind."[63] And before Noll, even as historian Richard Hofstadter savaged the Christian "evangelical spirit" as contributing mightily to a more general trend of "anti-intellectualism in American life," he nonetheless identified the central villain as a *departure from* rather than a *faithfulness to* the early modern spirit and ethos of New England Puritanism. For Hofstadter, what led to a decline in American religious life was a failure to maintain Puritanism's "delicate balance between intellect, which was esteemed as essential to true religion in New England, and emotion, which was necessary to the strength and durability of Puritan piety."[64]

A burden of this book is to recapture something of that "delicate balance." Spiritual formation in a Reformation key takes seriously the biblical insight that born-again believers are marked by a fruitful synergy between head and heart. Indeed, Joel Beeke and Mark Jones observe that "the genius of genuine Reformed piety is that it marries theology and piety so that head, heart, and hand motivate one another to live for God's glory and our neighbor's well-being."[65] Through regeneration, the Holy Spirit changes the heart and gives a new spiritual appetite. For such a regenerate person, firing the mind with God's truth becomes the primary way to whet the appetite and stir up a greater taste and desire for God and the things of God. This is a theme that marks out Reformed piety, one to which we return again and again in the pages that follow.

---

63   Mark A. Noll, *The Scandal of the Evangelical Mind* (Grand Rapids, MI: Eerdmans, 1994), 36.
64   Richard Hofstadter, *Anti-Intellectualism in American Life* (New York: Vintage Books, 1962), 64.
65   Joel R. Beeke and Mark Jones, *A Puritan Theology: Doctrine for Life* (Grand Rapids, MI: Reformation Heritage Books, 2012), 849.

PART 2

THE REFORMATION
TRIANGLE

3

Scripture

Hearing from God

YOUR EXPERIENCE MAY VARY, but among many of the evangelical Christians I know, a new trend has been quietly gaining ground in recent years: feeling bad about the state of one's "quiet time." Whether the bad feelings flow from boredom and confusion while doing one's morning devotions or regret and melancholy after *not* doing them, guilt over the ubiquitous evangelical practice is palpable. In fact, a quick Google search for "quiet time guilt" yields thousands of hits. Spread across blogs, books, and Reddit threads, stories range from heavy-handed, quiet-time-prescribing youth pastors and autobiographical laments over past failures to keep a routine to accusations that a sort of legalism is ineradicably baked into the very idea of the quiet time. The quiet time even has its own entry on Wikipedia, an entry that conspicuously includes a section labeled "Criticism." I must confess to occasionally contributing to this sea of devotional discontent, offering smug remarks about the relative historical recency of the quiet time and unceremoniously abandoning more than one Bible-in-a-year reading plan somewhere between Leviticus and Numbers.

The guilt, the frustration, the confusion—it's all understandable really. That said, I don't think it's wise to suggest from there that the quiet time is inherently and irredeemably problematic. No, the Bible does not command a particular daily devotional routine with a prescribed number of minutes spent and chapters read. No, one should not feel excessive guilt about not necessarily conforming to any given devotional prescription. Yes, one's capacity to sustain certain spiritual disciplines quite understandably varies based on one's season and context. And yes, the kingdom of heaven is surely filled with untold numbers of born-again believers who lacked access in this life to either personal copies of Scripture or the ability to read them. But it's also true that the Psalter begins with a description of the blessed as those marked by delighting in and constantly meditating on God's word (Ps. 1:1–2), and this call to love Scripture and to be transformed by constant, lifelong engagement with it is a consistent biblical theme from Genesis to Revelation—one that applies to all believers in every time and place.

Moreover, for our present purposes, even if we don't want to use the term *quiet time*, we must recognize that the basic idea behind it is completely in step with the spirit and practice of historic Reformation piety. As mentioned earlier, John Flavel drew on Proverbs 4:23 to describe the Christian's spiritual life as a struggle to "keep the heart with God" under all life's changing circumstances. According to Flavel, "Here lies the very pinch and stress of religion."[1] But if this is such a difficulty, how do we overcome it? How do we *keep the heart*? Flavel had much to say on this point, but the primary pressing need was, he told believers, "Let the word of Christ dwell in you richly" (Col. 3:16):

> If you would thus keep your hearts as hath been persuaded, then furnish your hearts richly with the Word of God, which is their best preservative against sin. Keep the Word, and the Word will keep you.

---

1   John Flavel, *The Works of John Flavel* (London: Banner of Truth, 1968), 5:423.

. . . It is the slipperiness of our hearts in reference to the Word that causes so many slips in our lives. . . . We never lose our hearts till they have first lost the efficacious and powerful impressions of the Word.[2]

In offering this advice, Flavel was marching in time with the rhythms of historic Reformation Christianity and, we should be quick to add, the testimony of Scripture itself. Indeed, it is worth noting that Proverbs 4:23, the verse from which Flavel derives the phrase *keeping the heart*, is set within a passage that itself directly connects keeping the heart with internalizing divinely inspired words:

> My son, be attentive to my words;
>> incline your ear to my sayings.
> Let them not escape from your sight;
>> keep them within your heart.
> For they are life to those who find them,
>> and healing to all their flesh.
> Keep your heart with all vigilance,
>> for from it flow the springs of life. (Prov. 4:20–23)

In a Reformed context, then, when we talk about spiritual formation, we are always, in one way or another, talking about engaging with God's word. The reason for this is simple: Scripture is God's appointed means for communing with his people. And it is through communion with the living God that the people of God are conformed more and more to his likeness. As the Dutch theologian Herman Bavinck (1854–1921) explained, it is in Scripture that "God daily comes to his people. In it he speaks to his people, not from afar but from nearby. . . . Scripture is the ongoing rapport between heaven and earth."[3]

---

2 John Flavel, *The Whole Works of the Rev. Mr. John Flavel* (London: W. Baynes and Son, 1820), 5:504–5.

3 Herman Bavinck, *Reformed Dogmatics*, ed. John Bolt, trans. John Vriend (Grand Rapids, MI: Baker Academic, 2003), 1:385.

Thus the Bible is not just one tool among many in our spiritual formation tool kit, but rather, whether directly or indirectly, the *whole* of our spiritual formation flows out from our engagement with it. You read Scripture and hear God's voice addressed to you. You meditate on Scripture and think about what he has said. Then your prayers, your words back to God, are a response to his prior word to you, and your prayers, in turn, are profoundly shaped in both form and content by the words of Scripture. When you are with other believers, you exhort and encourage and rebuke one another according to Scripture. Likewise, when you examine yourself, you measure your vices and your virtues not according to the cultural standards of the moment but according to the eternal standards set forth in God's word. When you reflect on your life and the places God has providentially led you, you process and contextualize that journey within the promises and thought world of Scripture. For Reformation-minded Christians, spiritual formation cannot be reduced to Bible reading, but it can also never be separated from it.

Because spiritual formation in a Protestant context is thus always a word-based affair, there is a sense in which it feels improper to isolate Scripture within a single chapter in a book like this. It is a move that potentially communicates that engaging with God's word is simply one more strategy, technique, or discipline one might employ as part of one's larger pursuit of "spirituality." Sometimes this idea seems to be implied even within ostensibly Protestant literature on spiritual formation. Often such books enumerate various spiritual disciplines and include something like "Bible study" or "Bible reading" as one more item on the list alongside other options. The list from one such book looks like this:

There are many great spiritual disciplines—the prayer of examen, retreats, spiritual direction, service, fellowship in small groups, worship, giving, Bible study, devotional reading, centering prayer, fasting, Scripture memorization, *lectio divina*, confession, journaling, intercession, to name a few. They are each wonderful tools and gifts for us in our following of Jesus.[4]

The implication here, whether intended by the author or not, is that all the practices listed could be equally useful depending on the season, circumstances, and personality of the individual.

Now it should be said clearly that in practice the author quoted here and many others who write in a similar way seem to highly prize Scripture, and it strikes me as wholly unlikely that they would ever imagine a Christian walk that did not include regular engagement with God's word. And yet much discourse on spiritual disciplines and spiritual formation often seems to fall short of making unmistakably clear and explicit what was a definite nonnegotiable for the Reformers and their spiritual heirs: life with God is life with and in his word. Yes, all of life and the diverse range of our human experiences provide opportunities for spiritual growth. But as we discussed in chapter 1, the Christian call to "do all to the glory of God" (1 Cor. 10:31) and the endless variety of ways that God makes "all things work together for good" (Rom. 8:28) should be understood more broadly as part of our sanctification. Our spiritual formation represents a subcategory within that broader, all-encompassing holistic work of God, and it is confusing to lump potentially anything and everything a believer might experience or engage in under the rubric of spiritual formation. This is because, as the Reformers saw clearly, the Bible itself consistently identifies the word of God as the means we must use if we hope to be spiritually shaped and formed. If I want to be "like a tree planted / by streams of water / that yields its fruit in its season," then the answer is not to create an individualized pastiche of attractive disciplines from a list limited only by my imagination. Rather, the God-given means at

4   Peter Scazzero, *Emotionally Healthy Spirituality: Unleash a Revolution in Your Life in Christ* (Nashville: Thomas Nelson, 2011), 156.

my disposal is clear and is universally applicable: I need to take "delight in the law of the Lord" and meditate on it "day and night" (Ps. 1:2–3).

In this book, then, even as we explore several spiritual disciplines, or "means of grace," over the ensuing chapters, we want to always keep in mind the way that Scripture informs and undergirds every one of them.[5] One way we can mitigate inadvertently suggesting that Bible reading is simply one more potential help along the way is to situate this chapter on Scripture within a larger section we are calling the "Reformation triangle." At the heart of historic Protestant spiritual formation is a triangulated relationship between Scripture, meditation, and prayer. Taken together, these three can be conceived as a conversation between the believer and God: we hear from God through his word, we reflect on what we've heard in meditation, and we then respond to God in prayer. As we touch on here and explore more deeply in subsequent chapters, these three activities were so closely conjoined among early modern Reformed and Puritan authors that they would often be used interchangeably as though they were all actually components of one basic activity. Indeed, in early modern Protestant manuals of piety, one can find these three disciplines treated in varying orders, some starting with prayer as the first duty, others with Scripture reading, still others with meditation. What becomes clear is that the three activities are in some real sense treated as aspects of a single activity: communion with the living God.

In this chapter, we examine in three major movements the first and foundational piece of the Reformation triangle: hearing from God in Holy Scripture. First, we consider more generally the centrality of the word within a Reformation context, briefly revisiting some of the

---

5   From an early stage in the Reformation, Protestant theologians employed the term "means of grace" in connection with both conversion and progressive sanctification. Because we are interested here in the spiritual formation of believers, we will consider the means of grace primarily in terms of progressive sanctification. Richard A. Muller, *Dictionary of Latin and Greek Theological Terms: Drawn Principally from Protestant Scholastic Theology*, 2nd ed. (Grand Rapids, MI: Baker Academic, 2017), 213.

themes we have already explored in previous chapters. Second, we address concerns that some have expressed about the Reformation's insistence on placing God's word at the center of our spiritual formation. These concerns are as old as the Reformation itself but have gained fresh momentum in our contemporary context. Third, we turn our attention to the practicalities of Bible reading for spiritual growth, asking how early modern Protestants might teach and guide us on this crucial point.

The Centrality of the Word within Reformation Thought

In describing the religious culture of early modern Scotland, historian Margo Todd concludes that "Protestantism is above all a religion of the book." As she explains further,

> Particularly in the Calvinist version of the faith, the word—read, preached, sung, remembered and recited back at catechetical exercise or family sermon repetition—became the hallmark of communal worship and individual piety. . . . In principle and in practice, the word defined the culture of Protestantism.[6]

Todd is absolutely correct, and for those of us who would follow in the footsteps of the Reformers, ours too must be, in this sense, "a religion of the book." As noted in the previous chapter, the Reformation more generally reprioritized word over sacrament, shifting the emphasis of religious life away from the priest's celebration of the Mass and onto the people's partaking in the ministry of the word. This shift itself was a response to the Bible's own testimony about what God primarily uses to shape his people. Thus, while the medieval church stressed an ever more elaborate sacramental system, the Bible again and again calls to the faithful in every age, "Let the word of Christ dwell in you richly,

6   Margo Todd, *The Culture of Protestantism in Early Modern Scotland* (New Haven, CT: Yale University Press, 2002), 24–25.

teaching and admonishing one another in all wisdom" (Col. 3:16). As a result, Reformation ministers understood their calling not in terms of a priestly obligation to re-present the sacrifice of Christ in the Mass and hear confessions but rather in terms of the biblical call to "shepherd the flock of God" (1 Pet. 5:2) through the ministry of the word.

In the wonderful, representative early Reformation treatise *Concerning the True Care of Souls* (1538), the Strasbourg pastor Martin Bucer (1491–1551) conceptualized all pastoral ministry in terms of the need to shepherd different types of sheep, each with its own specific needs. So sometimes pastors need to bring lost sheep into the fold, while at other times they need to care for sick and wounded sheep or encourage healthy ones to persevere. But in every case, however varied the task or circumstance, Bucer insisted that the means to be employed was always and ever the same: the ministry of the word. Bucer described it like this:

> Now all this [i.e., all this pastoral work to different kinds of sheep]
> is to be achieved and attained solely through teaching, exhorting,
> warning, disciplining, comforting, pardoning, and reconciling to the
> Lord and his church: in other words the proclaiming of the whole
> word of God.[7]

So all this work, essentially everything the pastor is called to do, is conceptually gathered together by Bucer under this one great heading of word ministry. He categorizes all the various activities that might occupy a pastor's time under the one great activity of "proclaiming the whole word of God" and claims that a pastor's work is to be completed "solely" through this means.

This elevation of the word represented a tremendous shift from a medieval religious culture in which preaching was often infrequent, occasional, and disconnected from the ordinary rhythms of parish

---

7 Martin Bucer, *Concerning the True Care of Souls*, trans. Peter Beale (Edinburgh: Banner of Truth, 2009), 33.

ministry.[8] Every Reformer understood preaching and Scripture as the means through which God creates and builds his church, giving men and women new spiritual life and forming Christ in them (Gal. 4:19). At an ordination service for new Church of England ministers in 1582, the preacher Simon Harward (fl. 1572–1614) opened up Jesus's exhortation to "pray earnestly to the Lord of the harvest to send out laborers into his harvest" (Luke 10:2). What, wondered Harward, would it look like to be a true and faithful laborer in the Lord's harvest field? In developing his answer, he contrasted Reformation ministry with its late medieval Catholic predecessor, explaining that "to be a laborer in the Lord's Harvest, is not . . . to mumble up Masses, and to offer up sacrifice, for the quick and the dead . . . and remit sins at their own pleasure." Instead, Harward insisted, "To be a laborer in the Lord's Harvest, is, to feed the flock of Christ, with the heavenly food of his blessed word, as did the Apostles, Prophets and Evangelists, in the primitive [i.e., early] Church."[9] So for Reformation pastors, the task of building up disciples and shepherding the flock of God was to be accomplished through the means of preaching and teaching God's word.

If the above holds true for Reformation ministry on a corporate level, then we would expect to find something similar when we look at Reformation spiritual formation on an individual level. And indeed, as Protestantism developed its distinctively Bible-based approach to personal piety, Bible reading was increasingly placed at the center of the project. Historian Alec Ryrie argues that "it would be hard to exaggerate the weight which Protestants of all stripes put on Bible reading," an assertion borne out by the Reformers' intense labors to

---

8 It is certainly not the case that preaching was absent from medieval Christianity but rather, as historian Andrew Pettegree observes, that "its impact would have been very uneven. For most parishioners preaching was an occasional event, rather than part of the daily or weekly norm of religious observance." *Reformation and the Culture of Persuasion* (Cambridge: Cambridge University Press, 2005), 12. See also Nicholas Orme, *Going to Church in Medieval England* (New Haven, CT: Yale University Press, 2021), 247–53.

9 Simon Harward, *Two Godlie and Learned Sermons, Preached at Manchester* (London, 1582), n.p.

put Bibles into the hands of every Christian.[10] In John Calvin's Geneva, for example, the registers of the consistory—the administrative body responsible for enforcing church discipline—contain numerous examples of church leaders admonishing church members to abandon Roman Catholic devotional practices (e.g., the use of rosary beads) and to instead purchase Bibles and faithfully read them.[11] Likewise, in Reformation Scotland, authorities passed a law in 1579 requiring that all households reaching certain income thresholds purchase a Bible. In some areas, this requirement was extended to anyone who could read, irrespective of annual income.[12] Records from kirk sessions—the Scottish equivalent of Calvin's consistory—show a special interest among pastors in promoting biblical literacy among their people. Again and again, church leaders wanted to know whether their congregants were reading and wrestling with Scripture, frequently identifying "contempt of the word" as "the mother of error and iniquity" and the source of "the universal coldness and decay of zeal in all estates."[13]

Practically speaking, this Reformed emphasis on personal Bible reading required church leaders to promote literacy among their congregants. Early modern Protestants were, of course, well aware that many in their communities could not read, and it should be underscored that a word-based piety does not necessarily require that capacity. Both hearing the word and reading the word were and remain equally valid ways to encounter and engage with Scripture.[14] That said, early modern Reformers also understood that literacy was a great

---

10   Alec Ryrie, *Being Protestant in Reformation Britain* (Oxford: Oxford University Press, 2013), 270.

11   Philip Benedict, *Christ's Churches Purely Reformed: A Social History of Calvinism* (New Haven, CT: Yale University Press, 2002), 97.

12   Benedict, *Purely Reformed*, 510–11.

13   Todd, *Culture of Protestantism*, 24.

14   In this chapter, we are specifically focusing on *reading* the Bible. Yet this emphasis should not imply that those who, for a whole host of reasons, approach Scripture primarily through the *hearing* of the word are somehow outside the scope of the word-centric piety being described. Indeed, in our day the wealth of digital resources at our disposal opens up tremendous possibilities for those unable to read Scripture for themselves.

gift, and they sought to spread it as widely as possible. In Scotland, for example, the Reformers mandated a school in every parish, these centers of education being seen as "necessary instruments to come to the true meaning and sense of the will of God revealed in his Word."[15] All across the early modern Reformed world, a push for literacy and personal Bible reading was central to their religious vision. Over and against Roman Catholicism's teaching that "the reading of the Bible is not necessary for salvation, or even advisable for every one under all circumstances," Protestants maintained that Scripture was to be the primary means through which Christians—all Christians—were to be spiritually formed and nourished.[16] One study of households in the seventeenth-century French village of Metz found that more than two-thirds of Reformed households owned at least one book (usually a Bible), compared with only 21 percent of Catholic households. Research findings like these have led historian Philip Benedict to conclude that across the Reformation world, "many humble church members . . . did acquire acquaintance with Scripture" and that this represented "a new relation with the printed word characterized by the intensive reading and rereading of the Bible." Moreover, "in this domain, the Reformed differed from their Catholic neighbors."[17]

Another example that can help us appreciate the way Protestant Reformers prioritized individual Bible reading as the centerpiece of their spiritual formation program is the so-called Geneva Bible (1560). Though usually overshadowed by the more famous King James Version (1611), the earlier Geneva Bible represented a major milestone in both English Bible translation and the advancement of a distinctively Protestant approach to spiritual formation. As one scholar notes, "The Geneva Bible transformed the Bible-reading habits of the English and

15 Todd, *Culture of Protestantism*, 59.
16 Joseph Wilhelm and Thomas B. Scannell, *A Manual of Catholic Theology: Based on Scheeben's "Dogmatik,"* 2nd ed. (New York: Benziger Brothers, 1899), 1:60.
17 Benedict, *Purely Reformed*, 516–18.

the Scottish" and was a key "means by which non-specialist reading of the Bible became commonplace."[18] The book was the product of English-speaking exiles who had fled the anti-Protestant persecution of Queen Mary I and sought safety in John Calvin's Geneva. While there, they set to work on a new Bible for an English-speaking audience. The real significance of the Geneva Bible, however, comes not just from its expert translation work but from the way it came loaded with innovative features all aimed at helping everyday people better navigate the sacred text. This, for example, was the first English Bible to use the chapter and verse divisions with which we are all now so familiar. Each chapter begins with a summary statement to guide the reader, marginal notes throughout to help explain the Bible's "hard places," and a sort of index at the back. The book also includes illustrations and maps depicting, among other things, the layout of the tabernacle, the priestly garments worn by the Levitical high priest, and the path taken by the Israelites during their forty years of wilderness wanderings. All these helps were included to assist the "simple" or ordinary reader and to keep him or her from becoming "discouraged."[19]

In this sixteenth-century Bible project, we can feel the heartbeat of the Reformation vision for spiritual formation, a vision of every Christian hearing directly from God in his word and being shaped and formed thereby. To that end, the Geneva Bible's introductory letter to the reader states that the aim of the Christian life is to glorify God and that "this thing is chiefly attained by the knowledge and practice of God's word." Scripture is described as "the light to our paths, the key of the kingdom of heaven, our comfort in affliction, our shield and sword against Satan, the school of all wisdom, the glass wherein

18 Michael Jensen, "'Simply' Reading the Geneva Bible: The Geneva Bible and Its Readers," *Literature and Theology* 9, no. 1 (1995): 31. See also John Barton, *A History of the Bible: The Book and Its Faiths* (London: Allen Lane, 2019), 450; Christopher Hill, *The English Bible and the Seventeenth-Century Revolution* (London: Allen Lane, 1993), 56–62.

19 *The Geneva Bible: A Facsimile of the 1560 Edition* (Peabody, MA: Hendrickson, 2007), "To Our Beloved in the Lord."

we behold God's face, the testimony of his favor, and the only food and nourishment of our souls." In light of this eloquent testimony to the central and indispensable role of Scripture in the life of the believer, it is not surprising to find the Geneva Bible editors urging Christians, "Willingly receive the word of God, earnestly study it, and in all your life practice it, that you may now appear indeed to be the people of God."[20] That final line captures it perfectly: for the Reformers, the people of God are identified as such and differentiated from the world chiefly by their knowledge of and devotion to the word that God breathed out.

The connection, then, between this word-based piety and personal spiritual formation is clear: no real spiritual growth is possible apart from engagement with God's word. But what did this look like in the lives of actual Christian men and women? Consider the following passage taken from a sixteenth-century devotional book, *A Chrystal Glasse for Christian Women* (1591). Attempting to describe and commend "the godly life" of Katherine Stubbes (1570/71–1590), the book portrays a Christian woman whose walk with God is characterized above all by a lively, continuous, heartfelt engagement with God's word: "For her whole heart was bent to seek the Lord, her whole delight was to be conversant in the Scriptures, and to meditate upon them day and night." Notice how this description equates a heart wholly "bent to seek the Lord" with a person whose "whole delight was to be conversant in the Scriptures"; the two descriptions are functional equivalents. A Christian seeking God is, by definition, a Christian seeking God's word. Stubbes was so taken up with Scripture that "you could seldome or never have come into her house, and have found her without a Bible, or some other good booke in her hand." And even on those occasions "when as she was not reading," we are told that "she would spend her time in conferring, talking and reasoning with her husband of the Word

---

20 *Geneva Bible*, "To Our Beloved in the Lord."

of God, and of Religion: asking him, what is the sense of this place, and what is the sense of that? How expound you this place, and how expound you that? What observe you of this place, and what observe you of that?"[21] For Katherine Stubbes, Scripture was the lifeblood of her Christian faith. Whether she was reading it, meditating on it, or talking about it with another believer, the text was the primary locus of her religious devotion.

Likewise, preaching in 1662, the Puritan Thomas Brooks (1608–1680) exhorted his congregation to "make Christ and Scripture the only foundation for your souls and faith to build on."[22] Notice the way that "Christ and Scripture" are almost treated as one and the same, that these two things together are "the only foundation for your souls." Why does he speak this way? The rhetoric reflects a deep sense that Christ is known only in and through the word and that building on him means, functionally, that one builds on the word.

An Overemphasis on the Word?

At this point, we must pause to recognize and consider objections raised in response to the historic Protestant emphasis on the centrality of Scripture in spiritual formation.

Expressed Concerns

Some have wondered whether all this attention paid to words, to reading, and to the ideas expressed in those words might actually produce a deformed sort of Christianity, an overly cognitive, brittle sort of religiosity that fills the head without ever firing the heart. Perhaps when Puritan authors like Thomas Brooks seem to almost equate Scripture with Christ himself, they have elevated the Bible and a Bible-based piety to a lofty height it was never meant to occupy.

---

21 Philip Stubbes, *A Chrystal Glasse for Christian Women* (London, 1591), A2v.
22 Thomas Brooks, untitled sermon, in *Sermons of the Great Ejection: An Introduction to Puritan Preaching* (Edinburgh: Banner of Truth, 2012), 38.

Such objections to Protestant Christianity were frequently voiced during the Reformation era itself. One striking illustration of this phenomenon comes to us from a French Roman Catholic satire published in 1556. The work depicts a Catholic traveler who, having just returned home after visiting Reformed churches, is retelling all that he saw and heard among the Protestants. What is especially striking in his report is the way he unfavorably likens Protestant worship to going to school. When asked to "tell . . . about the state of their churches, and how they govern themselves within them," he gives the following description:

> It is just like being inside a school. There are benches everywhere, and a pulpit in the middle for the preacher. . . . The stained glass windows are just about all knocked out, and the plaster dust is up to the ankles. . . . As soon as they enter the church, each one takes care to choose a spot to sit as in a school, and they wait for the preacher to come into the pulpit. . . . And if anyone makes a prayer on entering the church, he is pointed to and scoffed at, and held to be a Papist and idolater. Likewise if he is accused of owning a book of hours or a rosary, or has images in his house, or rests on holidays, he is immediately called before the consistory for punishment.[23]

The author describes the Reformed worship service as being more like a classroom lesson than anything that he would ordinarily associate with church. Notice how he highlights both what is happening and what is not happening. First, what *is* happening is a strong emphasis on the word of God preached, the entire seating arrangement being like a classroom to best facilitate the reading of Scripture and the preacher's sermon. Second, what is *not* happening is much of the usual medieval Catholic piety that would have presented alternatives to the word—for

23 Anonymous, *Passevent Parisien, respondant à Pasquin Romain: De la vie de ceux qui sont allez demourer à Genève, et se disent vivre selon la réformation de l'Evangile* (1556; repr., Paris, 1875), quoted in Benedict, *Purely Reformed*, 492.

example, stained glass windows as a visual alternative to the text of Scripture. The implication is that the Reformed emphasis on the word is both inappropriate (more like a school than a church) and deficient in its capacity to spiritually form and nourish the worshipers (the author notes that anyone actually pursuing spiritual formation through, say, the use of a rosary, is dismissed as an idolater).

In our own day, some continue to criticize Protestants for overemphasizing the divine word and the mind to the detriment of the heart and the whole person. Sometimes this comes from Roman Catholic critics. While explaining his move out of evangelicalism into Roman Catholicism, sociologist Christian Smith describes a sense of "dissatisfaction with the heavily cognitive, often rationalist, nature of much of Protestantism." "Protestantism," he says, "is a religion of the head" in which "what matters most are holding the right beliefs" and "possessing, professing, and defending the right words."[24] Though technically Smith objects here to an overemphasis on ideas as opposed to an overemphasis on Scripture, it is hard not to connect the two, especially given Protestantism's historic shift away from a sacrament-centric toward a Scripture-centric piety. This connection becomes especially clear when, in the same section of the book, the antidote Smith offers to an overly cognitive piety is one in which the sacramental life of the church takes center stage:

> Is the heart of Christianity really about believing correct ideas? What about the movement of the body in communal liturgy? . . . What about ingesting the Body and Blood of Christ? What about water and oil and incense and color in abundance as part of worship and spiritual life? . . . Why shouldn't God's grace be mediated through a variety of material and bodily sacraments, including anointing of the sick and holy marriage?[25]

24 Christian Smith, *How to Go from Being a Good Evangelical to a Committed Catholic in Ninety-Five Difficult Steps* (Eugene, OR: Cascade Books, 2011), 48–49.
25 Smith, *Ninety-Five Difficult Steps*, 49.

Such criticism, however, is not limited to Roman Catholic polemicists. Among many evangelicals one can detect a rising tide of skepticism regarding the Reformation's emphasis on the priority of the word. For example, in his influential book *You Are What You Love*, James K. A. Smith calls evangelical Christians to reassess "the pedagogies by which we induct young people into the faith."[26] In practice, this means moving away from an emphasis on a historic Reformation word-based piety and toward something that is less "about what we know" and more "about what we love," an approach to discipleship that is "more tactile than didactic" and based not on a "merely didactic information transfer" but on "a kind of know-how, a knowledge you carry in your bones."[27] The examples Smith provides revolve around substituting the Reformation emphasis on God's word for various visual and kinesthetic stimuli. He commends, for instance, "a series of tapestries" on display at the Roman Catholic Cathedral of Our Lady of the Angels in Los Angeles.[28] He also describes the children's Sunday school area in an Episcopalian church in which "the usual flannelgraphs and Bible memory verse posters are conspicuously absent" and "in their place is something that feels like a worship laboratory of sorts." One highlight within this "worship laboratory" is an "image of a third-century statue of the Good Shepherd from the catacomb of Domitilla."[29] With reference to this latter example, Smith explicitly contrasts the efficacy of the image with what he depicts as the relative poverty of God's word:

> It is just the sort of image and metaphor that gets lodged in your unconscious as a child, an imaged truth you then carry with you for the rest of your life—into your teens and eventually into your twenties, when you might drift from the faith . . . making a hundred

---

26 James K. A. Smith, *You Are What You Love: The Spiritual Power of Habit* (Grand Rapids, MI: Brazos, 2016), 139.

27 Smith, *You Are What You Love*, 138, 139, 142.

28 Smith, *You Are What You Love*, 140.

29 Smith, *You Are What You Love*, 139, 141.

bad decisions. . . . Now that you're here, you're partly angry and partly embarrassed, so you have avoided the church like the plague. . . . But what catches you short on some lonely evening of despair isn't a doctrine that you remember *or all those verses you memorized from the book of Romans.* What creeps up on you is the inexplicable emergence of this image of the shepherd from the deep recesses of your imagination's storehouse.[30]

Smith seems to be saying, as he has suggested elsewhere in his writings, that the historic Protestant priority given to knowing God through Scripture is not just incomplete but actually fundamentally misguided; it represents a charge that word-based piety simply cannot form disciples and capture the human heart in the way that images can.[31]

Formulating a Response

What can be said in the face of these serious and troubling claims? At least three lines of response seem appropriate.

First, as a basic matter of historical inquiry, the suggestion that the word-based piety of the Reformation failed to capture the hearts of ordinary Christians is difficult to sustain. In her study *The Culture of Protestantism in Early Modern Scotland,* historian Margo Todd has sought to refute the common perception that Reformed Christianity "proved in the long run to be an abstract, intellectual religion of the

---

30 Smith, *You Are What You Love,* 141–42 (emphasis added).

31 In his earlier work, for example, James K. A. Smith critiques Protestantism's "overly cognitivist picture of the human person" that "tends to foster an overly intellectualist account of what it means to be or become a Christian." While he goes on to describe certain Reformed accounts as marginally better, in practice he says of the two approaches, "I don't think I'd notice much difference." *Desiring the Kingdom: Worship, Worldview, and Cultural Formation,* Cultural Liturgies 1 (Grand Rapids, MI: Baker Academic, 2009), 42–45. In his more recent writing, Smith spends less time on these themes but continues the same line of argumentation, claiming, for instance, that for those who are "spiritually sensitive . . . such attunement happens less through doctrinal treatises and more through the spiritual disciplines of the church's worship." *How to Inhabit Time: Understanding the Past, Facing the Future, Living Faithfully Now* (Grand Rapids, MI: Brazos, 2022), 18–19.

elite."[32] Drawing on an impressive array of church records, personal journals, sermon manuscripts, and printed devotional texts, Todd concludes that the picture of Calvinist word-centered Christianity as an exclusivist, inapproachably cognitive affair is false: "Where the life of the community could be organized around sermons and Bible-reading, and where the most ordinary could be regularly held to a public recitation of their faith, Calvinism became genuinely a religion of the people."[33]

Likewise, in their introduction to a recent collection of essays titled *Puritanism and Emotion*, historians Alec Ryrie and Tom Schwanda dismiss "the old stereotype of Puritan emotionlessness" and document how recent scholarship has definitively dethroned "the simplistic opposition between reason and emotion" that was once assumed to be true.[34] Along similar lines, Charles Hambrick-Stowe's study of Puritan spiritual formation in seventeenth-century New England has demonstrated that the "manner of New Englanders' devotional reading yielded emotional and spiritual fruit."[35] Moreover, moving beyond the Puritans, it is clear that the eighteenth-century revivals of the Great Awakening marked a fresh turn back to the preaching and Bible study so emphasized by the Reformers that helped reignite hearts across the Protestant world.[36] So on a fundamental, empirical level, when we ask the question "Is it actually true that in practice the Reformers' shift away from the sacramental, image-laden religious culture of medieval Catholicism had a deadening effect on the religious affections of laypeople?" the answer from historians working in these fields is a resounding no.

---

32 Margo Todd, quoting R. Po-Chia Hsia, *Social Discipline in the Reformation: Central Europe, 1550–1750* (London: Routledge, 1989), 154, in Todd, *Culture of Protestantism*, 83.

33 Todd, *Culture of Protestantism*, 83.

34 Alec Ryrie and Tom Schwanda, "Introduction," in *Puritanism and Emotion in the Early Modern World*, ed. Alec Ryrie and Tom Schwanda (New York: Palgrave Macmillan, 2016), 4–5.

35 Charles E. Hambrick-Stowe, *The Practice of Piety: Puritan Devotional Disciplines in Seventeenth-Century New England* (Chapel Hill: University of North Carolina Press, 1982), 159.

36 For an excellent survey of the evangelical revivals, see Mark A. Noll, *The Rise of Evangelicalism: The Age of Edwards, Whitefield and the Wesleys* (Downers Grove, IL: InterVarsity Press, 2004).

Second, it is important to see that in emphasizing a word-based piety and the study of Christian truth, early modern Protestants did not believe themselves to be sidelining or marginalizing emotions. Rather, as we already observed in previous chapters, they believed that the God-ordained means of enflaming the heart for God was to fill the mind with God's truth. J. I. Packer summarizes the spirituality of John Owen like this:

> God . . . moves us, not by direct action on the affections or will, but by addressing our mind with his word, and so bringing to bear on us the force of truth. Our first task, therefore, if we would serve God, is to learn the contents of "God's Word written." Affection may be the helm of the ship, but the mind must steer; and the chart to steer by is God's revealed truth.[37]

And what Packer observes in Owen's work holds true throughout the Reformed tradition more generally. In her study of John Calvin, historian Elsie McKee concludes that "although Calvin's theology is regarded as primarily intellectual, he himself put the greater weight on the heart; heart and head must go together but the heart is more important."[38] Drawing on historic Reformed writers such as Jonathan Edwards and Thomas Goodwin (1600–1680) and bringing their perspective to a contemporary evangelical audience, John Piper explains that "the mind serves to know the truth that fuels the fires of the heart."[39] The relationship between mind and heart is thus a circular one, the two mutually reinforcing each other: "Thinking feeds the fire, and the fire fuels more thinking and doing. I love God because I know him. And I want to know him more because I love him."[40]

---

37 J. I. Packer, *A Quest for Godliness: The Puritan Vision of the Christian Life* (Wheaton, IL: Crossway, 1990), 195.

38 Elsie Anne McKee, ed., *John Calvin: Writings on Pastoral Piety*, Classics of Western Spirituality (New York: Paulist, 2001), 3.

39 John Piper, *Think: The Life of the Mind and the Love of God* (Wheaton, IL: Crossway, 2011), 36.

40 Piper, *Think*, 89.

This perspective clearly informs the devotional writing of early modern Protestants and appears again and again throughout the Reformed tradition. Listen to how Charles Hodge beautifully explained the historic Reformed understanding of the relationship between head and heart in spiritual formation:

> It is most unreasonable to expect to be conformed to the image of God, unless the truth concerning God be made to operate often and continuously upon the mind. How can a heart that is filled with the thoughts and cares of the world, and especially one which is often moved to evil by the thoughts or sight of sin, expect that the affections which answer to the holiness, goodness or greatness of God should gather strength within it? . . . We cannot make progress in holiness unless we devote much time to the reading, and hearing, and meditating upon the word of God, which is the truth whereby we are sanctified. The more this truth is brought before the mind; the more we commune with it, entering into its import, applying it to our own case, . . . the more may we expect to be transformed by the renewing of our mind so as to approve and love whatever is holy, just and good.[41]

So while one is surely free to argue that Protestants have been wrong all along to teach that the way to the heart is through the mind, one cannot credibly accuse them of neglecting the importance of the imagination, the emotions, and the heart.

Third, and perhaps most important from a Christian perspective, if one does wish to refute the Reformation conviction that the way to the heart is through the mind, one must grapple with the fact that the Reformers' ideas here were derived from and thoroughly rooted in the testimony of Scripture itself. These ministers and theologians were

---

41 Charles Hodge, *The Way of Life* (Philadelphia: American Sunday School Union, 1841), 376–77.

attempting to take the Bible seriously when it taught them that it is the word that is "able to save your souls" (James 1:21), that "man lives by every word that comes from the mouth of the LORD" (Deut. 8:3), and that Christ sanctifies his bride "by the washing of water with the word" (Eph. 5:26). The psalmist declares that "the law of the LORD is perfect, / reviving the soul" (Ps. 19:7). The prophet Jeremiah testifies,

> Your words were found, and I ate them,
>   and your words became to me a joy
>   and the delight of my heart. (Jer. 15:16)

And the apostle Paul tells Timothy that his main job as a shepherd of the sheep is to "devote [himself] to the public reading of Scripture, to exhortation, to teaching" (1 Tim. 4:13).

Thus it is only because he first read Jesus's words in John 17:17—"Sanctify them in the truth; your word is truth"—that the Puritan Thomas Watson observed that "the Word is the medium and method of sanctification, and we come to it not only to illuminate but to consecrate us."[42] And so too today when a Catholic critic asks, "Is the heart of Christianity really about believing correct ideas?"[43] a Protestant can only reply with Paul's assertion that "if you confess with your mouth that Jesus is Lord and believe in your heart that God raised him from the dead, you will be saved" (Rom. 10:9). If one wishes to overthrow the Reformation emphasis on God's word standing at the center of a truly Christian approach to spiritual formation, then one needs to do more than simply celebrate the beauty of images and the richness of non-Protestant liturgical traditions. Rather, one must deal with the mountain of scriptural testimony that seems to suggest that a Reformation word-centered piety is actually at root simply biblical piety by another name.

---

42 Thomas Watson, *Heaven Taken by Storm: Showing the Holy Violence a Christian Is to Put Forth in the Pursuit after Glory*, ed. Joel R. Beeke (Grand Rapids, MI: Soli Deo Gloria, 2019), 122.

43 Smith, *Ninety-Five Difficult Steps*, 49.

Practical Matters

We have now seen that for Reformation-minded Christians, Scripture was not one potential avenue for engaging with God but rather the primary place where God meets with his people, speaks into their hearts, and conforms them to the image of Christ. Such reflections should encourage us to be men and women of the word. As subsequent chapters explore further means of spiritual formation—prayer, self-examination, Christian relationships, and so on—we observe how each of these is controlled by and flows out of our primary engagement with Scripture. But for now, what more can we say about the actual practice of Bible reading? What does it entail? How do we do it? Considering those Reformed Christians who have gone before offers tremendous value here, especially when we notice those places where their emphases and approach seem to differ from our own.

As considered in the introduction to this book, much of the value in listening to voices from the past flows from the reality that many of the cultural pressures and possibilities that formed and shaped them are rather different from those that are daily forming and shaping you and me. This means that our spiritual predecessors are sometimes attentive to things we take for granted or miss altogether. The result is often that Christians from former eras are strong in areas in which we are characteristically weak. The point is not, then, that whenever we perceive differences between ourselves and people from the past, we should conclude that they are necessarily in the right and we in the wrong. Rather, the point is that when differences show up between us and them, we should pause and ask whether their differing set of priorities might not represent a helpful corrective for us. If a group of seventeenth-century Christians teleported into the twenty-first century, I have no doubt that we, in turn, would also have some things to teach them, but since the arrow of travel only goes in one direction, we must focus our attention on learning from those who went before us.

Two caveats before we begin. First, note well that no piece of Scripture reading advice or guidance, whether old or new, functions as *the* all-encompassing magical key to immediately transform your walk as a Christian. Sometimes we fool ourselves into thinking that if I just read one more book or hear one more conference talk, *then* I will have it figured out. This is not true. This side of glory, we always "see in a mirror dimly" (1 Cor. 13:12), and no piece of spiritual counsel immediately untangles all knots. Second, note that this chapter on Scripture is just the first of three components that constitute what we are calling the "Reformation triangle"—that is, the nexus of Bible reading, meditation, and prayer, which for early modern Protestants fused together to constitute real communion with God. This means that much of the practical wisdom we seek in terms of *how* to read Scripture with spiritual profit is actually housed in chapters 4 and 5 as we consider meditation and prayer. With those reminders in place, let's consider three practical exhortations for reading our Bibles well and with a view toward spiritual formation. To read Scripture in step with the historic Reformed tradition, we must read *frequently*, *actively*, and *expectantly*.

Read Frequently

After once noting that he had been neglecting "humble, purpose-like reading of the Word," the Scottish Presbyterian minister Robert Murray M'Cheyne (1813–1843) asked in his diary, "What plant can be unwatered, and not wither?"[44] M'Cheyne's image of a person as a plant in need of watering captures nicely the relationship between Bible reading and spiritual growth, highlighting both the need for regular, frequent application and the slow organic nature of the subsequent effect.

When we survey early modern Puritan devotional manuals, we find that the exhortation to *daily* Bible reading was a near-universal norm. The Christian ideal was to "labor for the spirituall foode of the soule,

---

44   Quoted in Andrew A. Bonar, *The Life of Robert Murray M'Cheyne* (Edinburgh: Banner of Truth, 1960), 27.

which must be gathered every day out of the Word, as the children of Israel gathered Manna in the Wildernesse."[45] At the funeral of Elizabeth Gouge (1586/87–1625), the preacher praised "her piety, as it was the best of her graces, whereby all the rest were seasoned." And this life of piety was marked especially by "her set hours every day . . . spent in holy Devotions," during which, we are told, she "tied herself by a set daily task to read the holy Scriptures, whereby she was able readily to answer any question propounded about the history and doctrine of the Scriptures."[46]

To help cultivate this daily habit, the most frequent suggestion among the Reformed was to be sure to read your Bible in the morning when you awake. "As soon as we open our eyes in the morning," wrote the Dutch theologian Willem Teellinck, "we should also open our spiritual eyes."[47] The significance of beginning the day with God was pressed with special force, the idea seeming to be that the soul possessed a particular openness in those moments upon waking and that to harness this receptivity for God would help ensure a more God-honoring course in whatever followed throughout the day. Puritan pastor Richard Rogers (ca. 1550–1618) urged his readers, "Awake with God in the morning, and before all things give him your first fruits."[48] This sense of a special spiritual potency upon waking in the morning was well captured by the poet George Herbert (1593–1633):

> I cannot ope mine eyes,
> But thou art ready there to catch
> My morning-soul and sacrifice:
> Then we must needs for that day make a match.[49]

45 Dorothy Leigh, *The Mothers Blessing* (London, 1616), 5.
46 Nicholas Guy, *Pieties Pillar: Or, A Sermon Preached at the Funerall of Mistresse Elizabeth Gouge, Late Wife of Mr. William Gouge* (London, 1626), 48.
47 Willem Teellinck, *The Path of True Godliness*, trans. Annemie Godbehere, ed. Joel R. Beeke, Classics of Reformed Spirituality (Grand Rapids, MI: Reformation Heritage Books, 2006), 195.
48 Richard Rogers, *A Garden of Spirituall Flowers* (London, 1615), A2r.
49 George Herbert, *The Complete English Poems*, ed. John J. Tobin (London: Penguin, 2004), 56.

While beginning the day with God was the most common pre-scription, the close of the day before bed was also highlighted as a choice moment for returning to God's word. It was often observed that "Isaac went out to meditate in the field toward evening" (Gen. 24:63) and that David came before the Lord both evening and morning (Ps. 55:17). In *The Practice of Piety* (1611), one of the most popular devotional manuals of the seventeenth century, Lewis Bayly directed Christians to read Scripture, pray, and meditate again "at evening, when thou preparest thyself to take thy rest." For motivation, Bayly urged his readers to "remember that many go to bed, and never rise again till they be wakened and raised up by the fearful sound of the last trumpet; but he that sleepeth and wakeneth with prayer, sleepeth and wakeneth with Christ."[50] By pursuing daily devotion in the morning and often again at night, early modern Protestants bookended the day with God, acknowledging themselves to be made in his image, fallen in Adam, redeemed in Christ, and renewed daily by the Spirit.

Then, as now, however, such exhortations to daily Bible reading prompted in some a sense that life's demands were too onerous to accommodate such a time-consuming activity. The Puritan minister Isaac Ambrose (1604–1664), for example, discussed ways that differ-ent people in different seasons of life have more or less time for Bible reading, though he insisted that "all must set apart some time for this duty."[51] Likewise, the Puritan pastor Richard Greenham (ca. 1540–1594) acknowledged that questions about the correct amount of time to give to Bible reading do not allow for easy one-size-fits-all answers. Rather, getting it right requires wisdom, and Greenham even went so far as to say that some Christians err in holding themselves to too *high* a standard in this area: "We must not read always, and do nothing

---

50 Lewis Bayly, *The Practice of Piety: Directing a Christian to Walk, That He May Please God* (Grand Rapids, MI: Soli Deo Gloria, 2019), 133–34.

51 Isaac Ambrose, *Prima, Media, et Ultima: The First, Middle, and Last Things* (London, 1659), 2:478.

else, as some offending in the one extreme, are after driven by Satan to the other."[52]

In our own day, many of us feel acutely the pressures and busyness of our lives and wonder whether some of this might be a unique product of twenty-first-century cultural conditions. Certainly, this is a central theme in Anne Helen Petersen's bestselling book *Can't Even: How Millennials Became the Burnout Generation*. In a work that clearly struck a nerve with a wide readership, Petersen documents her own sense of exhaustion, fatigue, and the mounting "evidence that something inside me was, well, broken." Petersen explains:

> My to-do list . . . just kept recycling itself from one week to the next, a neat little stack of shame. None of these tasks was essential, not really. They were just the humdrum maintenance of everyday life. But no matter what I did, I couldn't bring myself to take the knives to get sharpened, or drop off my favorite boots to get resoled, or complete the paperwork and make the phone call and find the stamp so that my dog could be properly registered. . . . All of these high-effort, low-gratification tasks seemed equally impossible.[53]

In Petersen's analysis, all this "errand paralysis" and the mounting "everyday stresses of 'adulting'—a word adopted to describe the fear of doing or pride in completing tasks associated with our parents," stem, at least in large part, from the specific conditions of twenty-first-century life: "Adulting . . . is hard, then, because living in the modern world is somehow both easier than it's ever been and yet *unfathomably* complicated."[54]

---

52 Richard Greenham, *A Profitable Treatise, Containing a Direction for the Reading and Understanding of the Holy Scriptures*, in Kenneth L. Parker and Eric J. Carlson, *Practical Divinity: The Works and Life of Revd Richard Greenham*, St. Andrews Studies in Reformation History (Aldershot, UK: Ashgate, 1998), 341.

53 Anne Helen Petersen, *Can't Even: How Millennials Became the Burnout Generation* (Boston: Houghton Mifflin Harcourt, 2020), xvi.

54 Petersen, *Can't Even*, xvii.

Surely it is correct that every cultural moment comes with a particular set of stressors, and it is not wrong to observe and map out the topography of anxiety unique to our age. That said, it is also salutary for busy twenty-first-century Christians to note that feeling overwhelmed by life's demands is the common lot of fallen men and women living in a fallen world. The early modern Puritans felt this just as we did. Lewis Bayly, for instance, anticipated that his readers would chafe at his exhortation to read the Bible daily: "But it may be thou wilt say, that thy business will not permit thee so much time, as to read every morning a chapter." Both the complaint itself and the weary sense of being overwhelmed that stood behind it could have come from any one of the burned-out millennials interviewed in Petersen's *Can't Even*. Where the Puritans differed from us, then, was not in feeling the stress and pinch of life but in how they responded to it. While we are often quick to feel sorry for ourselves and to rehearse and meditate on our present troubles, the Puritans were quick to push themselves to press on and reprioritize the "light momentary affliction" of this life in view of the "eternal weight of glory beyond all comparison" (2 Cor. 4:17). To this end, listen to what Bayly said to Christians who complained that they were too busy for daily Bible reading:

> Remember that thy life is but short, and that all this business [i.e., the daily business threatening to crowd out one's Bible reading] is but for the use of this short life; but salvation or damnation is everlasting! Rise up, therefore, every morning by so much time the earlier: defraud thy foggy flesh of so much sleep; but rob not thy soul of her food, nor God of his service; and serve the Almighty duly whilst thou hast time and health.[55]

Such bracing rhetoric feels out of step with the kinder, gentler devotional culture of our present moment. Few of our devotional books

---

55 Bayly, *Practice of Piety*, 107.

address their readers with the sort of blunt, confrontational words that were common among the Puritans. When the Scottish minister Samuel Rutherford (1600–1661) wanted to persuade a congregant to "work for [his] soul" and take his spiritual duties more seriously, he prodded him to "think what you would give for an hour, when you shall lie like dead, cold, blackened clay."[56] Contemporary writing on spiritual formation, for better or worse, typically avoids that sort of strong prescription, preferring to emphasize flexibility in one's routine and to stress empathy and compassion for those feeling pressed and burdened. Much more typical of a twenty-first-century approach is Peter Scazzero's advice:

> A good rule to follow when dealing with tools and techniques [for spiritual formation] is this: If it helps, do it. If it does not help you, do not do it. . . . If reading the psalms helps you, then great. Do it. If reading the psalms has become routine and dead for you, then don't. . . . Remember grace, which reminds us there is nothing we can do or not do that would cause God to love us any more than he does right now.[57]

Now the point here is not to suggest that Bayly's stronger exhortation is obviously superior in every way to contemporary devotional writing that avoids this sort of rhetoric. Rather, the point here, as elsewhere in this book, is to note ways that saints from a previous era seem to speak with a different tone and tenor from what we have grown accustomed to. Once we note that difference, we can then ask whether those men and women from an earlier age might not have something to teach us, an emphasis that might correct or challenge us. And on the question whether daily Bible reading is a necessary element of healthy spiritual formation, it seems that the early modern Reformed might

---

56 Samuel Rutherford, *Letters of Samuel Rutherford* (Edinburgh: Banner of Truth, 1973), 63.
57 Scazzero, *Emotionally Healthy Spirituality*, 162.

offer a corrective word that we do well to hear, even as we might want to round off or soften places where they can seem excessively strident.

Read Actively

When early modern Reformed Christians approached Scripture, their efforts were marked at every turn by a commitment to active reading. By "active" here, I mean an approach to Bible reading that is strategic, intentional, and thoughtfully designed to maximize, at least from a human perspective, one's time in God's word. In the opening chapter of their classic mid-twentieth-century guidebook *How to Read a Book*, Mortimer Adler (1902–2001) and Charles Van Doren (1926–2019) taught that active rather than passive reading is the key to getting the most from our books: "Reading can be more or less active, and . . . the more active the reading the better."[58] Adler and Van Doren were not early modern Puritans, but their active approach to reading aligns well with the advice Puritan pastors regularly gave their congregations about reading their Bibles: a thoughtful, engaged approach to Scripture was far superior to one that was thoughtless and superficial. Our current cultural moment can make quiet concentration and sustained focus feel especially hard to come by. Such cultural conditions, then, give us all the more reason to take a cue from our spiritual predecessors and approach our Bible reading with intention and care.

Richard Greenham counseled that "we must keep an order in our readings, and not be now in this place, now in another: for order is the best help for memory and understanding."[59] Such an emphasis on order and consistency led Puritan pastors to recommend various Bible reading plans. Differing considerably in the amount of Scripture prescribed and the order in which biblical books were to be approached, Puritan Bible reading plans were really not all that different from the

---

58 Mortimer J. Adler and Charles Van Doren, *How to Read a Book*, rev. ed. (New York: Simon and Schuster, 1972), 5.

59 Greenham, *Profitable Treatise*, in Parker and Carlson, *Practical Divinity*, 341.

many plans popular among evangelicals today. Some, like Greenham, would simply start reading at the beginning and work their way to the end. A path cut from Genesis straight through to Revelation made the most sense, he reasoned, because "the Holy Ghost in wisdom hath set the best order to his own word."[60] Others drew up programs that would begin with what were considered the more straightforward books—the Gospel narratives, for instance—and build toward those considered more obscure, like the Song of Solomon. One of the most popular approaches, then as now, involved reading the entire Bible over the course of a year with daily readings taken from different genres. Some plans segmented the daily readings to ensure that certain sections—the Levitical ceremonies, for example—would be read less frequently than other sections—say, the Psalms. Indeed, a common feature of Puritan programs was a heavy emphasis on regularly moving through the Psalter. As historian Alec Ryrie notes, "The psalms were seen as a book apart, 'an Epitome of the whole Bible,' and they had a central role in expressing and in forming Protestant piety."[61] Amid the diversity of approaches, the constant seemed to be the importance of having some sort of plan in place so that when you opened your Bible, you knew exactly where to go.

The common counsel regarding the amount of Scripture to read each day stressed quality over quantity. While some did commend extremely large amounts of Bible reading (such as Samuel Fairclough [1594–1677], who allegedly read the entire Bible through four times a year for fifty years!),[62] most ministers would have likely agreed with Lewis Bayly's advice that "one chapter thus read with understanding and meditated upon with application, will better feed and comfort thy soul than five read and run over without marking their scope or sense, or making any use of them to thine ownself."[63] Likewise, Greenham

---

60 Richard Greenham, "English Manuscript 524," in Parker and Carlson, *Practical Divinity*, 206.
61 Ryrie, *Reformation Britain*, 275.
62 Ryrie, *Reformation Britain*, 271.
63 Bayly, *Practice of Piety*, 106.

warned, "He that readeth little after a good manner profiteth more than he that readeth much otherwise."[64] Similar advice can be found a century later from the eighteenth-century evangelical Anglican Henry Venn (1725–1797), who urged Bible readers "to read but a small portion at one time." Why would this be? Venn argued, "It is common for those who have the character of being very devout to set themselves such a quantity, suppose two or three chapters, to read every day; a much larger portion this than they can sufficiently attend to." Note well, then, that two or three chapters a day—an amount often exceeded in many of our contemporary Bible reading plans—was too much in Venn's estimate. While he acknowledged that reading less would slow our progress through Scripture, "the singular benefit of such a method will amply reward our pains and prove its preference, . . . and the knowledge of what we gain in this manner will come with a transforming efficacy."[65] This emphasis on slowing down and thoughtfully meditating on Scripture with an eye toward personal application is the focus of our next chapter. But for now, we can simply note that for these older guides, effective, heart-transforming Bible reading was always attentive, *active* reading.

Another way that early modern Bible readers took an active approach to Scripture was to read the Bible with pen in hand. Historian Kate Narveson has described the extent to which "godly writing is linked with Scripture reading." Often this involved collecting and transcribing into a notebook those "texts that addressed issues of personal concern."[66]

This marriage of godly reading and godly writing, along with much else that we've been discussing regarding *active* Bible reading, comes across clearly in the Puritan minister Nicholas Byfield's (1579–1622) *Directions for the Private Reading of Scripture* (1618). Byfield noted that

---

64 Greenham, *Profitable Treatise*, in Parker and Carlson, *Practical Divinity*, 341.

65 Henry Venn, *The Complete Duty of Man: or A System of Doctrinal and Practical Christianity*, in *The Emergence of Evangelical Spirituality: The Age of Edwards, Newton, and Whitefield*, ed. Tom Schwanda, Classics of Western Spirituality (New York: Paulist, 2016), 127–28.

66 Kate Narveson, *Bible Readers and Lay Writers in Early Modern England: Gender and Self-Definition in an Emergent Writing Culture* (London: Routledge, 2016), 19.

many otherwise godly Christians "complain of their not profiting in reading," and some even "afflict their hearts marvelously with grief and fear, because they cannot read with more comfort and profit." Byfield concluded that with many of these "the fault is not in their affection to the Word, so much as in their want of direction for their reading."[67] To that end, he offered several helps to guide the godly toward a more profitable, active approach to daily Bible reading.

Byfield's system consisted of two main components. First, he recommended a daily reading program for systematically moving through all the Scriptures. Second, he encouraged readers to follow his practice of regularly collecting and writing down those verses and passages that struck him as especially significant. To do this, he kept in his journal several thematically arranged lists of biblical texts. One list contained passages that comforted him, another included passages that convicted him, while still others featured passages that directed him toward godly living and passages that he did not yet fully understand. This practice not only encouraged an especially fruitful, active sort of Bible reading but also positioned Byfield for future blessing when he could return to the texts thus collected:

> Now these places so noted, not only serve for present use, but while I live, in any distress, I may have recourse to these, as so many wells of joy, and if in my grief one, or two, or ten of them did not comfort me: yet a thousand to one some of them will have spirit and life in them to refresh me again in any sorrows: Besides, it marvelously establishes my faith, when I remember, in how many distinct places of Scripture the Lord was pleased to comfort me in particular.[68]

Today we might not necessarily want to mimic Byfield's system exactly (all told, he kept a rather unwieldy thirty-one separate lists of

67 Nicholas Byfield, *Directions for the Private Reading of the Scriptures* (London, 1618), preface, n.p.
68 Byfield, *Private Reading*, preface, n.p.

memorable Bible passages). But the active approach to searching the Scriptures and the overarching goal of somehow marking, recording, and returning to those texts that "wonderfully fill [the] heart with secret refreshing, and sensible joy" represent a worthy goal for all of us. For Byfield, the worth of the system was to be measured not by its immediate results but rather, like all that goes into our spiritual formation, by its slowly unfolding impact over time:

> Look not at the profit of this course the first week, or month: but consider, how rich it will make thee at the year's end. I am persuaded, if thou fear God, thou would not sell thy collections for a great price, after thou hast gathered them, if it were but for the good, they may doe thee in the evil day, when it shall come upon thee.[69]

In a day like ours when speed and convenience are prized above most else, the slow, steady, active approach taken by Byfield and other Puritans may require us to recalibrate our spiritual sensibilities, but their consistent testimony to us is that the effort is worth it in the end.

Read Expectantly

Why is our Bible reading cold and lifeless? Perhaps we have too low a view of Scripture. By "too low" in this context, I am not referring to debates about inerrancy. Rather, I mean the "too low" view that can subtly creep into the Bible reading of even those with the highest view of Scripture's authority and inspiration. It's the view that has taken hold whenever I come to my Bible without a sense of expectation that herein I am meeting with the one who made me and sustains my every breath. Whatever my theological conviction regarding the nature of the Bible, I experientially fail to read it as that which is "perfect, / reviving the

---

69 Byfield, *Private Reading*, preface, n.p.

soul" (Ps. 19:7). At root, this attitude reflects a tacit antisupernatural approach to Scripture and naturalistic assumption that the book before me is, in fact, one like any other.

Here our early modern predecessors offer a powerful remedy for us because, again and again, they approached their Bibles expectantly—that is, they came to the word expecting to hear the voice of the triune God. "To provoke a diligent reading of the Word," exhorted Thomas Watson, "labor to have a right notion of Scripture." What is that "right notion" that we must "labor" to lay hold of? We must "read the Word as a book made by God Himself."[70] Likewise, the Dutch theologian Campegius Vitringa reminds us that "he who reads it hears God speaking to him: he converses with God and with Christ Jesus Himself."[71] This is a functionally high view of what Scripture actually is, and apart from it, we fail to engage Scripture as we ought. Isaac Ambrose began his treatment of Bible reading by underscoring this very point, writing that "reading the holy Scriptures . . . is nothing else but a kind of holy conference with God." By "conference," he meant something closer to what we mean by "conversation,"[72] and so "when we take in hand therefore the Book of Scriptures, we cannot otherwise conceive of our selves [than] as standing in God's presence, to hear what he will say unto us."[73]

If approaching the Bible is the functional equivalent of approaching God himself to commune with him, then such an exercise never proceeds fruitfully unless it is accompanied by earnest prayer, prayer that the same Spirit who breathed out the words of Scripture will bless the one who reads them. This is why Richard Sibbes urged Bible readers,

---

70 Watson, *Heaven Taken by Storm*, 12.

71 Campegius Vitringa, *The Spiritual Life*, trans. Charles K. Telfer (Grand Rapids, MI: Reformation Heritage Books, 2018), 120.

72 We will see this term again in chap. 8 when we consider how our relationships with other believers can advance our spiritual formation, looking specifically at the Puritan practice of spiritual "conference" among Christians.

73 Ambrose, *Prima, Media, et Ultima*, 2:477.

Beg of God to seal to our souls that it is the Word, and that he would sanctify our hearts to be suitable to the Word, and never rest till we can find God by his Spirit seasoning our hearts, so that the relish of our souls may suit to the relish of divine truths, that when we hear them we may relish the truth in them, and may so feel the work of God's Spirit, that we may be able to say, he is our God. And when we hear of any threatening, we may tremble at it, and any sin discovered, we may hate it. For unless we, by the Spirit of God have something wrought in us suitable to the word, we shall never believe the Word to be the Word. And therefore pray the Lord, by his Spirit to frame our hearts to be suitable to divine truths, and so frame them in our affections that we may find the Word in our joy, in our love, in our patience, and that all may be seasoned with the Word of God.[74]

This functionally high view of Scripture and the corresponding expectation that reading our Bible is communion with God returns us to the idea of the Reformation triangle, the mutually reinforcing relationship between Bible reading, meditation, and prayer. While discussing Bible reading, Isaac Ambrose could casually exhort readers to "be frequent and diligent in meditation of the Word," suggesting that reading and meditation are simply two sides of the same coin. Then, shortly thereafter, he included prayer in the same discussion, observing that "although Prayer and the Reading of the Word be two distinct exercises, yet they mutually help one another, and consequently are fit to be joined together." Before we begin to read our Bible, Ambrose insisted that we should be "awing the heart with due reverence of God before whom we stand," a form of meditation. And then, as we are meditating in this way, Ambrose directed us to be "lifting up the heart unto God in prayer, to open our eyes, to enlarge our hearts, to

---

74 Richard Sibbes, *Works of Richard Sibbes*, ed. Alexander B. Grosart (Edinburgh: Banner of Truth, 1973), 2:496–97.

incline our heart to his testimonies."[75] Thus we can see why the three elements—Bible reading, meditation, and prayer—fuse together when we take seriously the idea that the Lord is really present and we are coming to meet with him. In subsequent chapters on meditation and prayer, we explore this conceptual nexus in greater depth, but for now let us simply observe that while in abstraction we may wish to draw a neat line dividing Bible reading, meditation, and prayer, it is not so straightforward *experientially*, and that this triangle of disciplines makes sense when we take seriously the idea of engaging Scripture as actually engaging God himself.

Furthermore, the historic Reformed practice of expectant Bible reading led them to approach the practice ready to wrestle and struggle. If reading the Bible is a real communion with the living God, then one should not expect the process to be straightforward, as though we were operating a piece of machinery. Thus, Campegius Vitringa explained how the Holy Spirit works on our hearts as we read Scripture, "stir[ring] up every good affection" and supplying "the prudence and self-control necessary to face the attacks of Satan and the temptations of the world," and he went on to state emphatically that "these fruits should not be expected from merely opening up and perusing the Bible." Early modern Reformed authors were clear that the Bible is not a book of spells that can be recited to achieve a desired effect. Indeed, as we have already discussed throughout this book, part of the Protestant agenda was to move the church away from a medieval piety that had for many become cold, mechanical, and perfunctory. Thus, "reading scripture is not just pronouncing words aloud but carefully considering and reflecting on what is said." For Vitringa, godly readers must "suck the sweetness from the flowers as the bees do."[76]

The crucial elements in moving from a lifeless "pronouncing words aloud" to something more like a bee at work in a blossom are meditation

75 Ambrose, *Prima, Media, et Ultima*, 2:478–80.
76 Vitringa, *Spiritual Life*, 121–22.

and prayer. These are the subjects of our next two chapters, but for now, we can simply note the degree to which our Reformation authors acknowledged that Bible reading was not magical or mechanical. As central as Scripture is for Reformed spiritual formation, the Bible does not read itself nor dispense blessings on command like a vending machine, and so Christians who would read with profit must apply themselves prayerfully, diligently, and with the help of the Holy Spirit.

———

So where does all this leave us in relation to the classic evangelical "quiet time," a practice that for many of us comes fraught with experiences of failure, frustration, and guilt? No doubt, such feelings are sincerely held by genuine Christians and are often perfectly understandable. But whatever negative associations might arise in our hearts and minds when we hear the term *quiet time*, the reality remains that historic Reformation Protestants were simply following the Bible's own prescriptions when they placed God's word at the center of spiritual formation. Not only is regular engagement with Scripture the foundational discipline for personal piety, but as we see in subsequent chapters, the Bible also undergirds and informs any other spiritual discipline we might undertake. When we come to the word, we come to commune with the living God, to hear from him, and to be shaped and formed thereby. The Christian life from inception to completion is a Bible-infused life. Early modern Christians understood this, and their lives are examples for us to follow. For their part, they never used the term *quiet time*, but they nonetheless walked with God by daily leaning on his word.

One such early modern Christian was the seventeenth-century Puritan Katherine Clarke (1602–1671), about whom it was said that "there was no day that passed over her head (except Sickness, or some other unavoidable necessity hindered) wherein she did not read some portions of the Sacred Scriptures, both in the Old, and New Testament, and of the Psalms." She read her Bible frequently, but she also read actively and with a great expectation that God would meet her there: "In reading she took special notice of such passages as most concerned herself. . . . And in reading of them she used to transcribe such passages as most warmed her heart."[77]

That description of Katherine Clarke was written by her husband Samuel (1599–1683), who, after her death, discovered in her cabinet a piece of paper that, "by frequent using, was almost worn out." On the paper, tucked away yet always close at hand, Katherine had written out "several Texts of Scripture" she had regularly turned to throughout her life "in times of Temptation or Desertion."[78] One of the texts she had transcribed was Psalm 40:4:

> Blessed is the man who makes
>   the Lord his trust,
> who does not turn to the proud,
>   to those who go astray after a lie!

For Katherine Clarke, spiritual formation was a word-based affair. She understood that making the Lord her trust meant trusting in what the Holy Spirit has uniquely inspired and that the only way to not go astray after lies was to be daily grounded in the truth that only Scripture can provide.

---

77 Samuel Clarke, *The Lives of Sundry and Eminent Persons in This Later Age* (London, 1683), 2:154.
78 Clarke, *Lives*, 2:157.

4

Meditation

Reflecting on God

IN THE RAPIDLY GROWING ARENA of mental health services, Headspace sits as a global leader. Describing itself as "mak[ing] mental health support accessible to everyone," the company claims to help over one hundred million people per year spread across two hundred countries.[1] And although Headspace highlights a range of products and services, perhaps its most well-known offering is the popular Headspace meditation app. Featuring attractive contemporary design, high-profile collaborations with celebrities such as singer John Legend, and its noticeable lack of overtly religious language, the Headspace app has helped introduce the practice of meditation to a younger, upwardly mobile generation that might otherwise resist it.[2] Indeed, as a recent article in *Fast Company* reports, "Where meditation was once a niche religious practice, a glut of mindfulness apps and advocates have pushed it into the mainstream."[3] According to the Headspace

1 "About Headspace," Headspace, accessed July 22, 2024, https://www.headspacehealth.com/about.
2 Jenny Sugar, "Watch John Legend's Super Bowl Ad for Headspace," Popsugar, February 10, 2022, https://www.popsugar.co.uk/.
3 Ruth Reader, "Exclusive: Headspace and Ginger Plan Merger to Form a Mental-Health Power-house," *Fast Company*, August 25, 2021, https://www.fastcompany.com/.

app, "Meditation is a life skill" that can help practitioners "feel clearer, calmer, kinder, and sharper." The app has been downloaded over seventy million times and offers specific guided practices that, if used correctly, promise to help manage anxiety, cultivate compassion, and curb one's stress.[4]

Apps like Headspace both reflect and fuel an exploding twenty-first-century fascination with meditation, mindfulness, and mental health more generally. Yet these things are not new. When we examine early modern Protestant devotional literature, we find a similar interest in a practice that Reformed authors also called "meditation." And although in each case, of course, they mean something rather different, the two understandings of meditation aren't *completely* unrelated. Both today's high-tech, app-facilitated meditation and early modern Protestant meditation involve slowing down, refusing to be distracted by the ordinary rush of life, and focusing one's attention in a particular direction for a particular purpose. Both understandings of meditation recognize the human capacity to intentionally cultivate our interior world, and both trade on the insight that our reality is profoundly shaped by what we give our regular, sustained attention.

Where the two understandings part company, however, is the recommended object of one's attention and the specific purpose in view. The sort of meditation promoted today by Headspace and practiced for thousands of years by Eastern religions focuses on the manipulation of one's physiological state—one's breathing, posture, and so forth—with the aim of reaping specific mental and physical health benefits. Depending on which practitioner you speak with, such physiological manipulations can become quite elaborate. Consider the following passage in which the French writer Emmanuel Carrère describes his own attempt to understand contemporary meditation:

---

4 "Meditation Made Simple," Headspace, accessed July 22, 2024, https://www.headspace.com /meditation.

Dr. Yang taught us the rudiments of meditation by means of numerous diagrams, meridian pathways, normal breathing (Buddhist) and inverted breathing (Taoist), small and large circulation. . . . After that I practiced with another master, Faeq Biria, who gained his profound knowledge of Iyengar yoga from the founder himself, B. K. S. Iyengar. Faeq Biria goes further than Dr. Yang, and maintains that to start meditating you need at least ten years of assiduous practice. You have to have opened the pelvic region, opened the shoulders, aligned the *bandhas*, aligned the *chakras* and mastered all the techniques of *pranayama*, and only then does this grand, mysterious, transformative thing called meditation happen, and it happens on its own.[5]

By contrast, meditation as practiced and commended by the early modern Reformed had very little to say about mandatory physiological manipulations and was instead about directing one's attention toward God and his promises as revealed in Scripture with the aim of stirring up God-honoring affections. To meditate in this latter, biblical way is to follow Paul and to "think about" godly things (Phil. 4:8), to follow Mary in "treasur[ing] up" God's promises and "pondering" them in your heart (Luke 2:19), and to follow the Colossian Christians in "set[ting] your minds on things that are above, not on things that are on earth" (Col. 3:2). In other words, this sort of meditation involves directing one's thoughts Godward so that we can grow in personal godliness.

In the previous chapter, we introduced the Reformation triangle of Bible reading, meditation, and prayer. This trio of biblically prescribed spiritual disciplines belong together and reinforce one another, often blending so subtly into each other that they cannot easily be distinguished. As the Puritan Thomas Manton (1620–1677) explained, "Meditation is a middle sort of duty between the word and prayer, and hath respect to both."[6] Functioning as this middle duty, meditation

---

5   Emmanuel Carrère, *Yoga*, trans. John Lambert (London: Jonathan Cape, 2022), 17.
6   Thomas Manton, *The Complete Works of Thomas Manton* (London: James Nisbet, 1872), 17:272.

involves taking God's word to heart, chewing it over, pondering it, and working through its implications for every facet of life. Such thoughtful reflection on God's word to us in turn kindles a desire to respond back to God in prayer with words of our own—our praises, thanksgivings, laments, and supplications—thus completing the triangle. Of the three Reformation triangle disciplines, meditation has arguably been the most neglected in contemporary evangelical circles, and thus its recovery could potentially bring substantial benefit.

This chapter, then, explores the Reformation idea of meditation and does so along three main lines. First, we look at the meaning of meditation, trying to more precisely define just what early modern Christians were talking about when they recommended it so forcefully. Second, we consider the relevance of meditation in our contemporary context, exploring some of the ways that a recovery of Reformed meditation might helpfully redress some of our particular twenty-first-century problems. And third, we examine some of the nuts and bolts of actually putting meditation into practice.

The Meaning of Meditation

As our brief encounter with the Headspace app underscored, we can be fairly certain what Reformed Protestant meditation is *not*. We might have a more difficult time, however, determining exactly what it *is*. Reformed meditation has something to do with thinking about God and the things of God, but can we be more specific than that? Surveying early modern Protestant devotional literature, one finds many positive references to something called "meditation," but trying to pin down exactly what is in view can sometimes feel confusing. In part, this confusion reflects changing usage over time but perhaps also a degree of conceptual elasticity inherent within the idea itself. Among English writers, the word "meditation" is derived from the Latin *meditatio* and was in use from at least the thirteenth century as a generic description for pious devotional writing. So one would find popular books such as a 1496 English translation of the "meditations" of Bernard of Clairvaux (1090–1153), a collection of devotional reflections on spiritual topics.[7]

During the Reformation and post-Reformation periods of the sixteenth and seventeenth centuries, Protestants were happy to continue using the word both as a noun describing devotional writing and, increasingly, as a verb describing a spiritual practice commended to all believers. While preaching to Oxford ministerial students in 1553, for example, the Italian Reformer Peter Martyr Vermigli urged his hearers to meditate on Scripture, explaining that "whatever happiness we can have while we live here is locked up in the sacred letters" and that the way to unlock said happiness from those "sacred letters" was through meditating on the same. Vermigli described the practice in terms of "ponder[ing] as carefully as possible the words and sentences that occur" and insisted, citing Psalm 1, that such an activity was explicitly commanded in the Bible itself.[8]

Similarly, the Geneva Bible (1560) often used the word "meditation" and its derivatives where the Latin Vulgate had used *meditatio*. Such usage often occurs in the Psalms, as in Psalm 119—"I will meditate in thy statutes" (Ps. 119:48 GNV)—and of course, most famously, in Psalm 1, wherein the godly person is characterized as one whose "delight is in the law of the Lord, and in his law doth he meditate day and night" (Ps. 1:2 GNV). Psalm 1 and its strong emphasis on meditation had a special significance for early modern Protestants, as evidenced by the Geneva Bible's explanatory note indicating that "this Psalm" is set "first in manner of a preface, to exhort all godly men to study and meditate the heavenly wisdom."[9] From this usage one can see that, however they fleshed out its details, early modern Reformed Protestants understood the practice of meditation to be a clearly biblical duty.

7   Alec Ryrie, *Being Protestant in Reformation Britain* (Oxford: Oxford University Press, 2013), 110.
8   Peter Martyr Vermigli, *The Peter Martyr Library*, vol. 5, *Life, Letters, and Sermons*, trans. John Patrick Donnelly (Kirksville, MO: Thomas Jefferson University Press, 1999), 285.
9   *The Geneva Bible: A Facsimile of the 1560 Edition* (Peabody, MA: Hendrickson, 2007), 235.

As the tradition developed, this duty to meditate took on greater and greater significance, especially among Puritan devotional writers. But what exactly does the duty entail? Sometimes, perhaps especially in its earlier usages, meditation seems to be used as a near synonym for prayer. So, for example, the Geneva Bible translates Genesis 24:63 as follows: "And Isaac went out to pray in the field toward the evening." Interestingly, the Latin Vulgate had translated this verse using the word *meditatio*, and the later King James Version (1611) likewise used the word "meditate" to describe what Isaac was doing out in the field. And although the Geneva Bible translators opted for "pray" rather than "meditate," notice how they went on to further explain Genesis 24:63 in a corresponding marginal note: "This was the exercise of the godly fathers to meditate on God's promises, and to pray for the accomplishment thereof." So we can see here a tight connection between the practice of meditation and the practice of prayer, the two activities representing, in some sense, two aspects of the same underlying reality.

To press even further, some writers can even occasionally talk about meditation as though it were synonymous with communion with God more broadly, as though to describe a meditating Christian was simply to describe a Christian walking faithfully with God. When, for example, the Presbyterian minister John Ball (1585–1640) sought to prove that "the most holy" saints were those who "most abounded in meditation," he listed various biblical figures who modeled the practice. As we might expect, this list is highlighted by various individuals whom Scripture *explicitly* describes as having "meditated" (e.g., Isaac in the aforementioned Gen. 24:63; David in Ps. 119:48). But in addition to these explicit biblical "meditators," we also find a reference to Enoch, who is said to have "walked with God" (Gen. 5:22) and about whom Ball commented, "Enoch in his whole life walked with God, and had much talk and communion with him."[10] Thus, when

---

10 John Ball, *A Treatise of Divine Meditation* (London, 1660), 7.

considering Enoch's faithful walk with God and the close personal communion that this description suggests, Ball could assume that such spiritual closeness must have been supported and sustained by the practice of meditation.

But despite such examples of a more flexible usage, descriptions of meditation among the early modern Reformed, and especially among the English Puritans, do tend to center on the idea that godly meditation is essentially a sustained sort of thoughtful reflection. Indeed, when Protestants describe "meditation," they sometimes seem to mean little more than thinking about something. And in the context of Christian spiritual formation, that "something" must be the triune God of Scripture, his works, his ways, and his promises to his people. As Thomas Watson put it, meditation is "a serious thinking upon God."[11]

That seems straightforward enough, and yet if meditation simply means a bare "thinking about," then we might be left slightly puzzled by the intensity with which early modern Protestants recommended the practice and the significance and stress that they laid on it. For example, in his *Treatise of Divine Meditation*, John Ball argued that without meditation, "a Christian life cannot stand."[12] Similarly, Ball's Dutch near contemporary Wilhelmus à Brakel could describe meditation as the means by which an empty soul "seeks to be filled with substance" and an activity wherein "the very essence of sweetness is to be found."[13] And the same Thomas Watson who described meditation so straightforwardly as "serious thinking upon God" also then insisted that this practice was "a duty wherein the very heart and lifeblood of religion lies."[14] What does it mean to assign such a central role to a "duty" that, on its face, seems to mean little more than "thinking about things"?

---

11 Thomas Watson, *Heaven Taken by Storm: Showing the Holy Violence a Christian Is to Put Forth in the Pursuit after Glory*, ed. Joel R. Beeke (Grand Rapids, MI: Soli Deo Gloria, 2019), 23.

12 Ball, *Divine Meditation*, 49.

13 Wilhelmus à Brakel, *The Christian's Reasonable Service*, trans. Bartel Elshout (Morgan, PA: Soli Deo Gloria, 1995), 4:26, 30.

14 Watson, *Heaven Taken by Storm*, 23.

The real significance of meditation lies in its capacity to transform mere thoughts about God and the things of God into heartfelt, soul-stirring, life-transforming convictions about the same. While it is not wholly inaccurate to say that Protestant meditation more or less means "thinking about divine truth," to describe it in that way and leave it there could cause us to miss the significant role that meditation plays in our spiritual formation. This is because the thinking in view when we talk about meditation is not a bare, detached sort of thinking in the way that one might *think about* the best route home from the grocery store. Rather, meditation entails an intentional sort of reflection that seeks to build on a bare understanding of what the text is saying and press further into its personal significance for the reader. One might say that meditation attempts to move God's truth from our heads into our hearts. Consider how Joseph Hall (1574–1656) defined it in his influential work *The Arte of Divine Meditation* (1606): "Meditation is nothing else but a bending of the mind upon some spiritual object, through diverse forms of discourse, until our thoughts come to an issue."[15] So in one sense, according to Hall, meditation *is* simply "thinking about" something, and yet this thinking, this "bending of the mind," cannot be deemed a success "until our thoughts come to an issue."

Similar definitions can be found across a range of early modern Reformed authors, and what binds the disparate definitions together is a shared sense that meditation is a particular sort of thinking that moves toward personal application and transformation; it's a reflection on divine truth that goes somewhere—namely, toward spiritual refreshment and growth. Thus, Thomas Manton defines meditation as "that duty or exercise of religion whereby the mind is applied to the serious and solemn contemplation of spiritual things"—that is, thinking about divine truth. But notice that Manton doesn't leave it there as a bare sort of thinking; rather, he goes on to add that this

---

15 Joseph Hall, *The Arte of Divine Meditation* (London, 1606), 7.

"contemplation" is specifically "for practical uses and purposes."[16] An essentially similar but somewhat more elaborate definition comes from John Ball, who describes meditation as "a serious, earnest and purposed musing upon some point of Christian instruction, tending to lead us forward toward the Kingdome of Heaven, and serving for our daily strengthening against the flesh, the world, and the Devil."[17] So too, for Wilhelmus à Brakel, a Christian meditates not, strictly speaking, to learn new information but rather to press more deeply into "divine things with which he was already . . . acquainted" so as "to be kindled with love, to be comforted, and to be stirred up to lively exercise."[18]

That reference to hearts being "kindled" and "stirred up" likens the growth of godly affections or emotions to maintaining a fireplace. Such fireplace imagery, according to historian Alec Ryrie, was "by far the most common" way for early modern Protestants to explain what they were trying to achieve through spiritual exercises like meditation: they were trying to "stir up" the dimming embers of the heart so that fresh flame might spring into life. "In an age of central heating," explains Ryrie, " 'stirring up' has become a half-dead metaphor, but in pre-modern Britain it referred to something which everybody saw, or did, almost every day."[19] As a fire burns down, the visible flames diminish and eventually die out altogether, leaving behind only cinders dusted over with ash, a dull gray heap that can appear utterly lifeless. And yet, of course, the life is still there, and as the coals are stirred up, they can be coaxed back into blazing through the steady application of motion and oxygen. And that steady application, that stirring up, is what happens inside the heart when a Christian meditates on a promise of God. "Meditation," wrote Isaac Ambrose, "is as the bellows of the soul, that doth kindle and inflame holy affections."[20]

16 Manton, *Complete Works*, 17:270.
17 Ball, *Divine Meditation*, 3–4.
18 À Brakel, *Christian's Reasonable Service*, 4:25.
19 Ryrie, *Reformation Britain*, 67.
20 Isaac Ambrose, *Media: The Middle Things* (London, 1649), 274.

The image of dying embers revived is so effective because it captures both the sense of present coldness that Christians often experience and the lingering desire and latent capacity to recapture the lost flame. One can see both elements clearly on display in Thomas Manton's description of godly thoughts in meditation as "the bellows that kindle and inflame the affections" such that one might "blow up those latent sparkles of grace that are in the soul."[21] The "sparkles of grace" are always there in the regenerate heart, but they cool and dim, requiring that we call on the Lord and apply his prescribed means to kindle and recapture them. It's the dynamic on display when the psalmist declares his sincere "delight" in the commandments of God but then still must beg the Lord in the very next verse, "Incline my heart to your testimonies" (Ps. 119:35–36). On the deepest level, the Christian heart *does* delight in the things of God—whatever the outward appearance at any given moment, there *is* heat and life deep down in the embers—but drawn astray by the world, the flesh, and the devil, our affection grows cold, and we must continually pray that God would incline and reincline our hearts toward him, stirring up the coals and rekindling the flame. And for Puritan authors, a key means that God has given his people to accomplish that goal is the practice of meditation.

The Relevance of Meditation

Given the stress early modern writers laid on meditation as a revealed duty incumbent on all Christians and not an optional add-on, it is worth asking whether contemporary evangelicals have neglected or even forgotten altogether this once-esteemed practice. In his study of Puritan meditation, David Saxton suggests precisely this, arguing that large swaths of the contemporary church are marred by a "shallow spirituality" and that this shallowness has spread in large part because

---

21 Manton, *Complete Works*, 17:275.

"over the last century believers have lost a regular focus on Christian meditation."[22] Likewise, Marian Raikes laments that "although evangelicals do have their own godly heritage of meditation (in the Puritans), they have largely lost sight of it" and that "few evangelical pastors seem to be either teaching or modelling meditative skills."[23]

Surely these criticisms do not accurately describe every contemporary context, but when I reflect on my own experience of growing up in an evangelical church, they don't seem too far off the mark. I remember frequent encouragements to read my Bible but few if any mentions of meditation, and certainly no one was insisting on the centrality and necessity of it. And for better or worse, it's rather difficult to imagine too many twenty-first-century preachers following Thomas Manton in dedicating ten consecutive sermons to unpacking Genesis 24:63: "And Isaac went out to meditate in the field toward evening."

To the extent that contemporary evangelicals do neglect meditation, however, we do so at a significant spiritual cost. In the first instance, if meditation is a biblical duty, as the Puritans believed, then our neglect is actually disobedience. Moreover, if the Puritans were right about the crucial role that meditation plays in our spiritual formation, then our failure to meditate causes us to miss out on its heart-warming, piety-inducing, life-transforming power. But in addition to these significant motivations, it also seems that by recapturing the early modern Reformed emphasis on meditation, we would go a long way toward combatting some of the problems that particularly plague our twenty-first-century cultural moment. Let's consider two such dilemmas raised by our current cultural context: (1) the problem of an overly cognitivist approach to Christian discipleship and (2) the need to slow down in a sped-up world.

---

22 David W. Saxton, *God's Battle Plan for the Mind: The Puritan Practice of Biblical Meditation* (Grand Rapids, MI: Reformation Heritage Books, 2015), 1–2.

23 Marian Raikes, *A Step Too Far: An Evangelical Critique of Christian Mysticism* (London: Latimer Trust, 2006), 10.

Meditation Guards against Brains-on-a-Stick Christianity

As mentioned in previous chapters, a number of prominent voices have criticized evangelical Christianity for being too preoccupied with the head at the expense of the heart. "We often approach discipleship as primarily a didactic endeavor," warns James K. A. Smith, and then we end up acting "as if becoming a disciple of Jesus is largely an intellectual project, a matter of acquiring knowledge."[24] The sad result of this approach, argues Smith, is a "brains-on-a-stick" Christianity in which we become "narrowly focused on filling our intellectual wells with biblical knowledge, convinced that we can *think* our way to holiness—sanctification by information transfer."[25] When we start imagining discipleship as an exclusively cognitive exercise, we lose sight of the deeper biblical insight that human beings are defined ultimately not by what they know but by what they love: "It is my desires that define me. In short, you are what you love."[26]

This sort of critique identifies a very real problem: the bare acquisition of knowledge, even biblical knowledge, does not automatically entail the sort of holistic transformation Christians are called to. Whether it's the observation from James that "even the demons" believe some true facts about God (James 2:19), Paul's insight that there is a kind of "knowledge" that only "puffs up" (1 Cor. 8:1), or Jesus's pervasive critique of the Pharisees (e.g., Matt. 23) despite their well-stocked storehouse of religious information, the Bible acknowledges and warns against the very real possibility that one can know information about God without really *knowing* him at all. As Smith helpfully reminds us, the heart is indeed the key—hence the present book's ultimate goal to help Christians "keep [the] heart with all vigilance" (Prov. 4:23). So the question isn't whether a concern about a brains-on-a-stick Christianity

---

24 James K. A. Smith, *You Are What You Love: The Spiritual Power of Habit* (Grand Rapids, MI: Brazos, 2016), 2.

25 Smith, *You Are What You Love*, 3, 4 (emphasis original).

26 Smith, *You Are What You Love*, 9.

is legitimate—it is legitimate. The question is about finding the correct response to such a concern.

Some have proposed that the solution to an overly brainy Christianity is to deemphasize the role of thinking and learning in discipleship and to instead focus more attention on the role of the body in liturgy and ritual. We return to questions of embodiment and ritual in chapter 9, but for now, let's simply notice that Reformation-minded Protestants have long been well aware of the possibility that one might fill the head without firing the heart. But in responding to this very real danger, they did not deviate from the word-centric piety that they saw revealed in Scripture itself. Rather, they believed that the biblically provided solution to an overly brainy Christianity was found through the regular practice of meditation. John Ball, for example, could warn that those who "hear often" and "read much, but live not in the exercise of Meditation" would end up with an unprofitable sort of religious knowledge "which swimeth in the brain, but is not kindly rooted in the heart."[27] In other words, if you want to avoid a dried-out, unhelpful brains-on-a-stick faith, remember to meditate.

To develop this idea further, observe the way that Puritan authors distinguished between meditation and study. "The student's life," observed Thomas Watson, "looks like meditation but doth vary from it." Acknowledging that we might easily mistake the one for the other—both, after all, always involve thinking, and both often involve reading—Watson offered three key ways to distinguish between study and meditation. First, they "differ in their nature. Study is a work of the brain, meditation of the heart."[28] Watson's contemporary Nathanael Ranew (ca. 1602–1677), drew the same distinction, associating meditation not with "head work, but heart work."[29] So in meditation, then,

---

27 Ball, *Divine Meditation*, 39.

28 Thomas Watson, *Discourses on Important and Interesting Subjects* (Glasgow: Blackie, Fullarton, 1829), 1:203.

29 Nathanael Ranew, *Solitude Improved by Divine Meditation* (Grand Rapids, MI: Soli Deo Gloria, 2019), ix.

we have something that certainly looks like "head work"—involving as it does reading, pondering, reflecting deeply—and yet these authors insist that it is ultimately concerned with the heart.

Second, in Watson's analysis, study and meditation are distinguished by their "design." You study with an eye toward acquiring new knowledge, learning things that you didn't know before you started to read. With meditation, by contrast, you are reflecting more deeply on something you more or less *already know*. As Watson put it, study is about "finding out of a truth," while meditation is about "the spiritual improvement of a truth."[30] This helps explain why some early modern writers actually defined meditation in terms of reflecting on truth already acquired. Recall the definition quoted earlier from Wilhelmus à Brakel, in which meditation involves a Christian reflecting on "divine things with which he was already . . . acquainted" so as "to be kindled with love, to be comforted, and to be stirred up to lively exercise."[31] Thomas Manton made essentially the same point, explaining that "the end of study is information, but the end of meditation is practice, or a work upon the affections."[32]

Third, Watson distinguished between study and meditation by considering the end result of each: the former, on its own, does not lead to spiritual improvement, whereas the latter exists to do just that. As Watson memorably put it, while study is important, it "leaves a man never a whit better; it is like a winter sun that hath little warmth and influence." Meditation, by contrast, "melts the heart when it is frozen and makes it drop into tears of love."[33]

In assessing this distinction between study and meditation, we see that they are certainly related and that both are commended as good things. And in practice, one can imagine the two activities blending

---

30 Watson, *Discourses*, 1:203.
31 À Brakel, *Christian's Reasonable Service*, 4:25.
32 Manton, *Complete Works*, 17:269.
33 Watson, *Discourses*, 1:203.

seamlessly into one another, with one acquiring new information through studying the Bible and then immediately meditating on it without some artificial barrier or time delay separating the one activity from the other. But even if study and meditation functionally overlap, by drawing the distinction in this way, Puritan writers were able to acknowledge and respond to the fact that the bare acquisition of religious knowledge did not necessarily lead to a deeper spiritual life. Thus, by taking the distinction between them seriously, we can also take the brains-on-a-stick concern seriously without abandoning our commitment to being "transformed by the renewal of [the] mind" (Rom. 12:2). As historian Charles Hambrick-Stowe has observed in his study of Puritan piety, "The reading and study of religious texts, though an intellectual activity, did not primarily or finally have an intellectual end." Rather, insists Hambrick-Stowe, "the exercise of the rational faculty opened the way to a changed heart."[34] Thus, as we try to untangle the relationship between so-called "head work" and "heart work," it is crucial to grasp the role of meditation in holding the two together.

Meditation Forces Us to Slow Down in an Age of Speed

A second reason for twenty-first-century Christians to especially prioritize meditation is the way that the practice helps us slow down in an age increasingly obsessed with speed. Many cultural commentators have remarked on the rapidly accelerating pace of change in our digital age. Deluged with infinite scrolls of news updates, "curated" images, and hot-take tweets, the pace at which we are expected to absorb new information has so rapidly increased that the journalist Robert Colvile has dubbed our historical moment "the Great Acceleration."[35] Podcast

---

34 Charles E. Hambrick-Stowe, *The Practice of Piety: Puritan Devotional Disciplines in Seventeenth-Century New England* (Chapel Hill: University of North Carolina Press, 1982), 158.

35 Robert Colvile, *The Great Acceleration: How the World Is Getting Faster, Faster* (New York: Bloomsbury, 2016).

apps can seamlessly play back their recorded conversations at double (or even triple!) speed. Thanks to Spotify and Netflix, you no longer need to trek to the mall to get the latest music and movies but can instead instantly stream them. And once you've started watching that new Hollywood blockbuster, you may notice that the average shot length seems to be getting shorter. Film data researcher Stephen Follows calculated that the average shot length in the popular *Iron Man* films has decreased in each subsequent iteration, falling from 3.7 seconds in the original *Iron Man* to 3.0 seconds in *Iron Man 2* to a lightning-quick 2.4 seconds in *Iron Man 3*.[36] Amazon and other online retailers work tirelessly to increase the pace of both their deliveries to your doorstep and the shopping experience itself. Indeed, testing at Amazon revealed that delaying page-loading times by as little as one hundred milliseconds can significantly decrease the likelihood that a user will continue shopping, and internal research at Google concluded that slowing down search results by just half a second reduced subsequent web traffic by 20 percent.[37]

Life is getting faster. And while some might be inclined to dismiss this accelerating pace as neutral or even beneficial, there are good reasons to suspect that our habitual exposure to this hyper-paced world has serious consequences for our capacity to slow down and pay attention to things that really matter. Some have even suggested that our constant immersion in the mind-boggling-fast and seemingly infinitely interconnected world wide web is actually reshaping the very architecture of our brains. This was the basic premise of Nicholas Carr's widely discussed 2010 bestseller *The Shallows* and has been taken up more recently by researcher Gloria Mark, who argues that the internet's very "design unleashes the floodgates for distraction" and that "the organization of

---

36 Stephen Follows, "How Many Shots Are in the Average Movie?," Stephen Follows Decoding the World through Data, July 3, 2017, https://stephenfollows.com/.

37 Greg Linden, "Marissa Mayer at Web 2.0," Geeking with Greg, November 9, 2006, http://glinden .blogspot.com/.

the internet, with its nodes and links and ever-changing content, has shaped not just where we pay attention but also the frequency at which we shift our attention."[38]

For Christians, and particularly for those Christians committed to the sort of word-centric Protestant piety that we have been exploring in this book, these developments are troubling, to say the least. This is because Scripture calls us to think on God and the things of God, and such purposeful pondering does not lend itself to speed, efficiency, and the rapidity demanded by our always-on digital world. For the psalmist, God's promises and commandments were to be treated like honey, a rare treat surely meant to be savored rather than sped through:

> How sweet are your words to my taste,
>   sweeter than honey to my mouth! (Ps. 119:103; cf. 19:10)

Contrast that sense of slowing down to appreciate what really matters with this description of our fast-paced culture from author Johann Hari: "In some ways, we are increasingly speed-reading life, skimming hurriedly from one thing to another, absorbing less and less."[39]

If the Christian life is to be marked by a thoughtful giving thanks to God "in all circumstances" (1 Thess. 5:18) and an ever-growing awareness that our very lives and everything else besides comes "from him and through him and to him" (Rom. 11:36), then believers must surely want to resist any sense that we are somehow "speed-reading life" and "absorbing less and less." Meditation can help us with that because to practice it aright requires that we slow right down. One can do many things quickly, but meditation is, by definition, not one of them. Listen to how Thomas Manton described it:

38 Nicholas G. Carr, *The Shallows: What the Internet Is Doing to Our Brains* (New York: Norton, 2010); Gloria Mark, *Attention Span: Finding Focus for a Fulfilling Life* (London: William Collins, 2023), 146–47.

39 Johann Hari, *Stolen Focus: Why You Can't Pay Attention* (London: Bloomsbury, 2022), 32.

Meditate upon the word; do not study the word in a cursory manner, or content yourselves with a slight taste, or a little volatile affection; but ponder it seriously, that it may enter into your very heart. Hasty and perfunctory thoughts work nothing. Meat must be well chewed and digested, if you would have it turn into good blood and spirits. You must follow it close till it settle into some affection.[40]

Manton's food imagery was common among Puritan authors looking to describe meditation. If reading Scripture was likened to eating, meditation was compared to the digestive process through which food was transformed into the vital stuff of life. Meditation, wrote Nathanael Ranew, "is like the assimilating or digesting power, helping to concoct spiritual food, and turn it into spiritual nourishment."[41] And while it is possible to eat one's food quickly, digestion moves at its own, rather slower pace. So too with meditation: it is, by definition, something that cannot be accomplished in haste. To practice it *is* to slow down. It is to block out the rush of the urgent and new so that people can give their mind and heart to what is ancient and eternally significant.

The Practice of Meditation

At this point, if you're anything like me, you may be feeling a mild to moderate sense of frustration with the way our discussion of meditation has thus far lacked a certain nuts-and-bolts specificity. Perhaps as you've read the foregoing exploration of meditation's meaning and benefits, you've been nodding along in agreement, yet you've also been feeling a rising tide of impatience as you wonder when, if ever, we will get on with explaining just what exactly the person meditating is expected to actually *do*. Even once we understand that meditation involves an intentional reflection on divine truth with an eye toward stirring up godly affections, we might still ask what such a project should actually entail.

40 Manton, *Complete Works*, 6:106.
41 Ranew, *Solitude Improved*, ix.

I speak here from personal experience, and if your mind also gravitates toward such practically oriented queries, you may be disappointed with much of what early modern Protestant devotional literature has to offer, at least on this particular point. Puritan reflections on the topic of meditation are often long on general exhortations and rather short on concrete specifics. As historian Alec Ryrie has noted, even the most adamant Protestant proponents of meditation "scrupulously avoided being prescriptive."[42] So, for example, after waxing eloquent on the spiritual blessings of meditation and urging that all Christians do it, Wilhelmus à Brakel concluded his discussion with what might seem to be a surprising indifference toward precisely how his readers should put this vital duty into practice: "I do not wish to prescribe rules to you. Begin with it and you will experience yourself which way is best for you."[43] Thomas Manton struck a similar note when he warned his readers to "not bridle up the free spirit by the rules of method." Rather than worrying overly much about "rules and prescriptions," Manton recommended "voluntary and free meditations" and described any specific guidance given as "arbitrary directions" meant to be helpful but never binding: "We do not prescribe, but advise."[44] This sort of nonchalance with respect to prescriptive practicalities is precisely what historian Charles Hambrick-Stowe had in mind when he concluded that "Puritans were undogmatic about these matters and approached them in a utilitarian spirit."[45]

In large measure, such reticence to spell out exactly *how* one should go about meditating stemmed from a desire to avoid the excesses of Roman Catholic writers and to hew more closely to what the Bible explicitly commands. Though early modern Protestants felt confident that "meditation is a duty lying upon every Christian," they were well

42 Ryrie, *Reformation Britain*, 116.
43 À Brakel, *Christian's Reasonable Service*, 4:30.
44 Manton, *Complete Works*, 17:281.
45 Hambrick-Stowe, *Practice of Piety*, 163.

aware that Scripture did not provide a detailed roadmap.[46] And thus, although scholars debate the precise degree of overlap between early modern Protestant and Catholic approaches to meditation, it seems safe to say that Catholic authors typically felt more comfortable offering detailed, specific instructions than did their Protestant counterparts.[47]

This contrast becomes evident when one contrasts the hesitant attitude toward specifics displayed in the above quotation from à Brakel with the rather more elaborate instructions spelled out in classic Catholic works like Francis de Sales's (1567–1622) *An Introduction to the Devout Life* (1609) and Ignatius of Loyola's *Spiritual Exercises* (1548). *Spiritual Exercises*, for example, offers a roughly thirty-day-long program with detailed instructions and numerous directive meditations. Emphasizing its practical nature, one Jesuit scholar has described the book as "a manual to guide exercises . . . comparable to a book on 'how to play tennis.'"[48] Among Protestant devotional writers, one finds less on *how* to play and quite a bit more on *why* one would want to play. Committed as they were to *sola Scriptura*, Reformation-minded Protestants were reluctant to provide the sort of detailed directions sometimes found in Catholic devotional manuals, in part because they worried that doing so would inappropriately bind the consciences of their readers with extrabiblical prescriptions.

So if you are looking for a detailed, step-by-step how-to guide that ensures you are meditating "correctly," then our early modern Reformation guides may disappoint you. Even when they devoted an entire treatise or sermon series to the topic, these authors had a way of celebrat-

---

46 Watson, *Discourses*, 1:201.

47 For three slightly different readings of this issue, see Hambrick-Stowe, *Practice of Piety*, 25–39; Ted A. Campbell, *The Religion of the Heart: A Study of European Religious Life in the Seventeenth and Eighteenth Centuries* (Columbia: University of South Carolina Press, 1991), 42–44; Tom Schwanda, *Soul Recreation: The Contemplative-Mystical Piety of Puritanism* (Eugene, OR: Pickwick, 2012), 131–33.

48 George E. Ganss, "General Introduction," in *Ignatius of Loyola: The Spiritual Exercises and Selected Works*, by Ignatius of Loyola, ed. George E. Ganss, Classics of Western Spirituality (New York: Paulist, 1991), 50.

ing meditation at length while remaining rather vague about what one is actually meant to do. In Nathanael Ranew's imposingly large work *Solitude Improved by Divine Meditation* (1670), the author devoted many pages to the benefits of this "most noble self-entertainment," repeatedly urged his readers to practice it, and spent much of the book describing various topics on which one might profitably meditate (e.g., salvation, death, heaven)—all while falling short of anywhere clearly insisting that a person meditate in this or that specific fashion. Even when, toward the end of the book, Ranew eventually arrived at a section promisingly labeled "Of the directions relating to meditation . . . for such as would begin," what follows might be best described as an elaborate meditation on meditation rather than a step-by-step guide for the perplexed.[49]

So what is one to do? Can't we at least say *something* about the specifics of meditation? Well, yes. So long as we remember that the Puritans understood themselves to be "offering flexible guidelines and not rigid rules to be followed,"[50] we can indeed note some of those practical pieces of advice that recur regularly in Puritan writings on meditation. Here are five to help us get going.

Hold Meditation and Scripture Closely Together

Functioning as one-third of what we've labeled the Reformation triangle, meditation must be held in a close relationship with both Scripture intake and prayer. In the next chapter, we consider prayer directly and return to how all three spiritual disciplines work together in concert. But for now, we must underscore the degree to which Reformation meditation was always meditation on what God has revealed in his word. Most often, this means meditating directly on a passage of Scripture: we hear God's words to us in Scripture, and then we naturally turn to think about them, reflect on them, and apply them to our

49 Ranew, *Solitude Improved*, vii, 260.
50 Schwanda, *Soul Recreation*, 129.

own hearts. "Reading and meditation," wrote Thomas Watson, "must appear together." Indeed, the two activities so complement and complete one another that each can be said to derive its real benefit from its proximity to the other: "Meditation without reading is erroneous; reading without meditation is barren."[51]

Meditating directly on Scripture, then, ought to be the bulk and mainstay of our practice. Thus, assuming one already has a commitment to daily Bible reading as discussed in the previous chapter, meditation largely takes the form of spending deliberate moments reflecting on what one is reading that day. There are, however, other prompts for meditation encouraged by Reformed authors. In addition to directly meditating on a passage of Scripture, Reformed Protestant devotional manuals regularly encouraged Christians both to meditate on one's own life—thankfulness for one's blessings, sorrow for one's sins, wonder at God's providential leading, and so forth—and to meditate on God's glory as seen in creation. According to the Puritan George Swinnock (1627–1673), "God hath given us three books, which we ought to be studying whilst we are living: the book of conscience, the book of Scripture, and the book of the creature [i.e., creation]."[52] All three "books" are fit subjects for meditation, and we explore self-examination and deliberate reflection on the created order in chapters 6 and 7 respectively. Yet it is worth noting carefully that even when meditation is not quite so directly linked to, say, one's morning Bible reading, it is vital that the content of one's meditation closely reflects what the Bible has already given. To prevent our meditation "from degenerating into mere daydreaming on sacred themes," B. B. Warfield recommended that we "meditate chiefly with the Bible in our hands and always on its truths."[53]

51 Watson, *Heaven Taken by Storm*, 118.

52 George Swinnock, *The Works of George Swinnock* (Edinburgh: James Nichol, 1868), 2:417.

53 Benjamin B. Warfield, *Selected Shorter Writings of Benjamin B. Warfield*, ed. John E. Meeter (Nutley, NJ: Presbyterian and Reformed, 1970), 2:484–85.

Here is a point at which Protestant meditation differs, at least in emphasis, from its Roman Catholic counterpart. Writing on Puritan piety, historian Tom Schwanda notes that "the role of Scripture was essential in shaping Puritan meditation, though less influential for Roman Catholics."[54] For Roman Catholicism, this relative willingness to deviate from a strictly Bible-based approach to meditation can be seen in a greater openness to imaginatively re-creating biblical scenes in the mind, a process that tends toward adding potentially elaborate extrabiblical details. It also appears in a stress on extrabiblical content such as the Marian dogmas and the cult of the saints and in the way Catholic devotional guides allow the yearly cycle of the extrabiblical liturgical calendar to structure devotional practices more generally.

Distinguish between "Settled" and "Occasional" Meditation

Although it is true that Puritan authors did not insist on a one-size-fits-all approach to the practice of meditation, almost all of them found it useful to divide the practice into two basic types: there was a "deliberate," "solemn," or "settled" meditation and also a "sudden," "occasional," or "extemporal" meditation. As Nathanael Ranew explained it, "Meditation is either that which is more set and solemn, or that which is more sudden and short."[55] The bulk of our discussion in this chapter is concerned with so-called "settled" or "deliberate" meditation, in which one incorporates intentional reflection into his or her dedicated devotional times. But before returning to focus largely on settled meditation, we should say a word on its shorter, more spontaneous counterpart.

As Joel Beeke has observed, "Nearly every Puritan book on meditation mentions occasional meditation."[56] The term referred to the sort of brief, explicitly Christian thoughts and reflections that one might

---

54 Schwanda, *Soul Recreation*, 132.
55 Ranew, *Solitude Improved*, 87.
56 Joel R. Beeke, *Puritan Reformed Spirituality* (Darlington, UK: Evangelical Press, 2006), 75–76.

have all throughout the day. Such godly musings could arise seemingly unprompted or be triggered by one's surroundings and circumstances, the natural world often serving this function. Indeed, Reformed meditation on God's glory as displayed in his creation was so thoroughgoing that we return to the subject in greater depth in chapter 7. But for now, observe that one's "sudden" meditations could be linked to almost anything. Lewis Bayly, for example, suggested that getting dressed in the morning could be an occasion for remembering "that as thine apparel serves to cover thy shame, and to fence thy body from cold, so thou shouldst be as careful to cover thy soul with that wedding garment which is the righteousness of Christ."[57] And then again, at the end of the day, Bayly found ample material to prompt further "occasional meditation," this time on the themes of death, resurrection, and comfort in God's providential care:

> When thou seest thy bed, let it put thee in mind of thy grave. . . . [L]et, therefore, thy bed-clothes represent to thee the mould of the earth that shall cover thee; thy sheets, thy winding-sheet; thy sleep, thy death; thy waking, thy resurrection: and being laid down in thy bed, when thou perceives sleep to approach, say, "I will lay me down and sleep in peace, for thou, Lord, only makest me dwell in safety" (Psal. iv. 8).[58]

Bayly's morning and evening extemporaneous meditations nicely illustrate three hallmarks of "occasional meditation" more generally: the meditations were (1) brief, (2) prompted by some mundane occurrence, and (3) shaped, constrained, and inspired by Scripture, even though not necessarily arising in direct response to it. For Puritan devotional writers, such God-directed thoughts would be sprinkled throughout

---

57 Lewis Bayly, *The Practice of Piety: Directing a Christian to Walk, That He May Please God* (Grand Rapids, MI: Soli Deo Gloria, 2019), 104.
58 Bayly, *Practice of Piety*, 142.

the day, thus helping the Christian keep the heart throughout each day. As the Puritan William Benn (1600–1681) put it, "Keep it we ought with all diligence; watch it by night, and by day; at home, and abroad; when we are in company, and when we are alone, at all times, and in all places."[59] Occasional meditation helps us do just that.

Grab Hold of a Thought, and Don't Let It Go

At its core, meditation is about intentionally lingering over particular scriptural truths, promises, stories, and insights so that God's word by his Spirit might work in us, not as a dead letter but as that which "is living and active, sharper than any two-edged sword, piercing to the division of soul and of spirit, of joints and of marrow, and discerning the thoughts and intentions of the heart" (Heb. 4:12). To this end, many of the Puritans' most detailed instructions for meditation serve not, as we see in some Roman Catholic guides, to set forth a specific spiritual program to be enacted stepwise over time but rather to encourage readers to grab hold of specific God-honoring thoughts and then refuse to let them go, turning them over and over in the mind until eventually they work their way into the heart.

Peter Martyr Vermigli taught that "meditation . . . mainly consists in two things," both of which entail a closer engagement with the Bible:

> The first is that you ponder as carefully as possible the words and sentences that occur [in Scripture]. They are extremely fruitful and contain in themselves infinite delights. The second is that you search through the Scriptures for other passages that are related to the ones you have in hand.[60]

Practically speaking, this means that many specific Protestant instructions for meditation often amount to simply uncovering different angles

59 William Benn, *Soul-Prosperity* (London, 1683), 290.
60 Vermigli, *Peter Martyr Library*, 5:285.

and questions through which one might approach a text of Scripture. As Thomas Watson put it, "A wise Christian is like the artist," who "views with seriousness, and ponders the things of religion."[61] As a landscape painter carefully observes the nuanced colors of the subject at hand, the interplay of light and shadow, textures, shapes and contours, so too the Christian in meditation looks carefully at every aspect of divine truth.

To make roughly this same point, the Puritan William Fenner (1600–1640) likened meditation to a person thoroughly investigating a house. While one could learn something about the house and its contents by standing in the street and taking a look or even by "peeping in at the windows," you'd certainly learn a lot more if you were to "come nigh, and draw the latch, and come into the house, and go into the rooms, and look about them." This closer, sustained inquiry into a scriptural truth is what we do when we meditate on it. "Meditation pulls the latch of the truth and looks into every closet, and every cupboard, and every angle of it."[62]

The precise shape of such an inquiry, in practice, takes many forms. Often it involves sitting with a truth and allowing the mind to explore its different aspects and implications. Thus, upon reading the promise of Isaiah 1:18 that "though your sins are like scarlet, they shall be as white as snow," Thomas Watson sits with that image, refuses to rush on, and instead chews it over in his mind:

> Scarlet is so deep a dye, that all the art of man cannot take it out; but behold here a promise, God will lay the soul a whitening; he will make of a scarlet sinner a milk white saint. By virtue of this refining and consecrating work, a Christian is made partaker of the divine nature; he hath an identity and fitness to have communion with God for ever; meditate much on this promise.[63]

---

61 Watson, *Discourses*, 1:200.

62 William Fenner, *The Use and Benefit of Divine Meditation* (London, 1657), 2–3.

63 Watson, *Discourses*, 1:211–12.

There is nothing especially novel or creative about Watson's meditation here, but the sort of extended reflection he models does require that one slow down and think on the biblical imagery in a more sustained fashion than we are often accustomed to doing. Sometimes this process involves considering how the small words in a verse—the pronouns, the prepositions, the linking words—actually function, as when William Fenner asks, "Dost thou know that Jesus Christ dyed for sinners? Ponder it with the true drift of it, how that it is not to let men go on *in* their sins, but to save them *from* their sins."[64]

Many of the specific forms that godly meditation takes involve comparing one Scripture passage with another. As Vermigli put it, "Nothing is more helpful for explaining the Scriptures than the sacred letters themselves," and thus searching through the Bible for "passages that are related to the ones you have in hand" becomes "a useful and a joyous hunt, not for deer and boars, but for heavenly treasures, which we can take with us as food for our journey all the way to heaven."[65] So upon reading about a particular attribute of God, one might, for example, think about how that attribute relates to another revealed aspect of who God is: "Dost thou know God is mercifull? Ponder it with his justice."[66] This sort of Bible reading is active reading in the best sense of the word. As historian Kate Narveson notes, Puritans meditating on Scripture "did not simply sit down and ponder a passage of Scripture"; rather, "they began with a passage that acted as a magnet for like passages," such that "the process had a visceral force when the meditator confronted her soul with the accumulated texts."[67]

To do this well—indeed, to do it at all—we need to slow down our Bible reading. For some of us, this may mean reading fewer chapters each day than we have attempted in the past. As we saw in the previous

---

64 Fenner, *Use and Benefit*, 15 (emphasis original).

65 Vermigli, *Peter Martyr Library*, 5:285.

66 Fenner, *Use and Benefit*, 15.

67 Kate Narveson, *Bible Readers and Lay Writers in Early Modern England: Gender and Self-Definition in an Emergent Writing Culture* (London: Routledge, 2016), 97.

chapter, many older Protestant writers have been less interested in the volume of our reading and more interested in how we can get the most spiritual benefit out of what we do cover. With respect to meditation, Puritan authors give us no consistent, definitive answer regarding "how long" we ought to do it. In answering the "how long" question, they typically begin by stressing that the purpose of meditation is to warm the heart, and then they conclude that one must meditate for as long as it takes to warm up. So at one point in his writings, Thomas Watson indicated that even just fifteen minutes a day would "leave a mighty impression," but his substantive answer to the "how long" question was more pragmatic and less prescriptive: "Meditate so long till thou findest thy heart grow warm."[68]

Apply God's Truth to Yourself

Given this Puritan emphasis on meditating until "thy heart grow warm," it should not surprise us to discover that much of the practical mechanics of meditation revolves around figuring out how to apply biblical insights to our lives. In her study of early modern Protestant devotional practices, Narveson observes that for the Puritans, "knowledge was useless if it remained merely in the head." As a result, these believers worked to "feel the truth by applying their reading to their own hearts," learning to "read, re-read, and meditate, so that the Word is made part of one's being and transformed into the structures of experience."[69] Such a commitment to applying God's word was perhaps put most succinctly by John Ball when he declared that "application is the life of meditation."[70]

This aspect of meditation requires both scriptural knowledge and a Scripture-framed self-knowledge, and thus it blends quite naturally into the idea of self-examination, which we cover in greater detail in

---

68 Watson, *Heaven Taken by Storm*, 29; Watson, *Discourses*, 1:254.
69 Narveson, *Bible Readers and Lay Writers*, 90–91.
70 Ball, *Divine Meditation*, 132.

chapter 6. But for now, simply notice that most often the way that meditation "works" to stir up godly affections is by applying scriptural truth to one's life in a fashion not unlike what faithful preachers attempt to do each week from the pulpit. So this might involve taking hold of a biblical promise, thinking about ways that God has kept it for you in the past, and then actively turning with fresh trust to the God who will surely keep on keeping his promises in the future. In this spirit, the Puritan David Clarkson (1622–1686) exhorted his readers to "collect the promises; treasure them up; methodise them aright; meditate on them. . . . Gather them. They are the meat that you must live upon in this wilderness. . . . Be as careful to gather them as the Israelites to gather manna."[71] Meditation could also involve searching one's heart for sin and praying for forgiveness or pondering God's blessings and thanking him. Or it might involve meditating on the hope of the resurrection and future glory, reflecting on the ways that our present disappointments and sorrows are in fact helping prepare us for "an eternal weight of glory beyond all comparison" (2 Cor. 4:17).

In all this, whatever convoluted associations we might have with the word *meditation*, when we encounter early modern Reformed writers describing their understanding of the practice, we find Christian men and women who really are not doing anything more complicated than slowing down and reflecting honestly on the ways that biblical ideas intersect with their own hearts and lives. Reckoning with that baseline simplicity that sits at the heart of meditation brings us nicely to our final practical point.

Don't Overthink It

We would perhaps do well to conclude our "practical advice" by returning to the opening point of this section: many Reformed authors were reluctant to be overly prescriptive when talking about meditation.

---

71 David Clarkson, *The Practical Works of David Clarkson* (Edinburgh: James Nichol, 1865), 1:189.

If early modern Reformed Protestants were somewhat evasive when it came to the mechanics of how to meditate, we would be wise to recognize that this was ultimately a feature and not a bug. For in addition to the basic Reformation desire to avoid insisting on rules not found in the Bible, the lack of detailed instructions found in Protestant devotional manuals also simply reflects the nature of meditation itself. As we have already noted, meditation *is*, in large part, nothing more than an intentional sort of thinking. It's a thinking about God and the things of God with an eye toward personal application. There is nothing magical, mystical, or even especially complicated about it. When we meditate, we are using the same faculties that helped us understand the text in the first place, but we are then simply building on that understanding by deliberately considering more deeply how those biblical realities intersect with our reality.

As such, we need to be careful that our understandable desire to know more about exactly *how* to meditate does not betray an unhelpful assumption that "real" or "correct" meditation must involve some sort of secret technique accessible only to the spiritual elite. As Marian Raikes warns, one of the dangers of the mystical impulse throughout church history has been an "unbiblical tendency to 'classify' Christians . . . compounded by the division within mysticism into beginners, proficients and perfects, and by the concept of 'the mystical faculty' as a special divine gift."[72]

Rather than imagining that there is some secret, unspoken technique lying behind the many Puritan exhortations to meditate, we should recognize that perhaps the main value the Puritans found in distinguishing between the "head work" of reading and the "heart work" of meditation was the distinction itself. In actual practice, reading Scripture and meditating on Scripture bleed into one another, such that the two activities often become scarcely distinguishable at all. As

---

72 Raikes, *Step Too Far*, 22.

we see in the next chapter, prayer also becomes imperceptibly folded in, thus completing our Reformation triangle. But to note that this blending takes place in practice is not to nullify the value of drawing such distinctions in theory.

To distinguish between reading and meditation is to recognize that a bare intellectual comprehension of biblical texts is not enough. It is to guard against the temptation to imagine that letting "the word of Christ dwell in you richly" (Col. 3:16) can be accomplished merely through a mechanical approach to Bible reading in which more always equals better. Puritan writers were constantly trying to underscore this point, stretching the limits of their imagination to better convey this sense that Bible reading was not really complete until it was joined up with godly meditation: "Reading brings me meat, meditation brings forth the sweetness. Reading brings the coals to the wood, meditation makes the flame. Reading brings me the sword of the word, meditation whets it."[73]

The payoff here for us is to recognize that in simply distinguishing between reading and meditation, we are already halfway there. Approaching God's word with these two categories in your mind rather than just the single category of Bible reading (as I was taught growing up) will, all by itself, equip you to do the sorts of things that Puritan authors had in mind when they talked at length about meditation. So don't get caught up in the trap of overthinking the mechanics of meditation, but rather see it as the appropriate Spirit-wrought response to reading or hearing God's word: you hear from God in Scripture, and then you *think* about what he has said through meditation, applying it prayerfully to your own life.

What Do You Attend To?

As we've noted throughout this chapter, early modern Protestants placed a very high premium on meditation. Listen to how a group of

---

73 Ranew, *Solitude Improved*, 110.

seventeenth-century English Presbyterian ministers pleaded with their readers to pay more attention to this "neglected" duty:

> If thou wouldest have thy understanding enlightened with the knowledge of God, thy affections inflamed with the love of God, thy heart established with the promises of God, thy solitariness cheared up with the company of God, thy afflictions mitigated with the comforts of God; and if thou wouldest have thy thoughts, words and works regulated by the command of God, pray and consider, pray and meditate.[74]

Much of this insistence stemmed, as we've seen, from the way meditation functions as the God-appointed means through which ideas about God are transformed into love for God. But there is another side to it as well, one that is perhaps even more fundamental and is a fitting note on which to close this chapter. Namely, meditation is so important because of the reality that, to a significant extent, our reality is shaped and who we are is revealed by what we give our sustained attention to.

The literary critic Sven Birkerts writes that "what we attend to gives a picture of who we are."[75] And in her bestselling book *Rapt: Attention and the Focused Life*, author Winifred Gallagher makes a similar point, noting that "your life is the sum total of what you focus on." Listen to how she elaborates on this point:

> If you could look backward at your years thus far, you'd see that your life has been fashioned from what you've paid attention to and what you haven't. You'd observe that of the myriad sights and sounds, thoughts and feelings that you could have focused on, you selected a relative few, which became what you've confidently called "reality." You'd also be struck by the fact that if you had paid attention to other things, your

---

74 Samuel Cotes et al., "To the Christian Reader," in Ball, *Divine Meditation*, n.p.
75 Sven Birkerts, *Changing the Subject: Art and Attention in the Internet Age* (Minneapolis: Graywolf, 2015), 244–45.

reality and your life would be very different. Attention has created the experience and, significantly, the self stored in your memory.[76]

Birkerts and Gallagher are not writing here as Christians trying to think biblically. And yet the main thrust of their observations chimes nicely with the Bible's emphasis on the high degree to which our interior lives and the thoughts that we habitually entertain determine and reveal who we really are. The psalmist asks God, "Turn my eyes from looking at worthless things; / and give me life in your ways," suggesting that a mind preoccupied by "worthless things" is incompatible with enjoying life in God's ways (Ps. 119:37). Because Paul insists that spiritual formation comes from "the renewal of your mind" (Rom. 12:2), he instructs believers, "Set your minds on things that are above" (Col. 3:2). Unlike the "enemies of the cross of Christ," who have "minds set on earthly things" (Phil. 3:18–19), Paul urges Christians to "think about" and dwell on "whatever is true, whatever is honorable, whatever is just, whatever is pure, whatever is lovely, whatever is commendable," whatever is "excellen[t]" and "worthy of praise" (Phil. 4:8). And Jesus teaches that what truly "defiles" a person is not something external but rather what comes from a person's interior life:

> What comes out of a person is what defiles him. For from within, out of the heart of man, come evil thoughts, sexual immorality, theft, murder, adultery, coveting, wickedness, deceit, sensuality, envy, slander, pride, foolishness. All these evil things come from within, and they defile a person. (Mark 7:20–23)

As Richard Baxter noted, in Scripture "our thoughts are so considerable a part of God's service, that they are often put for the whole."[77]

---

76 Winifred Gallagher, *Rapt: Attention and the Focused Life* (New York: Penguin, 2010), 14, 2.

77 Richard Baxter, *The Practical Works of Richard Baxter: Selected Treatises* (Peabody, MA: Hendrickson, 2010), 221.

And if who we are is so closely tied to the thoughts we entertain, so closely bound up with what we give our sustained attention to, then what could be more important than cultivating the habit of pondering, thinking about, and dwelling on God and the things of God? That sort of habitual God-directed and God-honoring attention is precisely what we seek to cultivate when we cultivate the practice of meditation. This is what the Puritan Oliver Heywood (1630–1702) was getting at when he wrote that "holy thoughts form a great part of a Christian's devotion," such that "this exercise of thoughts is indeed a Christian's walking with God."[78] We exercise our "holy thoughts" most directly in meditation, and in so doing, we walk more closely with God.

---

[78] Oliver Heywood, *The Whole Works of the Rev. Oliver Heywood* (Idle, UK: John Vint, 1827), 2:278–79.

5

Prayer

Responding to God

AS INNUMERABLE SAINTS WILL TESTIFY, authentic Christian life
and ministry is fueled by prayer and impossible without it. For Francis
(1912–1984) and Edith Schaeffer (1914–2013), this insight became
real one morning around the family breakfast table when Francis turned
to his wife and asked a simple but troubling question:

> Supposing we had awakened today to find everything concerning the
> Holy Spirit and prayer removed from the Bible. . . . What difference
> would it make *practically* between the way we worked yesterday and
> the way we would work today, and tomorrow? What difference would
> it make in the majority of Christians' practical work and plans? . . .
> Isn't much work done by human talent, energy and clever ideas?
> Where does the supernatural power of God have a *real* place?[1]

As this conversation led to others, the Schaeffers became convinced
that their lives needed to be marked by a real reliance on prayer and

---

1 Edith Schaeffer, *L'Abri* (London: Norfolk, 1969), 64–65.

that their next ministry should be established as a lived testimony to "the reality . . . that God exists, and that He is the One who has, time after time, answered prayer in the midst of well-nigh impossible circumstances to bring about something out of nothing."[2] The result was the establishment in 1955 of L'Abri in the Swiss Alps, a unique ministry founded to be "a spiritual shelter for any in need of spiritual help" and committed to a radical reliance on prayer.[3] Practically speaking, this emphasis on prayer manifested itself in the Schaeffers' decision to refrain from advertising the work or actively soliciting monetary gifts: "We make our financial and material needs known to God alone, in prayer, rather than sending out pleas for money."[4]

As one reads more about L'Abri's growth and impact, it's hard not to be impressed by both the nature of God's provision for the ministry and the faith of the Schaeffers in response to it. As Edith remarked after one especially timely answer to prayer, "Chance? Coincidence? Luck? To us it was a tremendous instance of answered prayer, a wonderful demonstration of the existence of a Personal God who deals with His children as individual, meaningful personalities, and in an individual way."[5] The Schaeffers sought to consistently lean on and lean into prayer, relying on God and calling out to him in a manner consistent with what they claimed to believe: that God was actually there and would hear and respond to them when they cried out. And by all accounts they were successful in their attempt. As Anky Rookmaaker (1915–2003) would later recall, "What impressed me most during that first visit to L'Abri in Switzerland was that the Schaeffers *believed* in prayer."[6]

The story of Francis and Edith Schaeffer founding L'Abri stands out as a powerful example of a Christian couple maturing in their spiri-

2   Schaeffer, *L'Abri*, 17.
3   Schaeffer, *L'Abri*, 13.
4   Schaeffer, *L'Abri*, 16.
5   Schaeffer, *L'Abri*, 98.
6   Anky Rookmaaker, "Lifting Up Holy Hands," in *Francis A. Schaeffer: Portraits of the Man and His Work*, ed. Lane T. Dennis (Westchester, IL: Crossway, 1986), 158 (emphasis original).

tual life through a deeper understanding of what prayer is: prayer is real communication with a God who is actually there and really does listen. And in furnishing us with their example, they join a long list of Reformation-minded Christians who have walked a similar path, discovering for themselves the inestimable value of prayer. Roughly half a century before the Schaeffers enjoyed their insight into prayer's significance, B. B. Warfield could be found urging his students, "Above all else that you strive after, cultivate the grace of private prayer."[7] And if we jumped roughly another half century earlier, we would find the Victorian Baptist preacher Charles Spurgeon (1834–1892) urging the students at his Pastors' College to "make the most of prayer," for "prayer is the master-weapon." Spurgeon continued, "We should be greatly wise if we used it more. . . . All hell is vanquished when the believer bows his knee. . . . Prayer links us with the Eternal, the Omnipotent, the Infinite; and hence it is our chief resort."[8] All the way back to the early modern period, we find a great cloud of witnesses testifying to the significance of prayer for authentic Christian life and ministry.

In this chapter, we explore this subject further, considering its special significance, its definition, and how we can approach it in a way that is consistent with the Reformed tradition. Finally, we consider prayer as it sits within our Reformation triangle, joining Scripture intake and meditation as that which fundamentally constitutes our communion with God.

The Significance of Prayer in Reformed Spiritual Formation

Across all major expressions of historic Christianity, prayer plays a central role in spiritual formation. In this the Reformers and their successors were no different, and it is difficult to overstate the significance

---

7 Benjamin B. Warfield, *Selected Shorter Writings of Benjamin B. Warfield*, ed. John E. Meeter (Nutley, NJ: Presbyterian and Reformed, 1970), 2:482.

8 C. H. Spurgeon, *An All-Round Ministry: Addresses to Ministers and Students* (London: Banner of Truth, 1960), 313–14.

they have historically assigned to prayer. In the preface to his *Discourse of the Work of the Holy Spirit in Prayer* (1682), John Owen declared that it would be "altogether needless" to begin his book with any general comment on "the necessity, benefit, and use of prayer in general." The reason for this was not that Owen lacked interest but rather that he assumed that the absolute centrality of prayer within the Christian life was a matter of such widespread, unquestioned agreement that any further comment on his part would be superfluous: "All men will readily acknowledge that as without [prayer] there can be no religion at all, so the life and exercise of all religion does principally consist therein."[9] Owen's assumption that prayer represented "the life and exercise of all religion" was widely shared among Reformation-minded early modern Christians. As historian Alec Ryrie summarizes, "Private prayer was the lifeblood of Protestant piety, the central love affair between God and the believer."[10] When early modern Protestants wrote on the Christian life, they devoted large swaths to the subject. In John Calvin's *Institutes*, for example, one of the longest chapters treats prayer, stretching to seventy pages in the McNeill-Battles edition.[11] In the Westminster Larger Catechism, questions 178–96 are all taken up directly with the subject of prayer, and the words "prayer" or "pray" appear sixty-one times in total.

As one examines these lengthy treatments of prayer, it quickly becomes clear that the amount of attention given to the subject was duly proportionate to the high regard in which it was held. Prayer, wrote the Dutch theologian Wilhelmus à Brakel, is "the very essence of religion."[12] His contemporary Campegius Vitringa assigned prayer "the first place

---

9   John Owen, *The Work of the Holy Spirit in Prayer*, in *The Complete Works of John Owen*, ed. Lee Gatiss and Shawn D. Wright, vol. 8, *The Holy Spirit—The Comforter*, ed. Andrew S. Ballitch (Wheaton, IL: Crossway, 2023), 23.

10   Alec Ryrie, *Being Protestant in Reformation Britain* (Oxford: Oxford University Press, 2013), 257.

11   John Calvin, *Institutes of the Christian Religion*, ed. John T. McNeill, trans. Ford Lewis Battles, Library of Christian Classics (Philadelphia: Westminster, 1960), 2:850–920 (3.20.1–52).

12   Wilhelmus à Brakel, *The Christian's Reasonable Service*, trans. Bartel Elshout (Morgan, PA: Soli Deo Gloria, 1995), 3:459.

among the means of promoting sanctification."[13] And for the Scottish pastor Robert Bruce (1544–1631), prayer was best described as "the life of the soul," that which "makes faith lively," and "the best gift that ever God gave man."[14] Perhaps the clearest indication of prayer's importance within Reformed piety can be seen in a striking metaphor sometimes used to explain its form and function: prayer is like breathing. "What is praying?" asked the Puritan Thomas Blake (1597–1657). He answered, "Prayer is the breathing of the soul."[15] "Take away prayer," wrote Richard Sibbes, "and take away the life and breath of the soul. Take away breath and the man dies; as soon as the soul of a Christian begins to live he prays."[16] The comparison to breathing highlights both the importance of prayer (without it one cannot sustain life) and the naturalness of it. Just as a living human being, under normal circumstances, breathes quite naturally without too much thought or worry, a real, live, born-again believer, under normal circumstances, is ever inclined to pray—prayer is simply what a Christian naturally does. Using a somewhat different image, the Puritan William Bridge (1600–1670) captured this same combination of necessity and naturalness when he described prayer as "the Christian's element": "As the fish lives in the water as in its element, and dies when it is out, so a Christian lives in prayer as in his element, and his heart dies when he is out of it."[17]

But why, we may ask, do Reformed theologians place such a high premium on prayer? A long list of reasons could be put forward. John Calvin suggested that "words fail to explain . . . how many ways the exercise of prayer is profitable."[18] And yet out of the many answers one might give, two seem especially significant. First, prayer is essential

---

13 Campegius Vitringa, *The Spiritual Life*, trans. Charles K. Telfer (Grand Rapids, MI: Reformation Heritage Books, 2018), 114.

14 Robert Bruce, *Sermons upon the Sacrament of the Lords Supper* (Edinburgh, 1591), n.p.

15 Thomas Blake, *Living Truths in Dying Times* (London, 1665), 100–101.

16 Richard Sibbes, *The Complete Works of Richard Sibbes* (Edinburgh: James Nichol, 1863), 6:96.

17 William Bridge, *The Works of the Rev. William Bridge* (London: Thomas Tegg, 1845), 2:102.

18 Calvin, *Institutes*, 2:851 (3.20.2).

because it is the vehicle through which we express praise and thanksgiving to God, and giving these to God seems as properly basic to the Christian life as prayer itself. In the Psalms, David offers a portrait of a godly man or woman when he states,

> I will bless the LORD at all times;
>   his praise shall continually be in my mouth. (Ps. 34:1)

Praise, blessing, and thanksgiving express themselves concretely as prayer, and these elements are interwoven accordingly: "Rejoice always, pray without ceasing, give thanks in all circumstances; for this is the will of God in Christ Jesus for you" (1 Thess. 5:16–18). In response to the question "Why do Christians need to pray?" the Heidelberg Catechism answers, "Because prayer is the most important part of the thankfulness God requires of us."[19] If we human beings are made in God's image, live in God's world, and daily enjoy innumerable blessings given to us, not by chance but by the gracious provision of the one from whom and through whom and to whom are all things (Rom. 11:36), then it makes perfect sense that our lives should be brimming over with thanksgiving and praise to that God. And when such thanksgiving and praise move out of the realm of abstraction and become actual and real for us, the form they inevitably and naturally take is prayer.

Second, prayer is of supreme significance within the Christian life because it is largely in response to our prayers that God has promised to bless us. "It is . . . by the benefit of prayer," wrote Calvin, "that we reach those riches which are laid up for us with the Heavenly Father."[20] This dynamic of asking God for blessing and then receiving the blessing we asked for is so basic to a biblical understanding of prayer that we can sometimes overlook it if we aren't careful. In some evangelical

---

19 "Heidelberg Catechism," in *Creeds, Confessions, and Catechisms: A Reader's Edition*, ed. Chad Van Dixhoorn (Wheaton, IL: Crossway, 2022), 328 (q. 116).

20 Calvin, *Institutes*, 2:851 (3.20.2).

circles, this danger is heightened when an admirable concern to avoid any appearance of a "prosperity gospel" focused on "health and wealth" potentially morphs into a failure to really appreciate what is actually a quite pronounced biblical connection between requests made to God in prayer and blessings received from God in return. Certainly, Jesus teaches this principle repeatedly. Whether he is expressly stating it (e.g., John 15:16), telling parables to suggest it (e.g., Luke 18:1–8), or using his own paradigmatic prayer to model it (Matt. 6:9–13), our Lord repeatedly and forcefully teaches that it is in and through our prayers that we receive good gifts from our Father in heaven. As Calvin put it, "Nothing is promised to be expected from the Lord, which we are not also bidden to ask of him in prayers." As a result, Christians must "dig up by prayer the treasures that were pointed out by the Lord's gospel, and which our faith has gazed upon."[21]

And while the temptation to focus on the gifts at the expense of the giver will always be with us, the biblical paradigm continually portrays our crying out to God for support, for blessing, for guidance—indeed, for "every good gift" (James 1:17)—as the God-appointed and God-honoring means through which we express and cultivate our childlike dependence on our "Father who is in heaven," the one who delights to give "good things to those who ask him" (Matt. 7:11). Writing in his journal in 1640, the New England Puritan Thomas Shepard (1605–1649) recorded his desire "not to live by providence only, but by prayer." In other words, Shepard realized that God's promise to provide for his children was in large measure to be realized in the Christian's life through the means of persistent prayer. God delights to give "good things *to those who ask him*" (Matt. 7:11), and thus, to expect the "good things" apart from the asking was to sit outside the biblical pattern. "I saw it my duty not only to pray," wrote Shepard, "but to live by prayer and begging, for I observed how some of God's people did go." To live like this is not

---

21 Calvin, *Institutes*, 2:851 (3.20.2).

necessarily to fall into the snare of the prosperity gospel; rather, it is to live as a child of God who is ever dependent on his heavenly Father:

> Hence I saw I was not to live by providence only, but by prayer (1) for myself, body, soul; (2) for my children and family, at home and abroad; (3) for the churches. Hereupon I asked the question, Would the Lord have me live by prayer thus? And I saw that he would have me because he gave me a heart framable to his will therein. And it did much refresh me to think that the Lord should desire me to live thus as if he took delight in my sinful prayers.[22]

Not only is it not wrong, then, to expect that God will bless us in response to our prayers, according to the nineteenth-century Princeton theologian A. A. Hodge (1823–1886), such an expectation is one of the nonnegotiable, "true conditions of acceptable prayer." If we would truly pray according to Scripture, wrote Hodge, "we must believe that we do and will obtain blessings by means of prayer which we would not attain without it."[23] We can see, then, that the supreme significance of prayer flows directly out of its unique function within the Christian life. Prayer facilitates the flow of thanksgiving and praise up to our Father in heaven, and in turn, it opens the channels of his blessing to flow back down to us.

What Is Prayer?

Having given some thought to how prayer functions within the Christian life and why the Reformed tradition has valued it so highly, we would be wise to now circle back and ask the most basic question of all: What exactly *is* prayer? The simplest and most straightforward way

---

22 Thomas Shepard, *God's Plot: Puritan Spirituality in Thomas Shepard's Cambridge*, ed. Michael McGiffert, rev. ed. (Amherst: University of Massachusetts Press, 1994), 94.

23 A. A. Hodge, *Evangelical Theology: A Course of Popular Lectures* (Edinburgh: Banner of Truth, 1976), 89–90.

to define prayer is as a person talking to God. The English Reformer Thomas Becon (1512–1567), whom scholars have identified as having authored the very first English Protestant treatise devoted exclusively to prayer, published a catechism in 1548 in which he defined prayer as "an earnest talk with God."[24] If Christians confess that God is personal, both capable and desirous of real relationship with his creatures, then to talk to him should be as natural as it is necessary.

As Campegius Vitringa helpfully noted, "It is a characteristic of God to 'hear prayer' (Ps. 65:2)."[25] We read in Genesis 4:26 that shortly after the fall, "people began to call upon the name of the LORD," and throughout Scripture the faithful are described as both hearing from God and speaking to him in return. The Psalms overflow with cries to God such as "Give ear to the words of my mouth" (Ps. 54:2) and corresponding praises such as "On the day I called, you answered me" (Ps. 138:3). Scripture assures us that "when the righteous cry for help, the LORD hears" (Ps. 34:17). The connection between inclusion among God's people and confidence that God will hear one's prayers is very tight: it is precisely because "the LORD has set apart the godly for himself" that David can immediately conclude, "The LORD hears when I call to him" (Ps. 4:3). Indeed, the entire Christian life itself begins with hearing God's word and responding back with words of repentance and faith: "When they heard this they were cut to the heart, and said to Peter and the rest of the apostles, 'Brothers, what shall we do?' And Peter said to them, 'Repent and be baptized every one of you in the name of Jesus Christ'" (Acts 2:37–38).

God has addressed us through his word, and we respond to him through our prayers. Or as William Ames put it, "In hearing the word we receive the Will of God, but in Prayer we offer our will to God, that it may be received by him."[26] Scripture and prayer thus work together

---

24 Ryrie, *Reformation Britain*, 99.
25 Vitringa, *Spiritual Life*, 116.
26 William Ames, *The Marrow of Sacred Divinity* (London, 1639), 244.

to create a conversational, or "dialogical," dynamic that lends structure to our communion with God and growth in grace.[27]

As with our ordinary conversations, our conversations with God in prayer will vary in length and intensity as our changing circumstances dictate. The English Puritans thus distinguished between "two kindes of prayer": there were times of set and focused, or "solemne," prayer—what happens, say, during our quiet time—and then there were also short, spontaneous prayers uttered throughout the day, "the secret and sudden lifting up of the heart to God, upon the present occasion."[28] The latter sort of spontaneous praying was understood to be a necessary part of a Christian's spiritual life and often understood as both a means to and a mark of a more general spirit of prayerfulness that would begin to permeate one's entire life and outlook. Indeed, it is spontaneous prayer, as the Puritan John Downame (1571–1652) explained, that helps the believer "pray without ceasing" (1 Thess. 5:17):

> It is not enough that we use daily these set solemn, and ordinary prayers, but we must, as our Saviour injoyneth us, Pray always, and as the Apostle speaketh, continually, and without ceasing. That is, we must be ready to pray, so often as God shall give us any occasion, . . . craving God's blessing when we undertake any businesse, and praysing his name for his gracious assistance, . . . craving his protection at the approaching of any danger, and his helpe and strength for the overcoming of any difficulty which affronteth us in our way.[29]

Moreover, these two kinds of prayer were understood as mutually reinforcing. They went together, and either one would quickly wither in

---

27 This dynamic also characterizes corporate worship. For a discussion of the "dialogical principle" in worship, see D. G. Hart and John R. Muether, *With Reverence and Awe: Returning to the Basics of Reformed Worship* (Phillipsburg, NJ: P&R, 2002), 95–97.

28 William Perkins, *The Whole Treatise of the Cases of Conscience* (Cambridge, 1606), 282.

29 John Downame, *A Guide to Godlynesse* (London, 1629), 209–10.

the absence of its counterpart. Spontaneous prayer, it was said, should supplement and enhance our settled prayer "as salt with meat."[30]

As we read the various definitions of prayer scattered throughout the Reformed tradition, we find elaborations on the idea of prayer as talking to God, even as we don't find anything fundamentally at odds with it. Thus, William Bridge defined prayer as "that act and work of the soul, whereby a man doth converse with God."[31] Likewise, according to John Calvin, to enter into prayer is to "enter conversation with God," a conversation "whereby we expound to him our desires, our joys, our sighs, in a word, all the thoughts of our hearts."[32] Such communication is not overly formal and impersonal, but rather, it is an "intimate conversation" in which believers find the living God "gently summoning us to unburden our cares into his bosom" and inviting us "to pour out our hearts before him."[33] Sometimes the metaphor was slightly tweaked, as when Matthew Henry (1662–1714) described the Bible as "a letter God has sent to us" and prayer as "a letter we send to him," but the emphasis was always on prayer as a way for the believer to communicate and dialogue with the living, personal, and ever-present triune God.[34]

Such prayer, by its very nature, encompasses the entirety of the Christian life, shaping and being shaped in turn by the breadth and depth of redeemed experience. "I understand prayer in a broad way," wrote Campegius Vitringa. "It refers to everything we communicate to God."[35] Such communication includes our praises, our petitions, and our thanksgivings. It includes expressions of joy, lament, and anger. As we communicate to God in prayer, we confess our sins, intercede on

---

30 William Gouge, quoted in Ryrie, *Reformation Britain*, 147.
31 Bridge, *Works*, 2:102.
32 Calvin, *Institutes*, 2:853 (3.20.4); John Calvin, *Instruction in Faith*, trans. and ed. Paul T. Fuhrmann (Philadelphia: Westminster, 1949), 57.
33 Calvin, *Institutes*, 2:854–55 (3.20.5).
34 Matthew Henry, *Directions for Daily Communion with God* (London: William Tegg, 1866), 12.
35 Vitringa, *Spiritual Life*, 115.

behalf of others, and cry out to God for his miraculous intervention amid trial and storm. In response to the question "For what things are we to pray?" the Westminster Larger Catechism (1647) suggests that the scope of our prayer should be as wide and deep as life itself: "We are to pray for all things tending to the glory of God, the welfare of the church, our own or others' good."[36] Sometimes our communication with God is eloquent and profound, as when we take the lofty expressions of the Psalter as our own; at other moments we "do not know what to pray for as we ought" and must lean on those Spirit-wrought "groanings too deep for words" (Rom. 8:26). Yet in all moments, our prayers communicate the full range of our Christian experience and represent an ongoing conversation with the God in whom "we live and move and have our being" (Acts 17:28).

Approaches to Prayer

If one cultivates this abiding sense of prayer as a real, personal conversation between God and the believer, then a certain approach to prayer is the inevitable result. At the same time, insofar as one thinks about prayer as "the converse of the soul with God," such a definition also rules out, or at least problematizes, certain other approaches to prayer.[37] For Reformation-minded Protestants, this concept has historically meant a positive emphasis on prayer that self-consciously engages both mind and heart and a corresponding suspicion of anything that would compromise that ideal. As the Reformers and their theological heirs have considered various accumulated Christian traditions regarding how best to pray, their challenge has been to align a Protestant approach to prayer with their wider theological vision. The various attempts to meet this challenge have not always yielded a consistent result—consider, for example, the fierce intra-Protestant disputes over the validity and

---

36 "Westminster Larger Catechism," in Van Dixhoorn, *Creeds, Confessions, and Catechisms*, 402 (q. 184).

37 Charles Hodge, *Systematic Theology* (Peabody, MA: Hendrickson, 2003), 3:692.

desirability of set or prewritten prayers in worship. For our purposes here, we can usefully focus on three major Protestant priorities that combine to shape an approach to prayer that is consistent with the spirit of the Reformation: prayer must be thoughtful, heartfelt, and tightly tethered to Scripture.

Prayer Must Be Thoughtful

If prayer is to be conversation with God in any meaningful way, then it must be a thoughtful affair. By this we mean that a person's prayers usually consist in thoughtfully chosen words that would, in theory, be intelligible and coherent to a third party listening in. If I sit down for a conversation with a friend, I assume that he and I will be able to understand what the other one has to say. If we can't do that, for whatever reason, then it will be difficult to regard whatever follows between us as a "conversation" in the normal sense of the word. So too for Protestants at prayer. As John Calvin put it, "We must unquestionably feel that, either in public prayer or in private, the tongue without the mind must be highly displeasing to God."[38] Citing the apostle Paul's comment that "I will pray with my spirit, but I will pray with my mind also" (1 Cor. 14:15), William Ames insisted that we pray "not only . . . with the Spirit, but with understanding," a thoughtful approach to prayer that demands giving attention "to God to whom we pray, to the thing about which we pray, and to the prayer itself."[39]

Perhaps the clearest way to understand what we mean by "thoughtfulness" in prayer is to contrast the Reformed approach with some of its alternatives. As we touched on previously, a diverse range of theologians and devotional writers throughout Christianity's history have advanced an approach to piety broadly characterized as "mysticism." According to Bernard McGinn, a leading scholarly authority on Christian mysticism,

38 Calvin, *Institutes*, 2:896 (3.20.33).
39 William Ames, *The Marrow of Theology*, ed. John Dykstra Eusden (Grand Rapids, MI: Baker, 1997), 259.

the "mystical element in Christianity" pertains to "the preparation for, the consciousness of, and the reaction to the immediate or direct presence of God."[40] Though a full discussion of mysticism lies well beyond the scope of this book, it is worth noting here that for many Christian mystics, their search for that "immediate or direct presence of God" led them to reassess the relationship between spiritual growth and the use of a rational, thoughtful, word-centric approach to prayer. The problem is not that mystical writers found *no place* for Scripture and thoughtfully chosen words. Rather, the problem has been *where* the mystics have often placed them within the spiritual journey. Mysticism has tended to view thoughtful, word-centered piety as pertaining to a less advanced stage in one's spiritual development. As one advances through discrete, successive stages in spiritual formation—typically three such stages—thoughtfully chosen words become less important as the mystic enjoys "the conscious sharing in God's own life and power and almost complete self-forgetfulness."[41]

As Jason Baxter explains in his *Introduction to Christian Mysticism*, to reach "unmediated contact with God," "you have to pass through the prior stages of purgation of the heart and purgation of the mind."[42] And while such a journey typically begins with the word-centered disciplines like petitionary prayer, Bible reading, and thoughtful meditation on said reading, the goal for the would-be mystic is not to remain at those relatively lower levels forever:

Mysticism believes that this infinite fountain for which our souls thirst is God, but God cannot be contained within the creation he made, nor can he be comprehended fully within human language

---

40 Bernard McGinn, *The Presence of God: A History of Western Christian Mysticism*, vol. 2, *The Growth of Mysticism: From Gregory the Great to the Twelfth Century* (London: SCM, 1994), xi.

41 Harvey D. Egan, *An Anthology of Christian Mysticism*, 2nd ed. (Collegeville, MN: Liturgical Press, 1991), xix.

42 Jason M. Baxter, *An Introduction to Christian Mysticism: Recovering the Wildness of Spiritual Life* (Grand Rapids, MI: Baker Academic, 2021), 8.

and rationality, by which we represent that creation in our minds. Thus, mysticism is an ascent through rationality toward the edge of language, and when we have arrived at the periphery of language, we walk over the edge and fall into the "darkness of unknowing," as Dionysius calls it, which is not ignorance but a way of knowing that is higher and deeper than our customary rational consciousness. In other words, mysticism is made up of a "learned ignorance," as Nicholas of Cusa calls it.[43]

Baxter goes on to describe "the mystical quest" as one that "ventures out into a space beyond language and even beyond 'knowing.' "[44] And while expounding the mystical piety of the twelfth-century monk Guigo II (1114–ca. 1193), Baxter describes "a four-step reading process . . . that leads from the mere 'letter of the word' to the experience of God." Thus, for Guigo and other mystics, "the process of meditating on scriptural words leads to a state of longing where speech comes to an end."[45]

A similar attempt to elevate prayer above the ordinary human reliance on thoughtfully chosen words can be observed in the Eastern Orthodox tradition of hesychasm (derived from a Greek word for "stillness") and its use of the so-called "Jesus Prayer." Echoing the cry of blind Bartimaeus in Mark 10:47, the "Jesus Prayer" consists in a single, brief petition: "Lord Jesus Christ, Son of God, have mercy on me a sinner." In and of itself, such a prayer could hardly raise any objections. In practice, however, Eastern Orthodox hesychasts have used the repetition of this text as a means to transcend language itself and move to a form of prayer in which "there is no longer the need for either words or methods."[46] As with other forms of mystical prayer,

---

43 Baxter, *Christian Mysticism*, 9.
44 Baxter, *Christian Mysticism*, 10.
45 Baxter, *Christian Mysticism*, 140–41.
46 Dumitru Staniloae, *Orthodox Spirituality: A Practical Guide for the Faithful and a Definitive Manual for the Scholar*, trans. Archimandrite Jerome and Otilia Kloos (South Canaan, PA: St. Tikhon's Orthodox Theological Seminary Press, 2002), 282.

the process is conceived in terms of discrete stages through which one passes from words to wordlessness. The Orthodox theologian Kallistos Ware describes the process like this:

> Normally three levels or degrees are distinguished in the saying of the Jesus Prayer. It starts as "prayer of the lips," oral prayer. Then it grows more inward, becoming "prayer of the intellect," mental prayer. Finally the intellect "descends" into the heart and is united with it, and so the prayer becomes "prayer of the heart" or, more exactly, "prayer of the intellect in the heart." At this level it becomes prayer of the whole person—no longer something that we think or say, but something that we are. . . . So the Jesus Prayer begins as an oral prayer like any other. But the rhythmic repetition of the same short phrase enables the hesychast, by virtue of the very simplicity of the words which he uses, to advance beyond all language and images into the mystery of God.[47]

Again, as with the mystics described above, the point here is emphatically not that Eastern Orthodoxy has no interest in thoughtfully chosen words and ordinary petitionary prayer. To the contrary, theologian John Chryssavgis describes his own Eastern Orthodox liturgy as one in which "we make petitions and offer intercessions in prayer," prayers in which "we unite our will and our mind, our word and our mouth, our problems and our priorities, as well as our emotions and our passions with the very content and ultimate intent of liturgy, namely 'the life of the world' (John 6:51)."[48] This certainly sounds like a context in which prayers are composed of thoughtfully chosen words. And yet as Chryssavgis explains, there is a clear sense within Orthodoxy that

---

47 Kallistos Ware, *The Orthodox Way*, rev. ed. (Crestwood, NY: St. Vladimir's Seminary Press, 1995), 123.

48 John Chryssavgis, *Light through Darkness: The Orthodox Tradition* (London: Darton, Longman and Todd, 2004), 47.

a higher form of spiritual life exists, a spirituality in which the master practitioner can transcend those ordinary, thoughtfully chosen words: "God is a mystery beyond understanding and experience. So silence is a fitting way of addressing God in prayer through an image-less, word-less attitude whereby one no longer says prayers but becomes prayer."[49]

It is here that a Reformed approach to prayer parts ways with these other traditions and insists instead that words, whether God's word to us or our words back to him, are not preparing us for some deeper, greater wordless experience of God's unmediated presence but rather *are* the means through which we commune with God. From a Reformation perspective, nothing like the mystical progression from words to wordlessness is commended in Scripture, and thus nothing like it should be commended to Christians. Marian Raikes's caution to us at this point is helpful:

> It is entirely wrong so to devalue words. After all, from the very beginning, God has revealed himself as a God who speaks, who makes himself known through words, and who has made us in his image as beings who communicate through words. Cyprian (the third-century bishop of Carthage) rightly said: "in prayer you speak to God, in reading God speaks to you." It is precisely in petition-with-thanksgiving that we most recognise our complete dependence on our Creator. Evangelicals are therefore right to regard so-called "higher forms" of prayer with suspicion and extreme caution.[50]

As Raikes's quotation of Cyprian (ca. 200–258) suggests and as we have mentioned already, there is a tight connection between the requirement that our prayers should be composed of thoughtfully chosen words and our definition of prayer as talking to God. By keeping this

---

49 Chryssavgis, *Light through Darkness*, 82.

50 Marian Raikes, *A Step Too Far: An Evangelical Critique of Christian Mysticism* (London: Latimer Trust, 2006), 41.

connection in view, we can also guard against a potential misunderstanding that might arise when one starts to connect true prayer with thoughtful prayer. Namely, it is important to note that in thinking about prayer in this way, the Reformed tradition is not attempting to limit authentic praying only to the most articulate and well spoken among us. To say that the heart of prayer is conversation with God and that meaningful conversation implies thoughtful engagement is not at all to imply that a prayer must reach a certain standard of eloquence, precision, or coherence before it can be considered a "real" prayer. The criterion of thoughtfulness simply implies a basic level of intellectual engagement with and connection to what we are saying, not rhetorical brilliance.

Furthermore, we must also acknowledge the reality that believers encounter times and seasons when they go to pray and yet find that words fail. We return in more detail to this theme of spiritual difficulty in chapter 10, but for now, and specifically with reference to prayer, we should note that the Puritans and other early modern Protestants were well aware of such struggles and did not see them as inherently compromising their basic principle that prayers should ordinarily consist of coherent, intelligible petitions and praises. Puritan pastors readily offered encouragement to Christians who found themselves unable to pray, often citing Paul's own encouragement to such individuals in Romans 8:26: "Likewise the Spirit helps us in our weakness. For we do not know what to pray for as we ought, but the Spirit himself intercedes for us with groanings too deep for words." Some might be inclined to take this verse as presenting biblical support for the idea of a sort of wordless prayer. Note, however, that the situation Paul describes represents a special case in which the power of the Holy Spirit compensates for the believer's weakness. "The main point of the paragraph," writes New Testament commentator Tom Schreiner, is that "believers should take tremendous encouragement that the will of God is being fulfilled in their lives despite their weakness and inability to know what to pray for."[51] This means that in Romans 8:26 prayer is God's merciful response to our low moments, our moments of weakness and failure when "we do not know what to pray for *as we ought*." This is precisely the opposite of mystical traditions that understand wordless prayer as the highest form of spiritual communion with God.

Reformation-minded pastors have thus understood prayers composed of thoughtfully chosen words as the biblical norm, but they see the kindness of God in bearing with us in and through our weak and wordless moments. Consider the following pastoral counsel from Richard Sibbes:

> God can pick sense out of a confused prayer. These desires cry louder in his ears than your sins. Sometimes a Christian has such confused thoughts that he can say nothing but, as a child, cries, "O Father," not able to express what he needs, like Moses at the Red Sea. These stirrings of spirit touch the heart of God and melt him into compassion towards us, when they come from the Spirit of adoption, and from a striving to be better.[52]

Here Sibbes reminds us that prayer is ultimately not about anything that might be construed as human performance but rather, at the most fundamental level, about a Holy-Spirit-led outflow of a heart that yearns for God and the things of God—an insight that leads nicely into our second mark of a Reformation approach to prayer.

Prayer Must Be Heartfelt

In addition to thoughtful prayer, the Reformers prioritized heartfelt prayer. To address God with carefully chosen words is important, but it is not sufficient. If those carefully chosen words do not express something

---

51 Thomas R. Schreiner, *Romans*, Baker Exegetical Commentary on the New Testament (Grand Rapids, MI: Baker, 1998), 446.

52 Richard Sibbes, *The Bruised Reed* (Edinburgh: Banner of Truth, 1998), 50–51.

of our inner reality, then our prayers are dishonest and false. Such yearning for sincerity in spiritual matters sits at the heart of the Reformation, a movement that might be reasonably understood as an attempt to take seriously the biblical insight that fallen men and women are prone to "honor [God] with their lips, / while their hearts are far from" him (Isa. 29:13). External rectitude and the outward appearance of Godliness mean less than nothing if unaccompanied by a corresponding movement of the heart, and in many ways this tension between what is going on without and what is going on within becomes especially prominent when we consider prayer.

Reacting against a medieval religious culture that often seemed to prize mechanical repetition of particular prayers over and against sincere, heartfelt crying out to God, early modern Protestants laid great stress on Jesus's warnings against empty, repetitious prayers: "And when you pray, do not heap up empty phrases as the Gentiles do, for they think that they will be heard for their many words" (Matt. 6:7). In practice, one consequence of this emphasis was "a surprisingly broad consensus that 'Prayer must be SHORT' and 'thy words must be few.' "[53] But whatever the actual length of any given prayer, the more important point was that one's prayers must actually reflect one's desire for and interest in God and the things of God. John Calvin warned "the godly" against "presenting themselves before God to request anything unless they yearn for it with sincere affection of heart."[54] This typifies a Reformation approach to prayer that is reflexively wary of anything that starts to look as if one is "just going through the motions." It was in this connection that Thomas Watson told the story of a man who taught his bird to repeat the Lord's Prayer. Reflecting on this account, Watson concluded that merely "to say a prayer is not to pray."[55] Writing

---

53 Ryrie, *Reformation Britain*, 152.
54 Calvin, *Institutes*, 2:857 (3.20.6).
55 Thomas Watson, *Heaven Taken by Storm: Showing the Holy Violence a Christian Is to Put Forth in the Pursuit after Glory*, ed. Joel R. Beeke (Grand Rapids, MI: Soli Deo Gloria, 2019), 20.

on prayer and the sixteenth-century English Protestant William Perkins, Stephen Yuille identifies "sincerity" as "the prerequisite of true prayer," a point that Perkins himself expressed as follows: "We must learn this one thing which Christ principally intends, to wit, in all holy duties to avoid hypocrisy, endeavoring to do them with all simplicity and sincerity of heart."[56] To better grasp what Perkins had in mind here, it is again helpful to contrast heartfelt, sincere prayer with approaches to prayer that seem decidedly lacking in this respect.

In the Middle Ages, for example, laypeople were typically encouraged to memorize and recite prayers written in Latin, a language that very few laypeople would have understood. In his study *Going to Church in Medieval England*, historian Nicholas Orme notes that all adult Christians were encouraged to memorize the Lord's Prayer (more commonly known as the Paternoster, from the Latin for "Our Father"), the Apostles' Creed, and the Ave Maria (the text of which is derived from Luke 1:28, 42), and that these "three texts were meant to form the basis of people's prayer until the Reformation." And while technically church officials "did not normally prescribe the language . . . in which they should be said," after surveying the evidence, Orme concludes that "there can be little doubt that the 'default' language was Latin."[57] Thus, the typical medieval Christian was encouraged to pray by simply reciting a form of words, repeating a series of syllables that, even if memorized perfectly, would not have been intelligible to the person reciting them. To make matters worse, Orme observes that the repetition of these prayers was "increasingly seen as a measurable way of earning spiritual merit," and thus, "they came to be said in multiples: the more the better."[58] This is a fine example of both the more

---

56 J. Stephen Yuille, "William Perkins on the Lord's Prayer," in *Taking Hold of God: Reformed and Puritan Perspectives on Prayer*, ed. Joel R. Beeke and Brian G. Najapfour (Grand Rapids, MI: Reformation Heritage Books, 2011), 69–70.

57 Nicholas Orme, *Going to Church in Medieval England* (New Haven, CT: Yale University Press, 2021), 180–81.

58 Orme, *Going to Church in Medieval England*, 182.

general spirit of "arithemetical piety" that the Reformation sought to do away with and the sort of approach to prayer that the Reformers would have understood as lacking the genuine heart engagement that real prayer requires.[59]

All this raises the question, of course, about how one actually prays sincere and heartfelt prayers. It's easy enough to warn against hypocritical and empty prayer, but how exactly does one arrive at its opposite? If Reformation piety was allergic to anything that seemed like vain and hollow repetition, then clearly one couldn't simply work one's way to authentic prayer through dogged determination alone. And yet Puritan devotional manuals are full of reminders that prayer is a daily duty that one must not neglect. Any attempt to square this circle will quickly return us back to the basic dynamic for Reformed spiritual formation discussed in chapter 2—that our growth in grace both demands our vigorous use of the means of grace and at the same time must be attributed not to our effort but to the Spirit's work in us. Early modern Protestant writing on prayer reflects this dynamic especially well, capturing what historian Alec Ryrie has described as the "two faces of Protestant prayer." What were these "two faces"? One was "childishly easy" and the other "impossibly difficult." Ryrie explains it like this:

> Easy, in that the mechanical business of saying prayers could scarcely be more so; difficult, in that it was the heart, not the mouth, which mattered. Difficult—indeed, impossible—in that true prayer came from the Spirit, not from yourself, but easy for the same reason, for all you needed to do was allow the Spirit to speak through your own sighs and groans. Difficult because nature revolted against it, and easy because grace made it possible.[60]

---

59 Francis Oakley, *The Western Church in the Later Middle Ages* (Ithaca, NY: Cornell University Press, 1979), 118.

60 Ryrie, *Reformation Britain*, 107.

The heartfelt prayer commended by the Reformers is prayer made in and through the Holy Spirit. The apostle Paul urges believers to be "praying at all times in the Spirit" (Eph. 6:18), an exhortation that captures both our responsibility to actively take hold of prayer as a means of grace—it is, after all, an exhortation—and our complete dependence on God at every point.

Prayer Must Be Tightly Tethered to Scripture

The third major mark of a Reformation approach to prayer is that it must always be tightly tethered to Scripture. When we talk to God in prayer, we come with an awareness that it is his word that initiates the conversation and makes it possible in the first place. We who "were dead in . . . trespasses and sins" had neither taste nor capacity for communion with our Maker until "God, being rich in mercy, because of the great love with which he loved us, even when we were dead in our trespasses, made us alive together with Christ" (Eph. 2:1, 4–5). As a result, it makes perfect sense that even as we bring our words to God in prayer, it must be his word to us that sets the agenda. Among early modern Protestants, this commitment to the priority of Scripture as a guide and rule for prayer shaped concrete prayer practices in a number of different ways, excluding some practices, encouraging others, and leaving many to the judgment of the individual Christian.

The excluded practices are, in some ways, the most obvious. Discontinuities are often easier to spot than continuities, and the list of things that the Reformers wanted to do away with prompted some of their most spirited polemical output. Thus, when they wrote on prayer, they spent a great deal of energy decrying traditional practices that they believed to be unbiblical or at least extrabiblical. We have already touched on some of these, namely, mystical approaches to prayer designed to transcend ordinary language and the repetitious use of set prayer texts that, at least in practice, often seemed disconnected from the heart of the one praying. The Reformers' chief objection to such things was their lack of biblical warrant. Another example of a prayer practice disallowed on these grounds was the Roman Catholic notion of the intercession of the saints—the idea that one can entreat the saints in heaven to pray on our behalf. In a lengthy section of his *Institutes*, John Calvin critiqued this idea as fundamentally unbiblical and in so doing set out the basic Reformed requirement that any approach to prayer (or to any spiritual practice for that matter) must be derived from Scripture itself:

> Then who, whether angel or demon, ever revealed to any man even a syllable of the kind of saints' intercession they invent. For there is nothing about it in Scripture. . . . Surely, when human wit is always seeking after assistance for which we have no support in God's Word, it clearly reveals its own faithlessness.[61]

Thus, the Reformed commitment to explicitly biblical patterns of prayer excludes a great many possible practices. But the story is not entirely a negative one of critique and exclusion. By seeking to pray in ways that are tightly tethered to Scripture, the Reformed tradition has also developed a rich, positive vision for what it means to pray faithfully. We have already unpacked a great deal of this positive vision, describing prayer as an ongoing, comprehensive conversation with God, a conversation marked by heartfelt sincerity and accomplished primarily through thoughtfully chosen words. The Reformed have understood prayer in this way because they have believed such a vision to be explicitly taught in Scripture itself.

The priority of Scripture in and for prayer is also seen, for example, in the way the tradition has emphasized the Lord's Prayer (Matt. 6:9–13) as a model or template for our own prayer life. Unlike some Christian traditions, the emphasis has not necessarily been on the need

---

61 Calvin, *Institutes*, 2:879 (3.20.21).

to pray the set text of the Lord's Prayer over and over again, but rather, as Calvin said, in the Lord's Prayer Jesus himself shows us the kind of prayer we ought to make: "He prescribed a form for us in which he set forth as in a table all that he allows us to seek of him, all that is of benefit to us, all that we need ask."[62] Thomas Watson insisted that the Lord's Prayer "contains the chief things that we have to ask, or God has to bestow" and that it should thus serve as "the model and pattern of all our prayers."[63] For this reason, the major Reformed catechisms and works of divinity all spend a great deal of time analyzing each of the individual petitions in the prayer, looking to better understand what sorts of requests are in and out of step with God's will as expressed in Scripture.

But thinking beyond this extensive use of the Lord's Prayer, at every turn we find evidence that Puritan prayer was dominated by Scripture. Whether they were quoting the Bible directly, paraphrasing and adapting it for personal application, or simply letting the priorities of a given text shape the priorities of a given prayer, Puritans modeled a commitment to praying God's own words back to him.[64] By infusing their prayers with Scripture, Puritans were able to better ensure that the things for which they prayed were in keeping with God's will. Fidelity to God's revealed will was a key mark of a true and effectual prayer, or as William Gurnall (1616–1679) put it, "To pray in faith is to ask of God, in the name of Christ, what He hath promised." If we pray out of step with God's revealed will in Scripture, then, in effect, warned Gurnall, "we subject God's will to ours, and not ours to his."[65]

Thus, Scripture functions to both exclude certain prayer practices and give shape and substance to others. But additionally, we should also note ways that the Reformed commitment to Scripture as a guide

---

62 Calvin, *Institutes*, 2:897 (3.20.34).
63 Thomas Watson, *The Lord's Prayer* (London: Banner of Truth, 1960), 1–2.
64 Kate Narveson, *Bible Readers and Lay Writers in Early Modern England: Gender and Self-Definition in an Emergent Writing Culture* (London: Routledge, 2016), 52–55.
65 William Gurnall, *The Christian in Complete Armour* (London: William Tegg, 1862), 657.

to prayer left some questions unresolved, relegating their answers to the category of things indifferent, areas where individual believers would need to determine a sensible pattern for themselves. The sorts of things that fall into this category typically arise from practical questions about which the Bible has little to say but, owing to their very nature, demand some sort of practical answer.

We might ask, for instance, what we ought to do with our bodies while praying. One has to do *something* with one's body at all times, including prayer times. So in that sense, the question of bodily posture cannot be avoided, and one offers a de facto answer to it out of necessity each time one prays. And yet the Bible does not insist on any particular posture for prayer, and thus the matter must be left to individual wisdom. This tension between the reticence to prescribe on matters where the Bible stays silent and the inescapable need to do *something* with our bodies while praying is evident in early modern Protestant discourse on the subject. As historian Alec Ryrie points out, on the one hand, kneeling was overwhelmingly the most commonly adopted posture for prayer. At the same time, "gestures in prayer were universally agreed to be 'meane & indifferent thynges' and within the devotional literature of the early modern period phrases like 'any decent' or 'some reverend gesture' became the norm."[66]

In this respect, Wilhelmus à Brakel is representative in that he begins his discussion by noting that physical movements "do not attribute worthiness and fortitude to prayer" and that "saints have prayed in various bodily postures; that is, being prostrate, sitting, and standing." And yet immediately after seeming to dismiss the subject, he nonetheless goes on to note that kneeling seems the most common scriptural posture, and he thus concludes that this "humble physical posture" is a helpful way to "glorify God both in our bodies as well as with our souls."[67] Notice, it's not so much that the Reformers found bodily posture an

66 Ryrie, *Reformation Britain*, 171.
67 À Brakel, *Christian's Reasonable Service*, 3:467–68.

unimportant consideration—clearly, they thought it worth their time and attention—but rather, they were hesitant to bind the consciences of their readers or hearers in a way that Scripture did not.

A similar attitude can be uncovered regarding other concrete specifics as well. For example, how many times per day should one turn to God in prayer? Answers vary, but typically, as with Bible reading and meditation, the morning was most highly prized, the evening was seen as very good if you could manage it, and some writers would also recommend a midday prayer for good measure. But in each instance, these recommendations were qualified with various caveats. The advice given by Wilhelmus à Brakel is typical: "There is no express command as to the time of private prayer; however, the saints, with their custom, have given us an example to be imitated: It is to be done in the morning, at noon, and at night."[68]

Reformed Christians have consistently sought to tether their prayers to God's word. Whether this has come through patterning prayers on biblical models, defining prayer itself according to Scripture, or excluding a whole host of popular practices as extrabiblical and hence unacceptable, the biblical emphasis has remained a constant. And yet as we have discussed throughout this book, many evangelicals today feel drawn to spiritual practices that the Reformers would have dismissed as having little or no real grounding in biblical revelation. Such a drift often emerges when the subject of prayer is discussed.

The practice of "centering prayer," for example, has been popularized in recent decades by the Roman Catholic monk Thomas Keating (1923–2018). Centering prayer involves silence, stillness, and the use of a "sacred word" to help the participant disengage from his or her thoughts: "When you become aware that you are engaged with your thoughts, return ever-so-gently to the sacred word." Whatever one's opinion of Keating and his work, there is no denying that the practice

---

68 À Brakel, *Christian's Reasonable Service*, 3:465.

of centering prayer flows directly out of the mystical Catholic tradition that Keating represents. Furthermore, it is equally clear that centering prayer, at least as usually understood, is at best extrabiblical—that is, not taught in Scripture—and potentially unbiblical in its emphasis on transcending ordinary language in pursuit of a more immediate, intimate experience of God. According to Keating, centering prayer represents "a movement beyond conversation with Christ to communion with Him."[69]

And yet despite the many problems such an approach raises from a Reformational perspective, centering prayer is regularly mentioned as a recommended, or at least unobjectionable, option in books written by and for evangelical Protestants.[70] Such recommendations betray an openness to traditions that are at odds with our Reformation heritage and should be approached with caution.[71] Now to be clear, if you were to become persuaded that the Reformers were out of step with Scripture on a given point, then by all means, you should wrestle prayerfully and consider carefully what the Bible actually has to say. But as we've noted throughout this book, it is worrying to find Christians who profess a commitment to Scripture and the Reformed tradition naively and uncritically embrace approaches to spiritual formation that contradict that commitment.

---

69   Thomas Keating, "The Method of Centering Prayer: The Prayer of Consent" (West Milford, NJ: Contemplative Outreach, n.d.), n.p., https://contemplativeoutreach.org.uk/leaflets/Method Leaflet.pdf.

70   E.g., Simon Chan, *Spiritual Theology: A Systematic Study of the Christian Life* (Downers Grove, IL: InterVarsity Press, 1998), 150; Kenneth Boa, *Conformed to His Image: Biblical and Practical Approaches to Spiritual Formation* (Grand Rapids, MI: Zondervan, 2001), 183; Tony Jones, *The Sacred Way: Spiritual Practices for Everyday Life* (Grand Rapids, MI: Zondervan, 2004), 69–75.

71   For a sympathetic yet critical appraisal of centering prayer, see John Jefferson Davis, *Meditation and Communion: Contemplating Scripture in an Age of Distraction* (Downers Grove, IL: IVP Academic, 2012), 134–42. Also, though ultimately more optimistic about centering prayer than I would be, James Wilhoit presents a clear and well-researched assessment of the practice in "Contemplative and Centering Prayer," in *Embracing Contemplation: Reclaiming a Christian Spiritual Practice*, ed. John H. Coe and Kyle C. Strobel (Downers Grove, IL: IVP Academic, 2019), 224–40.

Putting Together the Reformation Triangle

In this and the previous two chapters, we have been circling around this idea of the Reformation triangle: the nexus of Scripture reading, meditation, and prayer. The three activities reinforce each other and merge into one another, both logically and temporally. Because they are so tightly intertwined, we can meaningfully describe them as three sides of the same basic thing: communion with God. And because each activity both supports and is supported by the other two, one could persuasively make the case that each one is the most important or foundational of the three. Indeed, early modern Protestant authors were not consistent in assigning one or the other pride of place.

Scripture reading could certainly be understood as the most important of the three because it involves actually listening to the voice of God. When the Creator who spoke the world into existence speaks again to his creatures, they must pay attention, and thus the good shepherd distinguishes his flock by their willingness to hear him and listen to what he says: "My sheep hear my voice, and I know them, and they follow me" (John 10:27). If God had not revealed himself through his word, we would not know about his saving work in Christ, and we would not have a relationship with him at all, for "faith comes from hearing, and hearing through the word of Christ" (Rom. 10:17). So too our ongoing growth in grace flows from meeting God in his word. Recall Robert Murray M'Cheyne's diary entry quoted in chapter 3, in which, after lamenting his lack of "purpose-like reading of the Word," M'Cheyne posed the question "What plant can be unwatered, and not wither?"[72] Thus, surely Scripture intake is the most important of the three.

Or perhaps not. Perhaps meditation is the most important. Meditation is the means through which true piety is nurtured and nourished. We would do well to remember Thomas Watson's claim that meditation

---

72 Andrew A. Bonar, *The Life of Robert Murray M'Cheyne* (Edinburgh: Banner of Truth, 1960), 27.

is "the very heart and lifeblood of religion."[73] He could talk that way because he knew that apart from meditation, the things we read about in Scripture might remain a bare sort of head knowledge, a collection of religious facts, lacking transforming power and spiritual vibrancy. Without real, Spirit-led meditation on God and the things of God, what we read in theology books might remain nothing more than the sort of "knowledge" that Paul warns against, the sort that only "puffs up" (1 Cor. 8:1). If meditation is the God-given duty through which divine truth moves from the head to the heart and actually changes us, then wouldn't one be correct to conclude that meditation is actually the most important of the three?

And yet as we've seen in this chapter, the importance of prayer cannot be understated. Perhaps prayer is the most important. After all, in some meaningful sense, Scripture intake and meditation are almost vehicles helping us finally arrive at prayer. It is arguably through prayer that we truly commune with God, calling on his name, praising him for his goodness, thanking him for his gifts, and crying out to him with every need, burden, and desire of the heart. If you take all that away, are you really left with any meaningful "communion" at all? If Richard Sibbes could describe prayer as "the life and breath of the soul," then shouldn't one consider prayer to be the most significant of the three disciplines that constitute the Reformation triangle?[74]

The reality, of course, is that each of the disciplines plays a vital role in the Christian life, each one is commanded in Scripture, and each one so complements and is complemented by the other two that to try and rank them is ultimately an unfruitful exercise. This bottom line is repeatedly brought out by early modern Protestant writers, who, as we've already seen, habitually fuse the disciplines together in an attempt to better capture something of what it means to "grow in the grace and knowledge of our Lord and Savior Jesus Christ" (2 Pet. 3:18).

73 Watson, *Heaven Taken by Storm*, 23.
74 Sibbes, *Complete Works*, 6:96.

Prayer and meditation are "inseparably linked in nature, going hand in hand together," wrote John Ball, and "the connection can no more bee severed, than two Twins, who live and dye together."[75] William Bridge described meditation as "the sister of reading" and "the mother of prayer," and he insisted that if one's "heart be much indisposed to prayer," then the key to moving toward vibrant prayer is meditation.[76] Tweaking the imagery slightly, Lewis Bayly maintained that "reading and meditating on the word of God, are the parents of prayer."[77] And when Richard Greenham gave advice on how to best engage with Scripture, he included meditation and prayer as "properties of reverent and faithfull reading and hearing." In this he nicely captured the word-centric nature of Protestant piety, conceptually folding all three aspects of the Reformation triangle together under this idea of being fed, nourished, and formed by God's word. In Greenham's mind, the idea of reading and meditating on Scripture only made sense when it was couched in prayer "in the beginning, in the middle, and in the end," for without prayer, "we can never use them [i.e., reading and meditation], nor have [any] blessing by them."[78]

When we come to our devotional times, then, our basic goal should be to commune with the living God through these three foundational spiritual disciplines, allowing each one to inform and flow into the other two. Sometimes we might be best served in this by formally segmenting our quiet time into sections: reading for a time, then deliberately meditating on what we've read, and then finally turning to pray over the word, using our meditations as fuel for petition, thanksgiving, and

75 John Ball, *A Treatise of Divine Meditation* (London, 1660), 4.

76 Bridge, *Works*, 3:132.

77 Lewis Bayly, *The Practice of Piety: Directing a Christian to Walk, That He May Please God* (Grand Rapids, MI: Soli Deo Gloria, 2019), 105.

78 Richard Greenham, *A Profitable Treatise, Containing a Direction for the Reading and Understanding of the Holy Scriptures*, in Kenneth L. Parker and Eric J. Carlson, *Practical Divinity: The Works and Life of Revd Richard Greenham*, St. Andrews Studies in Reformation History (Aldershot, UK: Ashgate, 1998), 339, 345.

praise. But we may also find that the primary benefit of this threefold division lies less in any concrete partitioning of our time and more in the way it informs and fuels the way we think about communion with God. It's not so much that we have three discrete practices that together add up to spending time with God. Rather, by allowing the three to inform each other, we come to understand our growth in grace in terms of conversational communion with the one who made us: he addresses us through his word; we think meditatively on what he's said; we respond back to him in prayer.

A lovely closing example of a Reformed Christian modeling this three-way fusion in her own devotional life comes to us from an account of Jerusha Edwards (1710–1729), who died at only age nineteen, the sister of the eighteenth-century North American theologian and pastor Jonathan Edwards.[79] The "uncommon strength and excellence of her character" was explained, in large part, by her impressive pursuit of piety:

> Her religious life began in childhood; and from that time, meditation, prayer, and reading the sacred Scriptures, were not a prescribed task, but a coveted enjoyment. Her sisters, who knew how much of her time she daily passed alone, had the best reason to believe that no place was so pleasant to her as her own retirement, and no society so delightful as solitude with God.[80]

Note that in this passage, Jerusha Edwards's "religious life" is essentially equated with the triumvirate of meditation, prayer, and reading the Bible. Like Reformed Protestants before and after her, Jerusha "kept her heart" primarily through this trio. In the chapters to follow, we explore how Scripture intake, meditation, and prayer inform other areas of life, but while we may extend the scope and reach of these three, we never move beyond them.

---

79 Not to be confused with Jonathan's daughter Jerusha, born in 1730 and named for her late aunt.
80 Jonathan Edwards, *The Works of Jonathan Edwards* (Peabody, MA: Hendrickson, 2006), 1:lxxxii.

PART 3

———————

WIDENING OUR SCOPE

6

Self-Examination

Looking Inward

MARILYNNE ROBINSON'S Pulitzer Prize–winning novel, *Gilead* (2004), tells the story of the Reverend John Ames, an aging congregational minister, pastoring in small-town Iowa during the mid-twentieth century. With his own death looming on the horizon, Ames pens a series of letters to his young son in which he reflects on family, life, and faith. It's a beautiful novel, well told and full of insight.

One of my favorite passages comes right at the beginning, a text in which Ames reflects on a life spent in the church, getting to know all sorts of people:

> That's the strangest thing about this life, about being in the ministry. People change the subject when they see you coming. And then sometimes those very same people come into your study and tell you the most remarkable things. There's a lot under the surface of life, everyone knows that. A lot of malice and dread and guilt, and so much loneliness, where you wouldn't really expect to find it either.[1]

---

1   Marilynne Robinson, *Gilead* (New York: Farrar, Straus, and Giroux, 2004), 6.

"There's a lot under the surface of life." As the novel unfolds, Robinson wonderfully illustrates and explores the truth of that statement through the prism of her character John Ames, a man with plenty of "under the surface of life" things.

Gilead is, of course, a work of fiction, but the profound depths of human experience the novel points to are very real to all of us, and the basic intuition that each life contains deep wells of memory, emotion, and meaning, wells that are often unexplored, or at least *under*explored, finds confirmation in Scripture. Often this takes the form of exposing unacknowledged human sin and revealing the fallen image bearer's capacity for destructive self-deception:

> The heart is deceitful above all things,
>   and desperately sick;
>   who can understand it? (Jer. 17:9)

A storm of scarcely perceived attitudes, assumptions, and motivations swirls underneath our outward actions, a condition that the twentieth-century theologian Francis Schaeffer described as "man . . . separated from himself." Schaeffer wrote,

> The more the Holy Spirit puts his finger on my life and goes down deep into my life, the more I understand that there are deep wells to my nature. . . . [W]e are more than merely that which is on the surface. We are like the iceberg: one-tenth above, nine-tenths below. . . . As the Holy Spirit has wrestled with me down through the years, more and more I am aware of the depths of my own nature, and the depths of the results of that awful fall in the garden of Eden. Man is separated from himself.[2]

---

2   Francis A. Schaeffer, *The Complete Works of Francis A. Schaeffer: A Christian Worldview* (Wheaton, IL: Crossway, 1994), 3:289.

As Schaeffer noted, much of what's "under the surface" is bad, "the results of that awful fall in the garden." But Scripture also speaks more positively of other sorts of "under the surface" realities, strong currents of grace, redemption, and providential care running through our lives that likewise go unnoticed unless we take the time to observe them. One mark of God's people is that they are a *remembering* people, a people who never forget and actively call to mind God's redemptive dealings with them: "You shall remember that you were a slave in the land of Egypt, and the LORD your God brought you out from there with a mighty hand and an outstretched arm" (Deut. 5:15). The God who was faithful yesterday will surely be faithful again today and tomorrow and the day after that.

This logic not only undergirds the broad, corporate remembering that God's people are called to but also informs the individual Christian, who, like David, is encouraged in Scripture to remember God's past faithfulness to him as fuel for present-day strength and hope. After calling on the Lord to deliver him from enemies who seek his life, David preaches to himself with a recollection of God's protection in the past:

But I will sing of your strength;
    I will sing aloud of your steadfast love in the morning.
For you have been to me a fortress
    and a refuge in the day of my distress. (Ps. 59:16)

Or imagine Ruth at the end of the book that bears her name: married to Boaz, holding her new son, and taking a quiet moment to ponder the improbable ways that God led her through grief and uncertainty, providentially providing for her at every bend in the road. Moreover, in the biblical cry to God that he "teach us to number our days / that we may get a heart of wisdom" (Ps. 90:12), we perceive that time is a gift, rapidly passing and of unknown duration, and it is thus our joyful duty to ponder and reflect on the days we've been given, considering carefully what we've done in the past with an eye toward what we might yet do in the future.

"There's a lot under the surface of life," and part of our spiritual formation is to try and unearth a little bit more of it each day. For the Puritans and other early modern Reformed Christians, such autobiographical excavation or self-examination was regarded as a key component of keeping the heart. "The Puritan teachers as a body," writes J. I. Packer, "constantly insisted that realistic self-knowledge is a *sine qua non* for living the Christian life."[3] Richard Baxter wrote at length on "the mischiefs of self-ignorance and the benefits of self-acquaintance," and John Owen concluded that "for a man to gather up his experiences of God, to call them to mind, to collect them, consider, try, improve them, is an excellent thing—a duty practiced by all the saints, commended in the Old Testament and the New."[4] Jonathan Edwards preached on "the duty of self-examination," and Campegius Vitringa spoke for the entire tradition when he declared that a Christian "will never regret this practice of self-examination."[5] For Reformation-minded evangelicals, self-examination is a key tool in our pursuit of spiritual formation, and in this chapter, we unpack and explore it.

And as this chapter does that, it also marks the beginning of part 3 of this book: "Widening Our Scope." Part 3 broadens out from the Reformation triangle of Scripture, meditation, and prayer to consider other God-given means for our spiritual formation that extend those core disciplines in various ways. But as we see in what follows, none of the topics explored in part 3 actually represent *alternatives* to Scripture,

---

3 J. I. Packer, *A Quest for Godliness: The Puritan Vision of the Christian Life* (Wheaton, IL: Crossway, 1990), 194.

4 Richard Baxter, *The Practical Works of Richard Baxter: Selected Treatises* (Peabody, MA: Hendrickson, 2010), 755; John Owen, *Overcoming Sin and Temptation*, ed. Kelly M. Kapic and Justin Taylor (Wheaton, IL: Crossway, 2006), 91.

5 Jonathan Edwards, *The Works of Jonathan Edwards*, vol. 10, *Sermons and Discourses, 1720–1723*, ed. Wilson H. Kimnach (New Haven, CT: Yale University Press, 1992), 481–92; Campegius Vitringa, *The Spiritual Life*, trans. Charles K. Telfer (Grand Rapids, MI: Reformation Heritage Books, 2018), 136–37.

meditation, and prayer; rather, when understood rightly, they represent different angles from which to view the Reformation-triangle disciplines and different contexts in which to practice them. Our present topic, self-examination, illustrates well this relationship between the Reformation triangle and the wider themes explored in part 3.

The first Reformation-triangle discipline, Scripture intake, clearly informs and facilitates any self-examination worthy to be called Christian. As you think about your life before God, Scripture provides the standard against which you measure your conduct, and Scripture contains the divine promises that allow you to both rightly interpret your past and look confidently toward your future. Likewise, prayer is inseparable from biblical self-examination. As you consider your life, you naturally thank God for his faithfulness, repent of sins discovered, and ask his ongoing blessing on the future. All these tasks are accomplished through prayer.

But of the three Reformation-triangle disciplines, it is arguably meditation that fits most neatly with what self-examination hopes to accomplish. Indeed, if asked to explain self-examination, one might well describe it broadly as a sort of meditation on yourself. In self-examination you are reflecting on the shape of your life, on God's providential care for you, on your growth in grace and godliness, on your conduct toward others, and on your indwelling sin and need for ongoing forgiveness and inward renewal.

Now, immediately upon hearing this, some might question the wisdom of meditating on yourself in this way. After all, if Thomas Watson defined meditation as "a holy exercise of the mind whereby we bring the truths of God to remembrance," then wouldn't thinking about *yourself*, rather than God, be moving in the opposite direction?[6] And clearly, some potential dangers are close at hand for the would-be self-examiner. When an older Richard Baxter reflected on the spiritual

---

6 Thomas Watson, *Heaven Taken by Storm: Showing the Holy Violence a Christian Is to Put Forth in the Pursuit after Glory*, ed. Joel R. Beeke (Grand Rapids, MI: Soli Deo Gloria, 2019), 23.

habits of his younger self, he concluded that he probably spent too much time in self-examination: "I was once wont to meditate on my own heart, and to dwell all at home, and look little higher; I was still poring either on my sins or wants, or examining my sincerity." Baxter didn't see this youthful heart-searching as an inherently bad thing—he said exactly the opposite—but with age he did come to realize that his former approach was a bit imbalanced:

> Now, though I am greatly convinced of the need of heart-acquaintance and employment, yet I see more need of a higher work, and that I should look [more] often upon Christ, and God, and heaven, than upon my own heart. At home I can find distempers to trouble me, and some evidences of my peace; but it is above that I must find matter of delight and joy and love and peace itself. Therefore I would have one thought at home, upon myself and sins, and many thoughts above upon the high and amiable and beatifying objects.[7]

Clearly, a Christian's inner world needs gospel balance. When that balance is lost, the believer needs to recover it, as Baxter here recorded himself doing.

In chapter 10, we return to questions of what to do when things seem to be going in the wrong direction spiritually. But for now, let's simply notice that while anything can be distorted or taken to excess, the practice of self-examination itself does not necessarily lead to bad outcomes. In fact, quite the opposite: self-examination is commanded in Scripture, and it has been a great blessing to generations of Christians who sought to pursue it in an intentional way. When Paul wrote to the Galatians, he included a call to self-examination: "Let each one test his own work" (Gal. 6:4). When Paul mentored Timothy, he stressed the need for his young protégé to "keep a close watch on [himself]"

---

7   Richard Baxter, *The Autobiography of Richard Baxter*, ed. N. H. Keeble (London: Dent, 1974), 113.

(1 Tim. 4:16). And when he addressed the church in Rome, he offered this piece of advice: "I say to everyone among you not to think of himself more highly than he ought to think, but to think with sober judgment, each according to the measure of faith that God has assigned" (Rom. 12:3). Paul's logic assumed that the Roman Christians would be engaged in serious, thoughtful self-assessment about how God had gifted them and who he was calling them to be.

And if we think about meditation a bit more, perhaps the biblical call to, in effect, meditate on yourself is not so strange after all. For while Christian meditation is certainly meant to be a careful reflection on God and the things of God, that reflection on divine things, as you may recall from chapter 4, is meant to lead toward application to one's own life and heart. So yes, Thomas Watson defined meditation as "a holy exercise of the mind whereby we bring the truths of God to remembrance," but he went on to add that upon recalling God's truths, we then "seriously ponder upon them and *apply them to ourselves*."[8] To fully "apply them to ourselves" requires what the Puritans and their successors called self-examination. In this chapter, we think more deeply about why we should practice self-examination and what it might look like in practice. To that end, what follows is divided into three main sections: first, we consider self-examination as it relates to the Christian's battle against sin; second, we look at self-examination in relation to God's providential dealings with us; and third, we explore practical ways to implement self-examination in our day-to-day lives.

Self-Examination and the Battle against Indwelling Sin

The most basic and clear-cut rationale for self-examination is that the practice assists believers in their fight against indwelling sin and their desire to grow in grace. If Christians want to "walk in a manner worthy of the calling to which [they] have been called" (Eph. 4:1), then they

---

8 Watson, *Heaven Taken by Storm*, 23 (emphasis added).

must understand both what that worthiness looks like and how their own lives do or do not conform to it. Understanding the shape and scope of Christian faithfulness comes from studying the Bible, but knowing where we stand in relation to that biblical standard comes from studying our own hearts.

Arguably, the most foundational starting point for such self-study involves asking whether we are actually Christians at all: "Examine yourselves, to see whether you are in the faith" (2 Cor. 13:5). For the Puritans, this question felt especially pertinent because they operated within a national church structure in which almost everyone had been baptized and church attendance was, at least in theory, compulsory. Within such a context, Christian nominalism and false profession would have been constant worries for Puritan ministers who took Jesus seriously when he foretold of the many outwardly religious people who would one day hear the words, "I never knew you; depart from me, you workers of lawlessness" (Matt. 7:23). And though this issue's precise relationship to pastoral practice is clearly different in a twenty-first-century Western context marked by rapid religious decline, the question whether one is actually in Christ is perennially pressing for believers in every age. For our purposes, with our focus on ongoing spiritual formation among believers, we move on rather quickly here, merely noting the fact that, in a real sense, the first question for a Christian's self-examination is less about the fight against ongoing, indwelling sin (a concept that assumes real conversion) and more fundamentally about whether one has actually been converted in the first place.[9]

But once I have been united to Christ through faith, what then? One of the great Reformation insights into Christian living was to fully grasp the pervasive and insidious nature of indwelling sin, the pull toward sin that remains in this life even among those who have been truly born again. As they studied their Bibles, the Reformers rec-

---

9   For wisdom on this most foundational question, see Mike McKinley, *Am I Really a Christian? The Most Important Question You're Not Asking* (Wheaton, IL: Crossway, 2011).

ognized "that Scripture everywhere proceeds from the assumption that sin remains a reality in believers to the very end of their lives."[10] And if indwelling sin is a permanent reality this side of glory, then it follows that Christians will find themselves in a constant battle against it. In fact, as John Calvin observed in his commentary on Romans 7, whether a person is fighting this battle is actually a key mark that distinguishes Christians from non-Christians:

> The great difference between the believers and unbelievers is, that the latter are . . . pleased with sin in their whole hearts, and, therefore, devote themselves to it without any real opposition, on the part of their affections, to iniquity and vice. . . . On the other hand, the pious, in whom the regeneration of God has commenced,[11] are so divided in their feelings as to breathe after God with the chief desire of their heart, to desire heavenly righteousness, and hate sin, but are again drawn back to earth by the remains of their flesh. . . . This is the Christian warfare and struggle mentioned by Paul (Gal. 5:17) between the flesh and the Spirit.[12]

Reformation-minded Christians have always taken seriously that sense of "warfare and struggle" against sin. Drawing on Paul's insistence that a Christian must "put to death the deeds of the body" (Rom. 8:13), early modern authors settled on the language of "mortification" and "vivification" to describe the process through which indwelling sin gradually meets its end and new spiritual life grows up to take its place. "In the best of saints there is something which needs mortifying," wrote

---

10 Herman Bavinck, *Reformed Dogmatics*, ed. John Bolt, trans. John Vriend (Grand Rapids, MI: Baker Academic, 2003), 4:262.

11 Note that for Calvin, the word "regeneration" is here used to mean what later Reformed theologians and evangelicals typically term "sanctification," that is, the ongoing, progressive work of the Holy Spirit to conform the believer to Christ.

12 John Calvin, *Commentary on the Epistle to the Romans*, trans. Francis Sibson (London: L. B. Seeley and Sons, 1834), 289–90.

Thomas Watson, "much pride, envy, and passion; therefore mortification is called crucifixion (Gal. 5:24), and is not done suddenly. Every day some limb of the body of death must drop off."[13] Here we find a key dynamic underpinning real spiritual formation, one that Sinclair Ferguson describes as "the very heart of Reformed piety."[14] Namely, we observe a dual reality within the believer according to which sin no longer rules the heart ("Sin will have no dominion over you," Rom. 6:14) and yet nonetheless remains an ongoing problem that must be fought against daily ("When I want to do right, evil lies close at hand," Rom. 7:21). If sin still ruled the heart, then there would be no real desire for nor possibility of mortification, and yet if sin were no longer present at all, then mortification would not be necessary. If we take this dynamic seriously, we can see rather quickly how self-examination must play a crucial role in the ongoing effort to mortify indwelling sin. You can't actively fight against sins of which you are unaware. Nor can you repent of sins that you have not yet called to mind. And while it's true that fallen men and women never perfectly know the depths of their sinful hearts—"Who can discern his errors? / Declare me innocent from hidden faults" (Ps. 19:12)—there is more than enough that can be known, and the Bible calls us to reflect on it and repent of it.

In this connection, we can identify at least three major ways that self-examination supports our battle against indwelling sin. First, as we acquire greater self-knowledge, we will be better equipped to guard against temptation. Among the English Puritans, perhaps no single author is more closely connected with this theme than John Owen, who famously warned believers to "be killing sin or it will be killing you."[15] Owen understood that though we are all sinners, God has made

---

13 Watson, *Heaven Taken by Storm*, 10.

14 Sinclair B. Ferguson, *Some Pastors and Teachers: Reflecting a Biblical Vision of What Every Minister Is Called to Be* (Edinburgh: Banner of Truth, 2017), 268.

15 Owen, *Overcoming Sin and Temptation*, 50.

us to differ, and thus, different temptations exert more or less allure for different Christians. Through self-examination, Christians come to better understand their characteristic weaknesses and vulnerabilities so that they can more effectively guard against them:

> Let him that would not enter into temptations labor to know his own heart, to be acquainted with his own spirit, his natural frame and temper, his lusts and corruptions, his natural, sinful, or spiritual weaknesses, that, finding where his weakness lies, he may be careful to keep at a distance from all occasions of sin.[16]

The same situation that might tempt one person to explode in sinful rage might tempt another to shrink back in sinful cowardice. Some hearts are provoked to idolatrous covetousness by the allure of the spotlight, whereas others naturally shrink from attention and would be far more vulnerable to the heart-warping pull of money, sex, or leisure. All of us are prone to wander, but the particular byways we are drawn to differ according to our individual makeup. Self-examination helps us better know ourselves and thus better guard our hearts.

Second, regular self-examination helps us spot creeping sins early before they develop into much more serious problems. George Swinnock is best known for his monumental, thousand-page dissection of the Christian life titled *The Christian Man's Calling*. In this epic work, Swinnock describes self-examination as "a special preservative against sin," and he vigorously drives home the point that to "call thyself often to account" plays a crucial role in warding off little sins before they turn into big ones:

> The ship that leaketh is more easily emptied at the beginning than afterwards. . . . A frequent reckoning with ourselves will pluck sin up

---

16 Owen, *Overcoming Sin and Temptation*, 201.

before it is rooted in the soul. Examination will help the Christian that hath fallen and bruised himself to heal the wound whilst it is fresh, before it is festered.[17]

In Swinnock's estimate, "this one advantage" or benefit of self-examination, even "if there were no more, is extraordinary."[18]

It's not hard to see why he would say that. Once a sin takes hold in our lives, it becomes harder and harder to control. In her research into the dynamics of adultery, the psychologist Shirley Glass reports that most extramarital affairs do not begin with a full-fledged intent to betray one's spouse and destroy one's marriage. Rather, adulterous desire creeps in slowly, small transgressions accumulating as a new relationship begins to squeeze itself into the emotional space that should have been reserved exclusively for husband and wife:

> Surprisingly, the infidelity that I'm seeing these days is of a new sort. It's not between people who are intentionally seeking thrills, as is commonly believed. The new infidelity is between people who unwittingly form deep, passionate connections before realizing that they've crossed the line from platonic friendship into romantic love. Eighty-two percent of the 210 unfaithful partners I've treated have had an affair with someone who was, at first, "just a friend." . . . People who truly are initially just friends or just friendly colleagues slowly move onto the slippery slope of infidelity. In the new infidelity, secret emotional intimacy is the first warning sign of impending betrayal. Yet, most people don't recognize it as such or see what they've gotten themselves into until they've become physically intimate.[19]

---

17 George Swinnock, *The Works of George Swinnock* (Edinburgh: James Nichol, 1868), 3:140, 142.
18 Swinnock, *Works*, 3:142.
19 Shirley P. Glass, *Not "Just Friends": Protect Your Relationship from Infidelity and Heal the Trauma of Betrayal* (New York: Free Press, 2003), 1–2.

Many of these marriages might have averted catastrophe if the spouses involved had been practicing the sort of searching self-examination commended by the Puritans. And the dynamic that Glass identifies in the case of adultery applies more widely to all sorts of sins. When given the opportunity, a small flicker of disordered desire can quickly lead to an uncontrollable blaze. It's the sort of progression that James describes: "Then desire when it has conceived gives birth to sin, and sin when it is fully grown brings forth death" (James 1:15). Self-examination is "a special preservative against sin," as Swinnock put it, in large measure because it helps us intercept a sinful impulse before it gets out of control.

The third way that self-examination helps us in our struggle against indwelling sin is by leading us to confession, repentance, and a renewed sense of gospel assurance. Scripture teaches both that Christians continue to sin even after conversion ("If we say we have no sin, we deceive ourselves, and the truth is not in us," 1 John 1:8) and that this ongoing sin requires ongoing confession before God ("If we confess our sins, he is faithful and just to forgive us our sins and to cleanse us from all unrighteousness," 1 John 1:9). This seems clear enough, but if we dig deeper into the logic of such repentance, it becomes evident that the very concept seems to presuppose a certain degree of self-examination. In Psalm 51, David can pray, "Cleanse me from my sin," because, as the next verse makes clear, he first comes to a measure of knowing himself: "For I know my transgressions, / and my sin is ever before me" (Ps. 51:2–3). In the main, to confess my sin requires that I first know my sin. And to know my sin requires meditating on my heart in view of God's law.

The beauty of such confessing and repenting before the Lord is that it leads to an assurance of real pardon in Christ and a clean conscience rooted in union with him. Archibald Alexander described "a good conscience" as "the most essential ingredient in that peace which Christ gives to His disciples."[20] That "good conscience" and gospel assurance is

---

20 Archibald Alexander, *Thoughts on Religious Experience* (Edinburgh: Banner of Truth, 2020), 197.

rooted in knowing that we truly "are in Christ Jesus, who became to us wisdom from God, righteousness and sanctification and redemption" (1 Cor. 1:30). His righteousness is mine as a free gift that no one can take away. Knowing that truth, I can, when I recognize indwelling sin in my life, confess and repent with confidence that my justification before God was never in doubt and that the same God who justifies me will also continue to forgive me and sanctify me.

Putting his finger on this very point, Richard Sibbes suggested that "the reason why many Christians . . . are so full of doubts" is because they omit the self-examination and mortification of indwelling sin that could actually lead them to a fuller sense of their union with Christ and the forgiveness and inner renewal that such union provides. "Labour to grow in knowledge and mortification," Sibbes wrote, "for in that way we come to assurance."[21] Likewise, for this reason, when Thomas Watson was asked the question "What shall we do to get assurance?" his very first recommendation was to "keep a pure conscience": "Let no guilt lie upon the conscience unrepented of. . . . Guilt clips the wings of comfort. He who is conscious to himself of secret sins, cannot draw near to God in full assurance; he cannot call God father, but judge."[22] And in this same spirit, the Westminster Confession urges believers to be regularly "examining themselves" so that "they may come to further conviction of, humiliation for, and hatred against sin, together with a clearer sight of the need they have of Christ, and the perfection of his obedience."[23] Self-examination leads to gospel assurance by exposing and convicting me of my sin, driving me to Christ for forgiveness, and empowering me by his Spirit to press for further renewal and growth.

In all this, we see a tight connection between self-examination and growth in godliness, a connection drawn out well by Psalm 119:59–60:

---

21   Richard Sibbes, *Works of Richard Sibbes*, ed. Alexander B. Grosart (Edinburgh: Banner of Truth, 1973), 7:212.

22   Thomas Watson, *A Body of Divinity* (Edinburgh: Banner of Truth, 1983), 257.

23   "Westminster Confession of Faith," in *Creeds, Confessions, and Catechisms: A Reader's Edition*, ed. Chad Van Dixhoorn (Wheaton, IL: Crossway, 2022), 214 (19.6).

When I think on my ways,
I turn my feet to your testimonies;
I hasten and do not delay
to keep your commandments.

For the heart alive to God, thinking prayerfully "on my ways" leads to thinking deeply about God's ways and the extent to which the two are either aligned or out of sync. When I realize my own misalignment, this in turn recalls the perfect obedience of Jesus and the way his thoughts, attitudes, words, and deeds were in perfect alignment with his Father's will (Luke 22:42). And when I do *that*, I'm led back to praise God for the gift of Christ's righteousness imputed to me, a gift that opens up space for me to "hasten and . . . not delay / to keep [God's] commandments" (Ps. 119:60), free from all fear of condemnation (Rom. 5:1).

Self-Examination and the Story of Your Life

In addition to using self-examination as a tool to call oneself to account and fight against indwelling sin, early modern Protestants could also widen the conceptual net of self-examination to include a more general sort of theologically charged self-reflection. This broader sense involves thinking deliberately about one's life as a story that God is writing. It involves training one's mind and heart to reframe life's apparent chaos as something orderly, purposeful, and imbued with divinely ordained meaning. Through such intentional reframing, early modern Protestants reinforced their sense of Christian identity and strengthened their confidence in God's good plan and purpose for their lives. According to historian Kate Narveson, this approach to piety and self-examination encouraged "a new mode of self-expression and self-fashioning."[24] Alec Ryrie concludes that this dynamic was one of the defining features of early modern Protestant devotion:

---

24 Kate Narveson, *Bible Readers and Lay Writers in Early Modern England: Gender and Self-Definition in an Emergent Writing Culture* (London: Routledge, 2016), 6.

Early modern Protestants . . . were incubating the novel idea that every Christian life story was, in fact, a story: a coherent and progressive narrative in which the Spirit providentially led the believer on a winding but sure path to Heaven. Understanding that narrative in any individual case was not easy, especially when the particular story was not yet over, but the principle that every life lived under God must have a coherent meaning of this kind was unshakeable. The effort to discern those meanings was one of the wellsprings of the diaries, biographies, and autobiographies which began to flourish in our period. It was one of Protestantism's greatest sources of consolation: even disasters and failures were embraced within God's plan. And it gave the Protestant life the distinctive, restless dynamism which . . . is one of its most pervasive qualities.[25]

To illustrate this way of thinking, consider the New England pastor Thomas Shepard, who referred in his diary to his own life as a story unfolding within the larger narrative arc of what he called "God's great plot." Historian Michael McGiffert explains that Shepard's use of this phrase reflected the "faith in divine design by which Puritans affirmed their sense of the moral order of existence in an age of revolutionary turmoil, defined their parts in the play of God's purpose, and affirmed the cosmic dimensions of their experience."[26] For Shepard, then, the events of his life, whether the unexpected death of a loved one or the simple pleasure of a walk in autumn, were not just things that happened to happen to him but were instead carefully arranged elements in "God's great plot." To consistently implement this way of seeing is to transform every victory into a good gift from your Father in heaven and every defeat into a divinely ordained trial intended for your ultimate spiritual growth.

---

25 Alec Ryrie, *Being Protestant in Reformation Britain* (Oxford: Oxford University Press, 2013), 409.
26 Michael McGiffert, ed., *God's Plot: Puritan Spirituality in Thomas Shepard's Cambridge*, by Thomas Shepard, rev. ed. (Amherst: University of Massachusetts Press, 1994), 3.

Around the same time but on the other side of the Atlantic, Richard Sibbes was being carried by similar theological currents when he urged Christians to be "well read in the story of [their] own lives." According to Sibbes, such "self-reading" encourages the Christian as she reflects on God's faithfulness and goodness displayed in her life: "Every new experience is a new knowledge of God, and should fit us for new encounters." And when facing difficult circumstances, the Christian who is "well read" in his life story can recall past experiences to draw fresh strength for today: "If we could treasure up experiments [i.e., past experiences], the former part of our life would come in to help the latter; and the longer we live the richer in faith we should be." To do this is to cultivate what Sibbes memorably termed a "sanctified memory," and it represents a key component of our spiritual formation.[27] Listen to how he prescribed such remembering as the antidote for temptation, fear, and worry:

> The way for a Christian to recover his ground in time of temptation, is for him to enter into God's sanctuary, and not to give liberty to his thoughts to range in, considering the present estate that he is in; but look to former experiences, in himself, in others; see the promises and apply them; it shall go well with the righteous, but woe to the wicked, it shall not go well with them.[28]

When Sibbes urged readers to "look to former experiences," he was suggesting that we read the entirety of our lives with an eye toward finding spiritual meaning in both its peaks and its valleys.

And though clearly framed here as a spiritual exercise, the "sanctified memory" commended by Sibbes in some respects resembles the sort of self-reflection that is common to all people, whether they are Christians or not. As humans made in God's image and living in God's world, we have a desire to think deeply about who we are, what we've

27 Sibbes, *Works*, 1:277.
28 Sibbes, *Works*, 7:67–68.

done, the places we've been, and the people we've met. As evidenced by photo albums, diaries, and memento-lined shelves, there is a widely held intuition that remembering the past is an important and often pleasurable part of being human. Even if we can't quite articulate why, most people share a vague sense that making meaning in the present somehow draws on memories of the past.

In that connection, consider this passage from the literary critic Sven Birkerts:

> I was lying in bed just before dawn, awake, as so often happens now—suddenly alert with the sensation of "This is it—this is my life!" which usually arrives and then just vanishes, but I lay there, eyes closed, and held it. And I knew right then that I could turn my mind to any part of my life and bring it alive. Anything: the water fountain at my first school, the feeling of walking with my friend in the pine woods near my house, bouncing up and down at the end of the diving board at Walnut Lake, waking in a tent on hard ground in a dew-soaked sleeping bag, knowing the weight of my newborn son when I held him up over my head. I could point my mind to anything in my life and *have* it—savor it there in the dark, even as I was telling myself that this must not be forgotten, that it absolutely has to be attended to, that my life will make sense only when every one of these things is known for what it was, or is.[29]

As Birkerts marvels at the human capacity to call to mind—almost as if by magic—images, experiences, and stories from one's past, he is struck by a sharp sense that his scattered memories must *mean something*, insisting that "attention [be] paid to the life, to the *fact* of the life, to events and people, their enormous mattering."[30] Birkerts is

---

29 Sven Birkerts, *Changing the Subject: Art and Attention in the Internet Age* (Minneapolis: Graywolf, 2015), 252–53.

30 Birkerts, *Changing the Subject*, 252.

moved by the apparently self-evident truth of his intuition that one's memories hold an intrinsic meaning. And yet he doesn't quite seem sure of what that meaning might actually entail. He asserts the reality of it, emphatically so, but shortly afterward, his essay ends, leaving the reader to wonder exactly where the "enormous mattering" that attaches to memory might be found.

Here, then, is where the distinction between Birkerts's secular remembering and Sibbes's "sanctified" version of the same come into sharp relief: for apart from the biblical conviction that there is a God who not only "works all things according to the counsel of his will" (Eph. 1:11) but also makes all those things work together for my good (Rom. 8:28), Birkerts's appeal to the "enormous mattering" of life rings hollow. Apart from the biblical doctrine of God's providence over all things, the "story of my life" isn't a story at all but is instead a string of random events, "a tale / Told by an idiot, full of sound and fury, / Signifying nothing."[31] Another secular writer, Michael Harris, is perhaps closer to the mark when he confesses that, unlike Birkerts, he simply cannot believe that the story of his life has any real narrative structure:

> The fragile idea that your life is a cohesive story (that you will find your Heathcliff or survive a journey to Mordor) . . . certainly isn't borne out by today's lived experience. Real life feels more like a Tumblr feed than a novel. Real life is random, overpowering, and scarcely knowable as it scrolls past our bewildered, blinking eyes.[32]

For Christians, however, the details of our lives *are* infused with "enormous mattering" because we believe that such details are orchestrated

---

31 William Shakespeare, *Macbeth*, ed. E. K. Chambers, Warwick Shakespeare ed. (Toronto: Morang Educational Company, 1907), 99 (5.5.26–28).

32 Michael Harris, *Solitude: In Pursuit of a Singular Life in a Crowded World* (London: Random House, 2018), 178.

by God himself. A Christian finds meaning in his or her life story because the Christian believes that God is the story's ultimate author. This isn't always easy, of course, and sometimes unearthing what God is doing in the story of our lives can be very difficult indeed. As Edith Schaeffer observed when thinking about her own story, "Trumpets don't blow in life . . . as they would if we were putting on a play with sound effects." One often confronts moments of profound confusion and uncertainty, moments in which all one can do is wait patiently on the Lord (Ps. 40:1). "Trumpets don't blow" on cue to mark out every providentially significant moment, as Schaeffer goes on to note, "but we hear the faint echo in memory as we look back."[33]

Thus, whatever difficulties might attend to the process of reflecting theologically on the story of one's life, confidence in the practice's ultimate value is rooted in the promises of God. In response to the question "What is your only comfort in life and in death?" the Heidelberg Catechism replies, in part, that my comfort flows from knowing that God "watches over me in such a way that not a hair can fall from my head without the will of my Father in heaven; in fact, all things must work together for my salvation."[34] This statement is predicated on both a strong doctrine of God's providence and a confidence that those who have been truly born again will persevere and be kept by God from falling away, two distinctively Reformed theological convictions that weave together to reinforce the idea that one's life is a meaningful narrative with purpose and direction.

It is such conviction that stands behind one of the great Puritan treatments of this theme, John Flavel's *The Mystery of Providence* (1678). In this treatise, Flavel argued that "it is the duty of the saints . . . to reflect upon the performances of providence for them in all the states, and through all the stages of their lives."[35] The phrase "performances of

---

33   Edith Schaeffer, *L'Abri* (London: Norfolk, 1969), 55.

34   "Heidelberg Catechism," in Van Dixhoorn, *Creeds, Confessions, and Catechisms*, 291 (q. 1).

35   John Flavel, *The Works of John Flavel* (London: Banner of Truth, 1968), 4:347.

providence" is drawn from Psalm 57:2, which the King James Version translates, "I will cry unto God most high; unto God that performeth all things for me." Thus, when Flavel urged that we "reflect upon the performances of providence," he was encouraging us to think about past instances of God's blessing, provision, and deliverance from difficulty in our lives. Clearly, this would include the great events of one's life—births, deaths, conversions, marriages, new jobs, fortunes won and lost—but because Flavel believed in a meticulous providence in which God "ordain[s] whatsoever comes to pass," he could also spot God's "performances of providence" in literally every twist and turn of life.[36] Because God ordains not just the ends but also the means by which those ends are reached, one must learn to see both God's kindness in providing you a lifelong friend and also God's wisdom in arranging the myriad details that allowed the two of you to meet in the first place—you both were enrolled in the same class at the same school during the same hour, you happened to strike up a conversation, you happened to also have shared a walk home, and so on and so forth—a sequence of "coincidences" that aren't coincidences at all when viewed in light of God's sovereign provision.

To this end, Flavel encouraged Christians to reflect on various "performances of providence" that God works in the lives of the saints. For example, one could reflect on the fact and circumstances of one's birth and upbringing—what a marvel to be born at all, so that "we cannot therefore but admire the tender care of providence over us, and say with the Psalmist, Psal. cxxxix. 13. 'Thou hast covered me in my mother's womb.' "[37] Or one might consider the many ways God has faithfully provided through all manner of difficulty or the gift of productive employment: "If God bless your labours, so as to give you and yours necessary supports and comforts in the

---

36 "Westminster Confession of Faith," in Van Dixhoorn, *Creeds, Confessions, and Catechisms*, 189 (3.1).
37 Flavel, *Works*, 4:364–65.

world by it, it is a choice providence, and with all thankfulness to be acknowledged."[38] Each friend and family member one knows or has known is a special gift from God to be remembered, considered, and delighted in. Flavel reminded those who have children that "to have comfort, and joy in them, is a special providence, importing a special mercy to us."[39] And of course, for the Christian, the single greatest "performance of providence" must be the fact and circumstances of one's conversion to Christ, "the most excellent benefit you ever received" and "a subject which every gracious heart loves to steep its thoughts in."[40]

In remembering all these "performances of providence"—and Flavel named these and many more besides—the Christian has an incredible resource for spiritual formation. The story of your life is the story of God at work such that "it hath been the pious and constant practice of the saints in all generations, to preserve the memory of the more famous, and remarkable providences that have befallen them in their times as a precious treasure."[41] There is a special joy to be found in rejoicing at God's goodness and faithfulness to us throughout the course of our lives if we will only take the time to remember and reflect. When thoughtful non-Christians like Sven Birkerts intuit that the shape of a life is invested, down to its tiny details, with an "enormous mattering," they are not wrong.[42] They are fumbling toward a truth, but it is a truth that eludes them insofar as they fail to realize, as John Flavel did, that the details of life matter because they are graciously ordered by the all-wise God and hence directed toward his glory and our good in ways we can only scarcely begin to discern in this life. In grasping something of that meaning, power, and divinely ordained purpose, we find a deep reserve of encouragement and delight, which Flavel captured well:

38 Flavel, *Works*, 4:389.
39 Flavel, *Works*, 4:398.
40 Flavel, *Works*, 4:376.
41 Flavel, *Works*, 4:347.
42 Birkerts, *Changing the Subject*, 252.

Let me tell you, there is not such a pleasant history for you to read in all the world, as the history of your own lives, if you would but sit down and record to yourselves from the beginning hitherto, what God hath been to you, and done for you: what signal manifestations and out-breakings of his mercy, faithfulness, and love, there have been in all the conditions you have passed through. If your hearts do not melt before you have gone half through that history, they are hard hearts indeed.[43]

Putting It All Together

As we have now seen, the call to self-examination takes two basic forms. First, as we search our hearts and consider our conduct, self-examination assists us in our fight against indwelling sin. One cannot easily repent of and be on guard against a sin that one does not first identify, and thus the entire logic of the Christian's ongoing repentance and striving for holiness assumes a baseline of self-awareness and self-examination. Second, self-examination also takes the form of a more holistic autobiographical review, an intentional reading of our own stories through which we learn to see God's hand in all life's plot twists and to reflexively give him thanks and praise for his providential care. Both forms are important, and they often intertwine. But how do we actually incorporate them into our spiritual formation? Let's consider three final thoughts to help us draw the threads of our discussion on self-examination together and move this discipline from theory to practice.

Self-Examination Is Not Self-Absorption

The first thing that must be said is that the sort of self-examination described in this chapter is not to be equated with a sinful self-absorption. Although pride, vanity, and preoccupation with oneself to the neglect of others are perennial temptations for fallen men and women, there

43 Flavel, *Works*, 4:416–17.

are reasons to think that in our current cultural moment, we are especially vulnerable to their destructive allure. After conducting extensive research on the habits, attitudes, and assumptions of Americans born between 1970 and 2000, the psychologist Jean Twenge concluded that "this is a generation unapologetically focused on the individual." Across a wide swath of cultural markers and contexts, Twenge observed that "young people have been consistently taught to put their own needs first and to focus on feeling good about themselves." As a result of her findings, she labeled this cohort "Generation Me." And while Twenge's analysis of "Generation Me" is not all negative—for example, she goes out of her way to avoid "suggesting that we return to the supposedly ideal days of the 1950s"—if there is any truth to her conclusion that ours is "a culture that teaches . . . the primacy of the individual at virtually every step," then Christians living in it need to especially resist the pull toward an unhealthy and possibly sinful focus on oneself.[44]

Jesus calls his disciples to radically deny themselves and bear their cross (Matt. 16:24), and Paul expects Christians to "count others more significant than [themselves]" (Phil. 2:3). So any interest we have in self-examination must begin with the recognition that the practice does not represent an unqualified license to make things all about me. When Puritans such as John Flavel insisted that "above all other studies in the world, study your own hearts," they were not recommending self-interest for the sake of self-aggrandizement.[45] Rather, they consistently underscored that a right sort of self-examination is ultimately centered on God, not the individual. But how is that possible when the practice is called *self*-examination?

It's possible because, as John Calvin observed, true knowledge of self is closely related to true knowledge of God, and the two are "joined by

---

44 Jean M. Twenge, *Generation Me: Why Today's Young Americans Are More Confident, Assertive, Entitled—and More Miserable Than Ever Before* (New York: Free Press, 2006), 2, 7, 8.

45 Flavel, *Works*, 5:421.

many bonds."[46] And so for a redeemed, regenerate individual guided by Scripture, reflecting on the one quickly leads to reflecting on the other. Thus, when a Christian searches his heart for indwelling sin, he is led by the Spirit to ask with the apostle Paul, "Who will deliver me from this body of death?" and then answers with Paul, "Thanks be to God through Jesus Christ our Lord!" (Rom. 7:24–25). Likewise, when a Christian reviews and reflects on the shape of her life, the exercise does not serve to inflate her sense of self but rather leads her to thank the giver for "every good gift" (James 1:17). When Paul remembered his own past difficulties, circumstances in which he and his companions "were so utterly burdened beyond [their] strength that [they] despaired of life itself," his self-examination showed him that one purpose in his suffering was to ultimately bring him out of himself and toward greater dependence on God: "That was to make us rely not on ourselves but on God who raises the dead" (2 Cor. 1:8–9). And by recalling God's help in the past, Paul found a confidence for the present moment that was rooted in God's strength and not his own: "He delivered us from such a deadly peril, and he will deliver us. On him we have set our hope that he will deliver us again" (2 Cor. 1:10).

For Christians, then, when we examine ourselves in the manner that the Bible models and our Reformation forebears commended, it actually has the paradoxical effect of diminishing our own sense of self-importance and heightening the power, presence, and reality of God in our lives. For this to happen, however, our self-examination must be tightly tethered to Scripture, which brings us to our second point.

Self-Examination Reflects Scriptural Promises and Priorities

Yes, self-examination is meditating on your own life and heart, but that doesn't mean it should ever drift away from Scripture. Whether we are looking to mortify indwelling sin or magnify our gratitude toward

---

46 John Calvin, *Institutes of the Christian Religion*, ed. John T. McNeill, trans. Ford Lewis Battles, Library of Christian Classics (Philadelphia: Westminster, 1960), 1:35 (1.1.1).

God by reflecting on his providential care for us, we would do well to follow the example of those who went before by framing any and all examination of self within a larger understanding of God's word.

To this end, when the Puritans searched for sin in their lives, they held their conduct up against a biblical standard. As historian Jonathan Willis explains, this often involved using the Ten Commandments, or Decalogue, as a measuring line:

> The Decalogue was . . . the primary tool employed for the ongoing process of self-examination, and the consequent identification and cataloguing of sinful behaviours. Because of their scripturally-attested capacity for revealing the enormity of human sin, the commandments were the ideal choice for humbling the proud and reinvigorating them with feelings of repentance and a renewed desire for amendment of life—a cycle which ideally resulted in the strengthening of faith, a process linked to the doctrine of assurance.[47]

Because the Reformed tradition understands the Ten Commandments to constitute a concise summary statement of God's moral law, no vice or virtue eludes their reach. This can be seen in the major Reformed catechisms, which typically contain an exposition of the Decalogue that unfolds the full implication of each command. So, for example, when considering the eighth commandment, the Heidelberg Catechism explains that in addition to the prohibition of theft, obedience to God's law at this point also requires "that I do whatever I can and may for my neighbor's good, that I treat others as I would like them to treat me, and that I work faithfully so that I may help the needy in their hardship."[48] One can thus effectively work through the Ten Commandments, with or without the help of a catechism, and review one's life and conduct

---

47 Jonathan Willis, *The Reformation of the Decalogue: Religious Identity and the Ten Commandments in England, c. 1485–1625* (Cambridge: Cambridge University Press, 2017), 233.
48 "Heidelberg Catechism," in Van Dixhoorn, *Creeds, Confessions, and Catechisms*, 326 (q. 111).

accordingly. Likewise, meditating on any passage of Scripture can provide an occasion for self-examination. Does my life match the virtuous conduct commanded or modeled here? Or, conversely, am I guilty of the sin decried or committed in the passage in question?

Similarly, when considering one's past experiences and exercising one's "sanctified imagination," the same logic applies. For John Flavel, a key rule to remember when practicing this sort of autobiographical self-examination was that "the word interprets the works of God," and thus "all providences have relation to the written word." For the purpose of our spiritual growth, it's not enough to simply muse on our past experiences because "providences in themselves are not a perfect guide. They often puzzle and entangle our thoughts; but bring them to the word, and your duty will be quickly manifested."[49] In practice, for Flavel, this involved an active, intentional attempt to correlate his own life experiences with biblical promises, demonstrating to himself that the truths of God's word are in fact *true* with reference to himself. Consider Jeremiah's warning:

Cursed is the man who trusts in man
   and makes flesh his strength,
   whose heart turns away from the LORD. (Jer. 17:5)

Meditating on this verse, Flavel challenged Christians to think about their own past experiences:

Consult the events of providence in this case, and see whether the word be not verified therein? Did you ever lean upon an Egyptian reed, and did it not break under you, and pierce as well as deceive you? O how often hath this been evident in our experience! Whatsoever we have over-loved, idolized, and leaned upon, God hath from

49 Flavel, *Works*, 4:419.

time to time broken it, and made us to see the vanity of it; so that we find, the readiest course to be rid of our comforts, is to set our hearts inordinately or immoderately upon them: for our God is a jealous God, and will not part with his glory to another.[50]

When thus framed at every point by Scripture, self-examination becomes a genuinely Christian and powerful means to further our spiritual formation.

Self-Examination Must Be Intentional

Finally, we must be intentional about our self-examination. If we don't actively decide to do it, we likely won't do it at all. To some extent, of course, this could be said about all spiritual disciplines. It's always easier to hit the snooze button than to get up on a cold winter's morning to pray. But with self-examination, in addition to the same general inertia that threatens to derail any challenging endeavor, we must also contend with the heart's sinful bent toward self-righteousness and pride. We often resist taking an honest look at ourselves because we are afraid of what we might find there. Puritan authors were quick to highlight this point, as in this vivid description from John Ball:

> Meditation is the searcher of the heart. . . . Meditation discovers corruption, and acquaints us with the rebellion of our hearts and lives, with our blindness, security, earthly-mindedness, and infinite other loathsome filthinesses. . . . [B]y Meditation wee look into every dark, filthy corner of our naughty hearts, and rake into that stinking channel, which is seldome stirred.[51]

Because such self-revelations can be so uncomfortable, Thomas Manton believed that "of all the parts of meditation," self-examination "is the

---

50 Flavel, *Works*, 4:421.
51 John Ball, *A Treatise of Divine Meditation* (London, 1660), 21, 22, 25.

most difficult, for here a man is to exercise dominion over his soul, and to be his own accuser and judge; it is against self-love and carnal ease."[52]

Knowing that our hearts might put up extra resistance to this practice should motivate us to take extra special care to intentionally pursue it. While some degree of self-examination can naturally work its way into all our quiet times, the wisdom of past saints suggests that times set apart specifically for this purpose can significantly aid our spiritual growth. As Thomas Watson said,

> Do we set time apart to call ourselves to account and to try our evidences for heaven? "My spirit made diligent search" (Ps. 77:6). Do we take our hearts, as a watch, all in pieces to see what is amiss and to mend it? Are we curiously inquisitive into the state of our souls? Are we afraid of artificial grace, as of artificial happiness?[53]

One could do this, for example, once a week, designating every Friday's quiet time as an intentional opportunity for self-examination. Another logical approach might be to pair a special period of self-examination with your church's celebration of the Lord's Supper. If that happens, say, once a month, then the Friday or Saturday before would be a natural time to examine yourself and would connect nicely with both historical practice and Paul's injunction to "let a person examine himself, then, and so eat of the bread and drink of the cup" (1 Cor. 11:28).[54] Another historically popular way to intentionally pursue self-examination would be to use a spiritual journal to keep both an account of ongoing struggle and victory with sin and also a record of God's providential care.

But however we choose to pursue this practice, we should do it with intention, getting "under the surface of life" and carving out

---

52 Thomas Manton, *The Complete Works of Thomas Manton* (London: James Nisbet, 1872), 17:268.

53 Watson, *Heaven Taken by Storm*, 63.

54 See, e.g., Lewis Bayly, *The Practice of Piety: Directing a Christian to Walk, That He May Please God* (Grand Rapids, MI: Soli Deo Gloria, 2019), 220–23.

moments dedicated to what Willem Teellinck described as the "habitual examination of our conduct to see how we have passed our days and how well it is with our hearts." For by doing so, Christians "raise their hearts, as it were, into the presence of God by holy self-examination in order to keep themselves continually in good order and ready for God's service."[55] Moreover, as we reflect on the shape of our lives as God has dealt with us, disciplined us, blessed us, and worked through innumerable circumstances to conform us to the image of Christ, we will grow in thanksgiving and gratitude to the one who "has done all things well" (Mark 7:37).

55 Willem Teellinck, *The Path of True Godliness*, trans. Annemie Godbehere, ed. Joel R. Beeke, Classics of Reformed Spirituality (Grand Rapids, MI: Reformation Heritage Books, 2006), 183.

7

The Natural World

Looking Outward

ONE OF THE BESTSELLING nonfiction books of the early twenty-first century has been *Spare* by Prince Harry, Duke of Sussex. According to the website Literary Hub, *Spare* sold more copies in 2023 than any other book published that year, and it's not hard to see why: royalty, riches, romance, and celebrity all converge to make Prince Harry's memoir the sort of book that many find irresistible.[1]

But beyond the glamor and unique life story of the book's author, *Spare* also reflects the cultural moment and changing religious context out of which it emerged. In a review for the *Wall Street Journal*, religious historian Dominic Green argues that one of the book's main themes is Prince Harry's growing connection to the natural world, a connection that, at least in Green's analysis, takes on a quasireligious significance. The memoir, Green writes, is "a spiritual autobiography—a New Age story of suffering and rebirth." For Harry, "managing nature is 'a form of worship' and environmentalism is 'a kind of religion.'" When out and about in forests and glens, Harry

---

1 Emily Temple, "These Are the Bestselling (New) Books of 2023," Literary Hub, January 4, 2024, https://lithub.com/.

feels "close to God." Indeed, by his own account, Harry's most for-mative religious experience as a teenager came not during the many Anglican worship services he was forced to attend but rather after shooting a stag in the woods and coming into direct contact with the life and death of a living creature, an experience he describes as "baptismal."[2]

And while Prince Harry might be a trendsetter in some respects, his interest in neopagan nature worship reflects much larger cultural currents. The United Kingdom's latest census data indicates that the fastest-growing religion in England and Wales is shamanism, a loosely defined spiritual phenomenon that reflects the "human desire to connect with the earth, the stars and ultimately 'that which is greater than ourselves.'"[3] Meanwhile, across the Atlantic, *National Geographic* reports that the number of Americans identifying as "pagan" has risen from 134,000 in 2001 to at least 1.5 million in 2023. And while it isn't always easy to capture exactly what people mean when they self-describe as "pagan," the common thread, according to comparative religions professor Sarah Pike, is that "pagans view the natural world as sacred. They celebrate the interconnectedness of all things, seeing humans, nature, and spiritual beings as part of a web of life."[4]

The tendency to look toward nature to provide what only God can offer has been with us since the fall, but as the West has moved further and further away from any meaningful connection to Christianity, the elevation of nature as a source of transcendent meaning has gained momentum. Many have traced this phenomenon back to nineteenth-century Romanticism and influential writers such as Johann Wolfgang von Goethe (1749–1832), who "developed a sacralized understanding

2 Dominic Green, "Prince Harry's Pagan Progress," *Wall Street Journal*, January 19, 2023, https://www.wsj.com/.

3 Alexander Alich, "Shamanism: What You Need to Know about the Fastest-Growing 'Religion' in England and Wales," *The Conversation*, January 5, 2023, https://theconversation.com/.

4 Christine MacIntyre, "Paganism Is on the Rise—Here's Where to Discover Its Traditions," *National Geographic*, March 22, 2023, https://www.nationalgeographic.com/.

of nature as 'God-Nature.' "[5] Or consider someone like Ralph Waldo Emerson (1803–1882), a leading light within the so-called transcendentalist movement who preached "a vision not of heaven but of a saved and regenerated world of nature. . . . Regeneration, not through Christ but through Nature, is the great theme of Emerson's life."[6]

Even outside the confines of self-declared shamans, neopagans, and transcendentalists, one doesn't have to look very far to find descriptions of spiritually transformative encounters with the natural world. Consider the following passage recorded by the polar explorer Richard Byrd (1888–1957) during the months he spent alone at an Antarctic weather station:

> The day was dying, the night being born—but born with great peace. Here were the imponderable processes and forces of the cosmos, harmonious and soundless. Harmony, that was it! That was what came out of the silence—a gentle rhythm, the strain of a perfect chord, the music of the spheres, perhaps. It was enough to catch that rhythm, momentarily to be myself a part of it. In that instant I could feel no doubt of man's oneness with the universe. . . . It was a feeling that transcended reason; that went to the heart of man's despair and found it groundless. The universe was a cosmos, not a chaos; man was rightfully a part of that cosmos as were the day and night.[7]

Wherever one looks for antecedents and sources, it's difficult to deny that a persistent theme over the past two centuries of Western history has been a growing enthusiasm for nature as a source of spiritual meaning. After surveying this history, religious studies professor Christopher Partridge concludes that modern culture has witnessed a marked

5   Christopher Partridge, *The Re-Enchantment of the West*, vol. 2, *Alternative Spiritualities, Sacralization, Popular Culture, and Occulture* (London: T&T Clark International, 2005), 49.

6   Robert D. Richardson, *Three Roads Back: How Emerson, Thoreau, and William James Responded to the Greatest Losses of Their Lives* (Princeton, NJ: Princeton University Press, 2023), 26–27.

7   Richard E. Byrd, *Alone: The Classic Polar Adventure* (New York: G. P. Putnam's Sons, 1938), 85.

increase in "re-sacralized, holistic interpretations of nature as infused with the divine, if not, in some sense, divine in itself."[8]

Given such trends within the post-Christian West, it might come as a surprise to learn that Christians themselves have also long maintained a strong, though rather different, sense of connection between spirituality and the natural world. Whereas for people like Prince Harry and Richard Byrd nature comes to be seen as a spiritual end in its own right, a fountain of mystical fullness that neither requires nor is capable of providing anything greater beyond itself, for biblically minded Christians the creation exerts a spiritual allure insofar as it draws our thoughts and affections toward the one who called it into being by the power of his word.

Consider, for example, the New England Puritan Anne Bradstreet (1612–1672), who has been described as "the mother of American poetry" and is widely celebrated among literary scholars for "her lively wit, driving intelligence, and maternal warmth."[9] Among the many significant themes that run through Bradstreet's work, one of the most intriguing is her appreciation of nature and her corresponding conviction that true delight in the natural world should inevitably lead to delight in God himself. In what is often considered her finest poem, "Contemplations," Bradstreet expressed her delight like this:

> I wist [i.e., know] not what to wish, yet sure thought I,
> If so much excellence abide below;
> How excellent is he that dwells on high?[10]

Across thirty-three stanzas, Bradstreet observed the world around her with a careful eye, allowing each new creational reality to draw her heart

---

8   Partridge, *Re-Enchantment of the West*, 2:50.

9   Jane Donahue Eberwein, "Anne Bradstreet (c. 1612–1672)," *Legacy* 11, no. 2 (1994): 161, 166; for more on Bradstreet's piety, see Jenny-Lyn de Klerk, *5 Puritan Women: Portraits of Faith and Love* (Wheaton, IL: Crossway, 2023), 89–110.

10 Anne Bradstreet, *The Works of Anne Bradstreet in Prose and Verse*, ed. John Harvard Ellis (Charlestown, MA: Abram E. Cutter, 1867), 371.

closer to the Creator who gave them shape and form. She meditated, among other things, on the rising sun, the changing leaves of an oak tree in autumn, and the flowing of a stream. In Bradstreet's vision, no aspect of creation was an inappropriate object for theological reflection—even lowly insects could serve to raise her thoughts and affections upward toward divine things:

> I heard the merry grasshopper then sing,
> The black clad Cricket, bear a second part,
> They kept one tune, and plaid on the same string,
> Seeming to glory in their little Art.
> Shall Creatures abject, thus their voices raise?
> And in their kind resound their maker's praise:
> Whilst I as mute, can warble forth no higher layes.[11]

Bradstreet's poetic talent might have been a rare gift among Reformation-minded Christians, but her interest in the intersection between nature and spiritual formation was not. In that respect, she was representative, not an outlier. Scholars have noted within the Reformed tradition a persistent "desire to carefully record and describe the glories of God's good creation. If creation is a theater, or mirror, of God's glory one could do no better than study diligently the splendors God has placed there."[12] Moreover, observers like Bradstreet not only grasped this relationship between God and creation conceptually but also worked to harness the insight as a vehicle to further their own spiritual formation.

This is an important point to recover because much of the current spiritual formation literature has neglected it. After surveying the various spiritual disciplines recommended in half a dozen books on

---

11 In this context, a "lay" is a brief lyric, typically sung. Bradstreet, *Works*, 373.

12 William A. Dyrness, *Reformed Theology and Visual Culture: The Protestant Imagination from Calvin to Edwards* (Cambridge: Cambridge University Press, 2004), 309.

spiritual formation, Evan Howard found that "none of the disciplines listed . . . mention nature."[13] Though that may come as a surprise in light of the tremendous attention paid to nature as a source and site of spirituality within mainstream popular culture, it reflects an opportunity for us to learn from our Reformed and Puritan forebears. Thus, our goal in this chapter is to explore this point, considering some of the different ways that Reformed thinkers such as Anne Bradstreet sought to "grow in the grace and knowledge of our Lord and Savior Jesus Christ" (2 Pet. 3:18) through biblically informed reflection on the world he has made. In what follows, we see that they found the natural world to reflect God's glory, teach God's truth, and aid in spiritual formation.

The Natural World Reflects God's Glory

That nature reflects God's glory is arguably the clearest and most straightforward way that the natural world fosters Christian growth. It is a fundamental axiom of biblical thought that God is the Creator of all that exists: "By faith we understand that the universe was created by the word of God, so that what is seen was not made out of things that are visible" (Heb. 11:3). And just as a painter's canvas reflects his or her particular vision, creativity, and way of seeing, so too God's creation reflects him, and through observing it, we can see and savor something of God's own glory. Thus the psalmist declares,

> The heavens declare the glory of God,
>   and the sky above proclaims his handiwork. (Ps. 19:1)

Or as the Belgic Confession memorably puts it, the "universe is before our eyes like a beautiful book in which all creatures, great and small, are as letters to make us ponder the invisible things of God: his eternal

---

13 Evan B. Howard, *A Guide to Christian Spiritual Formation: How Scripture, Spirit, Community, and Mission Shape Our Souls* (Grand Rapids, MI: Baker Academic, 2018), 106, 109.

power and his divinity, as the apostle Paul says in Romans 1:20."[14] Such a statement captures a general consensus among Reformed theologians about the spiritual value embedded within the natural world. "The Reformed tradition from Calvin to Edwards," writes historian Belden Lane, "has expressed an extraordinary delight in nature's beauty as a training ground for desiring God." Just as Anne Bradstreet did through her poetry, these theologians through their writings have "persistently discerned God's glory filling the earth," while being careful to also maintain "that God's being is never contained by anything within it."[15]

Lane's last point is significant because some scholars have suggested that Reformed authors have, from time to time, felt this sense of God's glory radiating throughout his creation so intensely that they drifted into moments of near-pantheistic rapture. Pantheism and its variations blur the distinction between the Creator and the creation, positing that the two realities are ultimately one and the same. Such pantheism can either be stated explicitly or be conveyed in a vague, ill-defined way, as in the passage cited above from the explorer Richard Byrd. In this connection, the influential mid-twentieth-century scholar Perry Miller wrote that the Puritans "always . . . verge so close to pantheism that it takes all their ingenuity to restrain themselves from identifying God with the creation."[16] And though the Puritans and other early modern Reformed theologians were decisively *not* pantheists, one can find statements that do strongly—even shockingly—stress the reality of God's connection with his creation.

For example, after cataloging opinions from various pagan authors on the relationship between the created order and whatever divine power might lie behind it, John Calvin wrote,

14 "Belgic Confession," in *Creeds, Confessions, and Catechisms: A Reader's Edition*, ed. Chad Van Dixhoorn (Wheaton, IL: Crossway, 2022), 79 (art. 2).

15 Belden C. Lane, *Ravished by Beauty: The Surprising Legacy of Reformed Spirituality* (New York: Oxford University Press, 2011), 25.

16 Perry Miller, *The New England Mind: The Seventeenth Century* (New York: Macmillan, 1939), 15.

> I confess, of course, that it can be said reverently, provided that it proceeds from a reverent mind, that *nature is God*; but because it is a harsh and improper saying, since nature is rather the order prescribed by God, it is harmful in such weighty matters, in which special devotion is due, to involve God confusedly in the inferior course of his works.[17]

Now I probably would not feel comfortable speaking that way from the pulpit—and, in fairness to Calvin, it sounds as if he's saying that he wouldn't either—but Calvin was clearly no pantheist. Yet the fact that he could write in this way at all testifies to the weight that he placed on the biblical notion that "the heavens declare the glory of God" (Ps. 19:1). He wanted to take this idea seriously, and he wanted to tease out just what it might mean for the Christian life.

But to understand the approach that Calvin and other Reformed authors took to this subject, notice one of the caveats he gave: he warned that strong statements about the creation reflecting the Creator "can be said reverently" but only if such statements proceed "from a reverent mind." In other words, only regenerate Christians, with "the eyes of [their] hearts enlightened" (Eph. 1:18) and wearing what Calvin called the "spectacles of Scripture,"[18] are able to properly discern the correct relationship between Creator and creation. Only the believer can truly and consistently observe "the sky above" and recognize that this starry expanse is neither devoid of divine presence nor to be equated with the Creator but is rather that which "proclaims his handiwork" (Ps. 19:1). For Calvin and other Reformed Christians, unbelievers might make many observations on the natural world, some of them surely full of insight, and yet insofar as they lack a "reverent mind," they inevitably fall into that Creator-creature confusion that Paul describes in Romans

---

17 John Calvin, *Institutes of the Christian Religion*, ed. John T. McNeill, trans. Ford Lewis Battles, Library of Christian Classics (Philadelphia: Westminster, 1960), 1:58 (1.5.5; emphasis added).

18 For Calvin's famous spectacles analogy, see Calvin, *Institutes*, 1:70 (1.6.1), 160–61 (1.14.1).

1:25: "They exchanged the truth about God for a lie and worshiped and served the creature rather than the Creator, who is blessed forever!"

So in this chapter, it is important to recognize that our focus, as throughout this book, is on the spiritual formation of converted Christians. When reading statements from Reformed authors regarding the spiritual value of looking at the creation, we must remember that certain practices that are edifying to Christians will not have precisely the same effect when carried out by non-Christians. Just as Calvin maintained that those in possession of a "reverent mind" could be spiritually nourished through reflection on the creation in ways that those lacking such a mind could not, our focus in all that follows is on Christians trying to think Christianly about creation and to grow in grace and wisdom as a result. As Archibald Alexander put it, "The universe, which to the atheist is full of darkness and confusion, to the Christian, is resplendent with light and glory."[19] We are thus in no way trying to establish—or even comment on—any sort of natural theology through which non-Christians might come to faith in the living and true God. In general, the Reformed tradition has been more pessimistic on this score than other Christian traditions, but that is not our concern here. Rather, we are interested in what good use spiritually minded believers, guided by Scripture, might make of observing the world around them.

For early modern Reformed authors, such good use began with recognizing that every aspect of the created order, from the sky above our heads to the dirt beneath our feet, presents us with an opportunity for wonder and praise. John Calvin conveyed this idea to his readers through a striking suite of metaphors, describing creation variously as a book, an image, a painting, a school, a mirror, a garment, and a theater.[20] Each of these metaphors carries a different nuance, but all

19 Archibald Alexander, "The Bible: A Key to the Phenomena of the Natural World," *Biblical Repertory* 5, no. 1 (1829): 107.

20 Diana Butler, "God's Visible Glory: The Beauty of Nature in the Thought of John Calvin and Jonathan Edwards," *Westminster Theological Journal* 52 (1990): 16.

capture the sense that nature is designed to point beyond itself and that it can be, for those with eyes to see, a potent source of illumination and delight. Indeed, as Calvin explained, "After the world had been created, man was placed in it as in a theatre, that he, beholding above him and beneath the wonderful works of God, might reverently adore their Author."[21] Though such an easy relationship between God, the world, and his image bearers was disrupted by the fall, it still behooves men and women to "contemplate God's works since" they have "been placed in this most glorious theater to be a spectator of them."[22] Just as a theater is purposefully built for enjoying the drama unfolding on stage, so too God has created forests, deserts, lakes, and rivers for humanity to behold and appreciate:

> Let us not be ashamed to take pious delight in the works of God open and manifest in this most beautiful theater. . . . [A]lthough it is not the chief evidence for faith, yet it is the first evidence in the order of nature, to be mindful that wherever we cast our eyes, all things they meet are works of God, and at the same time to ponder with pious meditation to what end God created them.[23]

Although the image of creation as a theater is the most well known of Calvin's metaphors, his others are, in some ways, more provocative. Of particular interest is the way several of them—notably, creation as painting, mirror, and garment—suggest the idea of seeing a thing truly but indirectly. If you look in a mirror, you really are looking at yourself, and yet you are not seeing yourself directly, your perception being mediated through the glass. You both see yourself and do not see yourself at the same time. In similar fashion, Calvin explored the paradoxical notion that God is both invisible to us and yet continuously seen through his creation:

21 John Calvin, *A Commentary on Genesis*, trans. John King (London: Banner of Truth, 1965), 64.
22 Calvin, *Institutes*, 1:72 (1.6.2).
23 Calvin, *Institutes*, 1:179 (1.14.20).

[God has] revealed himself and daily discloses himself in the whole workmanship of the universe. As a consequence, men cannot open their eyes without being compelled to see him. . . . [W]herever you cast your eyes, there is no spot in the universe wherein you cannot discern at least some sparks of his glory. . . . [T]his skillful ordering of the universe is for us a sort of mirror in which we can contemplate God, who is otherwise invisible.[24]

Alongside the mirror metaphor, Calvin also used the imagery of creation as a garment to make a similar point. When we see a human body draped in cloth, its shape and proportion are truly and accurately perceived, and yet we never actually see it directly. The application of such an image to God is suggested by Scripture itself:

Bless the Lord, O my soul!
O Lord my God, you are very great!
You are clothed with splendor and majesty,
    covering yourself with light as with a garment,
    stretching out the heavens like a tent. (Ps. 104:1–2)

Calvin picked up on the psalmist's garment imagery and developed it with striking effect:

In comparing the light with which he represents God as arrayed to a garment, he intimates that although God is invisible, yet his glory is conspicuous enough. In respect of his essence, God undoubtedly dwells in light that is inaccessible; but as he irradiates the whole world by his splendour, this is the garment in which He, who is hidden in himself, appears in a manner visible to us.[25]

24 Calvin, *Institutes*, 1:52 (1.5.1).
25 John Calvin, *Commentary on the Book of Psalms*, trans. James Anderson, vol. 4 (Edinburgh: Calvin Translation Society, 1847), 145.

Calvin insisted that "the knowledge of this truth is of the greatest importance," and it isn't hard to see why. For when we take these ideas seriously, we come to understand how we can see, at least indirectly, the unseeable God, an insight that both draws us closer to our Creator and infuses his creation with an almost unimaginable degree of significance and revelatory power:

> That we may enjoy the sight of him, he must come forth to view with his clothing; that is to say, we must cast our eyes upon the very beautiful fabric of the world in which he wishes to be seen by us, and not be too curious and rash in searching into his secret essence. . . . God . . . meets us in the fabric of the world, and is everywhere exhibiting to our view scenes of the most vivid description. . . . [H]e clothes himself with this robe for our sake.[26]

Through encountering the natural world, then, we are indirectly seeing, experiencing, and savoring something of God: he "meets us in the fabric of the world." This real but indirect enjoyment of God becomes the first main way that nature functions as a spur for spiritual formation. If spiritual formation involves a "conscious process by which we seek to heighten and satisfy our Spirit-given thirst for God," as we defined the term in chapter 1, then surely that formation is furthered by carefully reflecting theologically on and enjoying the beauty of creation. This is because insofar as the creation truly reflects God's glory and reveals God to us, it is satisfying to the soul. And yet insofar as that same encounter is indirect and mediated, it serves to excite our desire for a fuller, longer-lasting, and more direct divine encounter, pointing us ultimately toward our hope for a new heavens and new earth, where we "will see his face" (Rev. 22:4). The beauty of the inlet and the oak tree is, in a real way, God's beauty, and yet the glimpse we

---

26 Calvin, *Psalms*, 4:145–46.

receive is partial, fading, incomplete, and marred by imperfection. In our fallen world, "the creation waits with eager longing" (Rom. 8:19) for God's ultimate renewal, and our enjoyment of that creation stirs a similar sort of longing in our hearts.

Something of this dynamic is on display, for example, in the writing of Richard Baxter, who picked up the same language of creation as "fabric" when he exclaimed, "What a deal of the majesty of the great Creator doth shine in the face of this fabric of the world!"[27] Baxter celebrated the beauty of the earth and seized on it as an occasion for praise and thanksgiving:

> Surely, his works are great and admirable, sought out of them that have pleasure therein. This makes the study of natural philosophy so pleasant, because the works of God are so excellent. What rare workmanship is in the body of a man, yea, in the body of every beast, which makes the anatomical studies so delightful! What excellency in every plant we see, in the beauty of flowers; in the nature, diversity, and use of herbs; in fruits, in roots, in minerals, and what not! But especially if we look to the greater works; if we consider the whole body of this earth, and its creatures, and inhabitants; the ocean of waters, with its motions and dimensions; the variation of the seasons, and of the face of the earth; the intercourse of spring and fall, of summer and winter; what wonderful excellency do these contain![28]

For Baxter, this sort of meditation on creation was a source of delight, but he didn't end there. After stirring up his heart to enjoy the natural world as God's handiwork, he pressed into the idea that indirectly reflecting on God's glory must pale in comparison to directly experiencing the real thing, which his heart was ultimately yearning for: "Why think, then, in thy meditations, if these things, which are but servants

27 Richard Baxter, *The Practical Works of Richard Baxter* (London: James Duncan, 1830), 23:383.
28 Baxter, *Practical Works*, 23:383.

to sinful man, are yet so full of mysterious worth; what, then, is that place where God himself doth dwell, and is prepared for the just who are perfected with Christ!"[29]

The Natural World Teaches God's Truth

We come now to the second way that engaging with creation can further our spiritual formation: the natural world teaches God's truth. If the previous way of thinking about this subject could take Psalm 19:1 as its keynote—"The heavens declare the glory of God"—then this second way of approaching God's creation might adopt for itself Proverbs 6:6:

> Go to the ant, O sluggard;
>> consider her ways, and be wise.

The picture of ants instructing sluggards is perhaps not as familiar or as majestic as the glittering night skies invoked by Psalm 19, but the lesson of Proverbs 6:6 is crucial nonetheless. For in this verse and others like it, we learn that the structure and pattern of the natural world is meant to instruct us. The created order is exactly that, an *order*, and as such, each element has been carefully coordinated within the whole so that even the lowly ant carries a lesson for those willing to see it. Creational realities have not spilled out randomly without purpose; rather, they reflect the wisdom, design, and intention of the good God who made them. It's our job, then, to observe and learn.

If Calvin's theater and garment metaphors best conveyed the idea that creation reflects God's glory and should prompt our wonder and worship, then his description of creation as a school best communicates the idea that the natural world teaches God's truth. Expounding Psalm 19:4, he could describe the "heavenly bodies" themselves as "preaching

---

29 Baxter, *Practical Works*, 23:383–84.

the glory of God like a teacher in a seminary of learning."[30] Elsewhere he remarked that in the well-ordered world that God has designed, "even irrational creatures give instruction."[31] Others have similarly described nature as a school of learning for the godly. The Puritan Robert Cleaver (d. 1613), for instance, explained that the lazy fellow of Proverbs 6:6 was to sit in the "schoole" of the ants as God "makes them his master, that they should teach him, and hee should learne more wisedome and understanding."[32] Likewise, Richard Baxter took it as axiomatic that in the world that God has made, "every creature must become a preacher to us," so that "as the fish brought money to Peter to pay his tribute, so every creature would bring us a greater, even a spiritual gain."[33] And two centuries later, Charles Spurgeon made the same point with the same sort of metaphor, reminding his hearers that "never can the tiller of the ground open his eyes without learning something if he is willing to be taught."[34] Spurgeon was so enthusiastic on this point that he even published an entire volume of *Farm Sermons* (1882), each one insisting that the natural world is meant to function as a source of instruction for the people of God:

> Weeds and plants, frost and sunshine, green shoots and yellow ears, drills and reapers, hedges and ditches, foxes and sheep, drought and flood, waggons and horses, harrows and ploughs—all reveal some spiritual mystery concerning God and our own souls. Surely those men should learn much who find a schoolmaster and a lesson-book in every acre which they cultivate.[35]

30 John Calvin, *Commentary on the Book of Psalms*, trans. James Anderson, vol. 1 (Edinburgh: Calvin Translation Society, 1845), 313.

31 Calvin, *Institutes*, 1:69 (1.5.15).

32 Robert Cleaver, *A Brief Explanation of the Whole Booke of the Proverbs of Salomon* (London, 1615), 97.

33 Richard Baxter, *The Practical Works of Richard Baxter* (Ligonier, PA: Soli Deo Gloria, 1990), 194.

34 C. H. Spurgeon, *Farm Sermons* (London: Passmore and Alabaster, 1882), iv.

35 Spurgeon, *Farm Sermons*, iv–v.

Many within the Reformed tradition have embraced this sense that the earth itself and everything in it has been a rich source of spiritual instruction. Perhaps the name most strongly associated with this sort of thinking is Jonathan Edwards, who kept a notebook in which he recorded scores of "shadows of divine things." These divine shadows were cast by the natural realities all around him, each one providing spiritual insight and edification: "God does purposely make and order one thing to be in an agreeableness and harmony with another. And if so, why should not we suppose that he makes the inferior in imitation of the superior, the material of the spiritual, on purpose to have a resemblance and shadow of them?"[36] Something like this is arguably happening in biblical passages like Proverbs 6:6, in which the activity of the "inferior" ant bears an instructive resemblance to the superior activity of human beings cultivating diligence and zeal in their vocations. Edwards also justified his approach to the natural world by appealing to Jesus's own method of teaching: "Christ often makes use of representations of spiritual things in the constitution of the [world] for argument, as that the tree is known by its fruit" (Matt. 12:33).[37] So in this spirit, Edwards compiled observations on all sorts of creational realities, finding in the silkworm "a remarkable type of Christ" and concluding that through the constant alternation between day and night, "God teaches that we are to expect changes here, and must not expect always to enjoy a sunshine of prosperity."[38]

If one were to pursue seriously the idea that every bug, branch, and boulder has a lesson to teach, then it wouldn't take long to fill many books with such observations and insights. And indeed, long before Edwards began to keep his notebook of earthly pointers to heavenly truths, the seventeenth-century English Puritans were writing lengthy volumes organized around exactly this sort of principle. A classic example comes

---

36 Jonathan Edwards, *The Works of Jonathan Edwards*, vol. 11, *Typological Writings*, ed. Wallace E. Anderson and Mason I. Lowance Jr. with David Watters (New Haven, CT: Yale University Press, 1993), 53.

37 Edwards, *Works*, 11:57.

38 Edwards, *Works*, 11:59, 89.

from John Flavel, whose book *Husbandry Spiritualized: The Heavenly Use of Earthly Things* (1674) was designed to help Christians "walk with God from day to day" by taking "the several objects you behold" all around you in creation and transforming them into "wings and ladders to mount your souls nearer to him who is the centre of all blessed spirits."[39] To that end, Flavel drew spiritual lessons from everyday things like a rain shower in springtime, ripe corn gathered at harvest, and a farmer feeding his cattle.[40] Flavel's observations on the world around him were consistently simple, edifying, and straightforwardly biblical. He saw something and connected it to a truth he already knew from Scripture. To illustrate, consider Flavel's meditation upon spying an impressively large oak tree:

> What a lofty flourishing tree is here? It seems rather to be a little wood, than a single tree, every limb thereof having the dimensions and branches of a tree in it; and yet as great as it is, it was once but a little slip, which one might pull up with two fingers; this vast body was contained virtually and potentially in a small acorn. Well then, I will never despise the day of small things, nor despair of arriving to an eminency of grace, though at present it be but as a bruised reed, and the things that are in me be ready to die. As things in nature, so the things of the Spirit, grow up to their fulness and perfection by slow and insensible degrees. The famous and heroical acts of the most renowned believers were such as themselves could not once perform, or it may be think they ever should. Great things both in nature and grace, come from small and contemptible beginnings.[41]

There is nothing especially surprising or original in what Flavel has written. It is simply the fruit of a Christian attempting to think Christianly on what he sees all around him.

---

39 John Flavel, *The Works of John Flavel* (London: Banner of Truth, 1968), 5:6.
40 Flavel, *Works*, 5:77, 110, 170.
41 Flavel, *Works*, 5:197.

And just as Flavel found a teacher in the oak tree, so too have a host of Puritan authors found edifying instruction in everything from the changing of the seasons to the sight of two rams butting heads. Like Flavel, the Puritan Richard Steele (1629–1692) composed a series of reflections on agricultural life titled *The Husbandman's Calling* (1668), while his contemporary John Collinges (1623–1690) turned his eye toward the many spiritual lessons to be drawn from the craft of weaving in *The Weavers Pocket-book: or Weaving Spiritualized* (1675). In eighteenth-century New England, Cotton Mather (1663–1728) wrote a trio of titles in this vein: *The Religious Mariner* (1712), *The Fisherman's Calling* (1712), and *Agricola, or the Religious Husbandman* (1727). Each one of these volumes represents an attempt to take seriously the way the Bible presents the creation as one great, continual, endlessly fascinating display of God's wisdom, creativity, and kindness. They saw the world as God's world, an ordered, intentional place in which mountains are not merely the result of tectonic plates colliding but rather arise precisely "to the place that [God] appointed for them" (Ps. 104:8) and in which even as "young lions roar for their prey," they can be truly understood as "seeking their food from God" (Ps. 104:21). Their response to this splendor was to say with the psalmist, "I will sing praise to my God while I have my being" (Ps. 104:33), and a part of this praise was intentionally meditating on the wonder of the natural world as a teacher of God's truth.

The Natural World Aids in Spiritual Formation

Of all the subjects covered in this book, this one might be the most neglected—even more so than the neglected practice of meditation discussed earlier. In one sense, this seems counterintuitive. For whether we are considering David Attenborough's popular nature documentaries, the media's steady interest in ecological crises, or the hordes of selfie seekers posing in front of a favorite waterfall, vista, or unusual rock formation, our culture can seem almost obsessively interested in exploring and celebrating the natural world. Moreover, for many twenty-first-century Westerners, this appreciation of the great outdoors seems increasingly to be crossing over into more or less explicit forms of nature worship. At the same time, when I think about my own preaching, I can't remember the last time I creatively, imaginatively, carefully, and biblically reflected on how the things of this world reflect God back to us in the way that John Flavel did for his congregation. Your own experience may differ, but when I read Puritan pastors unfolding theological lessons from their everyday observations of nature, I feel as if I've been transported to another, rather alien, world.

Why might this be? In part, it surely reflects a modern lifestyle that disconnects us from the natural world. Our early modern predecessors were overwhelmingly situated within rural contexts, and most of them would have had direct, daily contact with agriculture. When they stepped outside, they were confronted with an outpouring of flora and fauna that we urbanites and suburbanites have to work hard to find. But it's more than that. Surely a part of me has also become more deeply attuned to the rhythms of secular modernity than I would care to admit. Does my disconnection from the mindset animating Edwards's "shadows of divine things" actually betray a sense in which I no longer believe deep down that the created world is coherent and indicative of God's character? Have we lost that sense of connection between Creator and creation? When it starts to rain, do I really believe as the psalmist did that in this very instance, it is God himself who "prepares rain for the earth?" (Ps. 147:8). Has the awareness of a deeply embedded telos within the creation itself and a vivid sense of an abiding, unbreakable continuity between the Maker and what he has made faded for twenty-first-century evangelicals?

If the answer to any of those questions is yes, or even maybe, then we need to return to the practices of those who went before us. To draw our thoughts on this theme together, here are four guidelines to bear in mind as we look to incorporate this older perspective on God's creation into our own pursuit of spiritual formation.

Read the Book of Nature according to the Book of Scripture

The first thing we need to remember is that meditating on the works of God in nature can serve us well only if controlled by Scripture at every point. When John Flavel published his own theological reflections on the created order, he made sure to remind readers at the outset that "the discoveries of God in the word are far more excellent, clear, and powerful" than anything one might learn from observing the rocks and rivers.[42] As mentioned earlier, contemporary culture is very happy to celebrate the wonder of the natural world, but it takes that celebration in anti-Christian directions because it lacks the insight that only the Bible can offer.

While the relationship between the non-Christian and general revelation is complicated and well beyond our scope here, we can conclusively state that any God-honoring meditation on creation is one that accords with and flows from God's word. Reformed theologians have long been comfortable affirming that God reveals himself through both the book of nature and the book of Scripture, but they have also never wavered in the conviction that the latter must control the former. Archibald Alexander explained it succinctly:

> The Bible furnishes the full and satisfactory commentary on the book of nature. With the Bible in our hands, the heavens shine with redoubled lustre. . . . Without the book of revelation, the book of nature would be as a volume sealed; but with this key, we can open its wonderful pages, and receive instruction from every creature of God.[43]

Practically, this must mean that while my reflections on the world around me can call to mind what I've learned from Scripture, illustrating it, amplifying it, and helping me apply it in fresh and invigorating fashion, I must not attempt to deduce any new or novel doctrines from

---

42 Flavel, *Works*, 5:7.
43 Alexander, "The Bible," 107–8.

my observations of the created order. And when we look at the sorts of lessons that early modern Protestants derived from nature, we find in the main that they stuck to this principle. So for us too, while the intensity of a summer thunderstorm might call to mind the infinitely greater reality of a God who is "glorious in power" and whose "right hand . . . shatters the enemy" (Ex. 15:6), we are not developing some sort of new theology of thunderclaps. We are simply allowing the vividness and immediacy of the storm to evoke a fresh appreciation of the God we know from Scripture itself.

For Jonathan Edwards, his meditations on nature were intended to "confirm the Scriptures" and draw out the "excellent agreement" between God's two books.[44] Earlier I referenced that Edwards found "a remarkable type of Christ" in the humble silkworm. Such a connection might seem fanciful on first blush, but when you read his explanation, it's clear that Edwards learned no new doctrine from the silkworm but rather found a striking illustration of doctrine he already knew from Scripture. Here are his comments in full:

> The silkworm is a remarkable type of Christ, which, when it dies, yields us that of which we make such glorious clothing. Christ became a worm for our sakes, and by his death finished that righteousness with which believers are clothed, and thereby procured that we should be clothed with robes of glory.[45]

From years spent immersed in his Bible, Edwards already knew and believed that Christians were clothed in Christ's imputed righteousness and that this great salvation was procured through Christ's death on the cross. The silkworm didn't teach him that theological truth, but in God's wisdom and kindness, he was powerfully reminded of it through this surprising channel.

44 Edwards, *Works*, 11:74.
45 Edwards, *Works*, 11:59.

Get Outside, and Go for a Walk

If we want to pursue spiritual formation through encountering God's creation, we cannot even begin until we make ourselves go outside. This is the first and most obvious step, but it's worth underscoring because the conditions of twenty-first-century life often seem to militate against it. When reading Puritan accounts of Christian piety, the twenty-first-century reader is perhaps struck by the frequency with which early modern Protestants refer to going outside for their devotional activities. Mary Rich, Countess of Warwick (1625–1678), for example, made it her regular practice to rise early and go to the woods for meditation and prayer.[46] Thomas Shepard referred to meditating while "walking in [his] garden," and each year Isaac Ambrose took time to retreat intentionally to the "sweet silent Woods," where he would enjoy "Spiritual refreshings" through "Prayer, and Meditation, and Self-Examination."[47] Jonathan Edwards's biographer George Marsden recounts that after finishing his dinner, Edwards would habitually "ride two or three miles to a secluded place where he would walk for a while." As he savored "the blue mountains that graced the horizon of the river valley" and "the views he could gain by climbing the surrounding hills," Edwards would take time to pray and to contemplate the giver of such delightful gifts.[48] In all these descriptions, we find a dynamic in which the natural world becomes both the object of the individual's meditation and the arena in which that meditation takes place.

Such early modern accounts are common and reflect an eagerness to step outside that many of us in the twenty-first century seem to lack. With our ultracomfortable, climate-controlled indoor spaces

46 De Klerk, *5 Puritan Women*, 72–73.

47 Thomas Shepard, *God's Plot: Puritan Spirituality in Thomas Shepard's Cambridge*, ed. Michael McGiffert, rev. ed. (Amherst: University of Massachusetts Press, 1994), 122; Tom Schwanda, *Soul Recreation: The Contemplative-Mystical Piety of Puritanism* (Eugene, OR: Pickwick, 2012), 83.

48 George M. Marsden, *Jonathan Edwards: A Life* (New Haven, CT: Yale University Press, 2003), 135.

and our cornucopia of entertainment options, it probably requires a bit of extra effort on our part to get off the couch and seek out a green space. Indeed, the subtitle of a popular book suggests that American children now suffer from "nature-deficit disorder."[49] And yet even if extra effort is required, we neglect this aspect of Christian formation to our detriment. In the seventeenth century's most popular devotional manual, *The Practice of Piety* (1611), Lewis Bayly recommended that "either before or after supper," the Christian should "walk into the fields and meditate upon the works of God," an activity of great value, "for in every creature thou mayest read, as in an open book, the wisdom, power, providence, and goodness of Almighty God."[50] As with each of the disciplines discussed in this book, pursuing this one requires intentional effort. One easy way to begin might be to designate one morning each week as a day to do your morning quiet time outdoors, whether sitting in the backyard or walking through a local park. This would be a small thing, but if the early modern Puritans are to be believed, it could yield great dividends.

Remember That Creation Also "Groans"

Much of our discussion here has revolved around nature as beautiful and harmonious and thus reflecting the beauty and harmony of its Creator. This is all biblical and true, and yet it is not the whole story. At creation, "God saw everything that he had made, and behold, it was very good" (Gen. 1:31). And one day, when God makes all things new, "no longer will there be anything accursed, but the throne of God and of the Lamb will be in it" (Rev. 22:3). But for us who now live in the time between creation and new creation, we cannot see the divine glory reflected in nature without also comprehending the curse that

---

49 Richard Louv, *Last Child in the Woods: Saving Our Children from Nature-Deficit Disorder*, updated ed. (Chapel Hill, NC: Algonquin Books of Chapel Hill, 2008).

50 Lewis Bayly, *The Practice of Piety: Directing a Christian to Walk, That He May Please God* (Grand Rapids, MI: Soli Deo Gloria, 2019), 201–2.

mars it. In God's kindness, man still can "bring forth food from the earth" (Ps. 104:14), but he must contend with "thorns and thistles" while he does so (Gen. 3:18). Yes, the "rivers clap their hands," and the "hills sing for joy together" (Ps. 98:8), testifying to God's already-established reign and rule, but they are also "groaning together in the pains of childbirth" (Rom. 8:22), heavy with the recognition that God's victory is not yet complete.

If we embrace the goodness of creation without also recognizing its fallen condition, we risk indulging in an overly sentimental and ultimately false understanding of the created order as we currently find it. A balanced view combines celebration of the natural world with a sober recognition that things are not as they ought to be. To pursue this approach, we should follow our forebears in recognizing that even nature in its fallen state still has much to teach us. Charles Spurgeon made explicit that "we may find instruction everywhere," even in corners of the natural world where the darkness seems most apparent: "To a spiritual mind, nettles have their use, and weeds have their doctrine. Are not all thorns and thistles meant to be teachers to sinful people?"[51]

Jonathan Edwards modeled well this balanced approach, refusing any conception of the natural world that was "sentimentally sweet." Instead, as George Marsden explains, "He saw all created reality as bittersweet contrasts, dazzling beauty set against appalling horrors, ephemeral glories pointing to divine perfections."[52] Edwards illustrated this perspective right at the beginning of his "Images of Divine Things" notebook, his very first entry identifying death in nature as a pointer toward God's ultimate judgment: "The agonies, the pains and groans and gasps of death, the pale, horrid, ghastly appearance of the corpse, its being laid in the dark and silent grave, there putrifying and

---

51   Charles H. Spurgeon, *Talks to Farmers: Inspiring, Uplifting, Faith-Building Meditations* (Nashville: Nelson Books, 2022), 2.

52   Marsden, *Jonathan Edwards*, 136.

rotting and becoming exceeding loathsome, and eaten with worms (Is. 66:24), is an image of the misery of hell."[53] And elsewhere, Edwards connected "the exceeding terribleness of the lion, tiger, crocodile and some other beasts" with "the infinite horror and amazement of those that fall a prey to the devil."[54] The lessons to be learned from nature's violence, decay, and danger surely contrast, often sharply, with those to be gleaned from its moments of exquisite beauty. Yet these differences do not annihilate the reality that God has things to teach us in every aspect of our life and world.

Seek Out the Extraordinary, but Also Savor the Mundane

Finally, as we look to incorporate a greater appreciation of the natural world into our spiritual formation, we should recognize that edification and wonder can be found in both the extraordinary and the mundane aspects of God's creation. With a little effort, we can discover incredible beauty within the natural world, and it's an effort well worth making. How many of us live near parks that we've never visited and trails we've never bothered to explore? In real life, however, not every sunset is dramatic nor every vista frame worthy, and if we only allow ourselves to appreciate God's creation when we're on vacation at Yosemite, we will miss out on a great many blessings.

Instead, we should strive to be like John Flavel, who found God-honoring inspiration from "the sight of many sticks lodged in the branches of a choice Fruit-tree," and Richard Steele, who was encouraged in his Christian walk through everyday realities like stones, sheep, and the sowing of corn.[55] We don't need a trip to the Grand Canyon to marvel at the creation if we can learn to emulate Jonathan Edwards, a man for whom every common moonrise and rainstorm was an occasion for discovery and delight in God:

---

53 Edwards, *Works*, 11:51.
54 Edwards, *Works*, 11:98.
55 Flavel, *Works*, 5:197; Richard Steele, *The Husbandmans Calling* (London, 1672), 141, 160, 147.

I often used to sit and view the moon, for a long time; and so in the daytime, spent much time in viewing the clouds and sky, to behold the sweet glory of God in these things: in the meantime, singing forth with a low voice, my contemplations of the Creator and Redeemer. And scarce anything, among all the works of nature, was so sweet to me as thunder and lightning. Formerly, nothing had been so terrible to me. I used to be a person uncommonly terrified with thunder: and it used to strike me with terror, when I saw a thunderstorm rising. But now, on the contrary, it rejoiced me. I felt God at the first appearance of a thunderstorm. And used to take the opportunity at such time to fix myself to view the clouds, and see the lightnings play, and hear the majestic and awful voice of God's thunder: which often times was exceeding entertaining, leading me to sweet contemplations of my great and glorious God.[56]

Or finally, consider the exhortation from Charles Spurgeon to see the whole of the created order as a gift from God and full of his glory:

I now bid you to see God in common things. He makes the grass to grow—grass is a common thing. You see it everywhere, yet God is in it. Dissect it and pull it to pieces; the attributes of God are illustrated in every single flower of the field, and in every green leaf. In like manner, see God in your common matters, your daily afflictions, your common joys, your everyday mercies. Do not say, "I must see a miracle before I see God." In truth everything teems with marvel. See God in the bread of your table and the water of your cup. It will be the happiest way of living if you can say in each providential circumstance, "My Father has done all this."[57]

---

56 Jonathan Edwards, *Personal Narrative*, in *The Works of Jonathan Edwards*, vol. 16, *Letters and Personal Writings*, ed. George S. Claghorn (New Haven, CT: Yale University Press, 1998), 794.

57 Spurgeon, *Talks to Farmers*, 170–71.

If we could adopt this perspective, it would transform the way we experienced the world around us, whether considering the extraordinary or the mundane. And the ultimate realization, of course, for the Christian, is that both the ordinary and the extraordinary are, in the end, one and the same, for both point us to God himself. So let us learn to see afresh that "everything teems with marvel" because everything comes from God.

8

Christian Relationships

Looking to One Another

ONE OF THE MOST IMPORTANT and, frankly, terrifying books in recent years is *Bowling Alone* (2000), by the Harvard social scientist Robert Putnam. Combing through a vast field of data, Putnam documents in devastating detail the decline of what he calls "social capital" in twentieth-century America. "Social capital" is a broad term that tracks the degree to which people do things together. The nation's social capital thus includes participation in civic life (town hall meetings, local elections, and school boards), community organizations (Boy Scouts, Rotary Clubs, and religious groups), and "the almost infinite variety of informal ties that link Americans—card parties and bowling leagues, bar cliques and ball games, picnics and parties."[1] The idea of "social capital" is not unique to Putnam, and a variety of authors before him have found it a helpful way of thinking about human relationships, suggesting that our multiple interconnections function as a vital resource requiring wise stewardship.

But what uniquely frightens about Putnam's work on social capital is the dramatic trend line he unearthed through his analysis: across

---

1 Robert D. Putnam, *Bowling Alone: The Collapse and Revival of American Community* (New York: Simon & Schuster, 2000), 27.

all these diverse contexts for human connection, Putnam found that from the mid-twentieth century onward, participation in every sort of collective activity was going down. Whether he looked at political, social, or religious spheres, the results consistently pointed to the fact that Americans at the end of the twentieth century were far less likely to do things with other people than were their mid-twentieth-century counterparts:

> The dominant theme is simple: For the first two-thirds of the twentieth century a powerful tide bore Americans into ever deeper engagement in the life of their communities, but a few decades ago—silently, without warning—that tide reversed and we were overtaken by a treacherous rip current. Without at first noticing, we have pulled apart from one another and from our communities over the last third of the century.[2]

And while the explanations for the erosion of social capital are multifaceted and open to debate, the ramifications of Putnam's conclusions are not: to the extent that his work accurately depicts the society in which we now find ourselves, we are in trouble.

Everyone knows that loneliness is painful, and scientific research increasingly indicates that people who lack meaningful social connection suffer physical consequences, in addition to the more well-known emotional sort.[3] Moreover, as Christians who know God's verdict that "it is not good that the man should be alone" (Gen. 2:18), we of all people should be acutely aware of our intrinsic need for social connection and the dangers lurking whenever we neglect it. Reading a report like Putnam's should alert us both to the danger in which we find ourselves and to the need for intentionality in build-

---

2   Putnam, *Bowling Alone*, 27.

3   See John T. Cacioppo and William Patrick, *Loneliness: Human Nature and the Need for Social Connection* (New York: Norton, 2009), 92–109.

ing relationships. If the texture of life in the twenty-first century is making it harder, not easier, to develop and sustain meaningful, life-giving relationships, then it would surely do us good to look to the wisdom of men and women from previous centuries for help and guidance.

That is precisely what we are doing in this chapter, thinking about how our early modern Protestant forebears approached Christian relationships as a critical means of fostering spiritual formation. One potential criticism of this book is that it is overly focused on the individual. And while it's certainly true that the present volume *is* largely concerned with the individual Christian who wants to grow in his or her personal walk with God, that interest in the individual should not be mistaken for a destructive *individualism*. The Puritan spirituality this book draws on has also been charged with fostering an unhealthy preoccupation with the individual. Yet this charge cannot withstand scrutiny, for when one reads Puritan authors, one finds that their individual pursuit of piety was never unrelated to their corporate experience of spiritual formation. As historian Dewey Wallace explains, "However much Puritan spirituality focused on individual experience, the spiritual life was lived in fellowship with other Christians and especially within the community of faith constituted by the congregation."[4] Christianity is an inherently corporate endeavor, and as we make plain in this chapter, a healthy Christian spirituality is one that is cultivated in community with others.[5]

In what follows, we first explore some of the primary contexts for Christian relationships, thinking about bonds forged within the home, the church, and beyond. Then we turn to the Puritan practice of "conference," a way they framed friendship as a specific means of Christian

---

4   Dewey D. Wallace Jr., "Introduction," in *The Spirituality of the Later English Puritans: An Anthology*, ed. Dewey D. Wallace Jr. (Macon, GA: Mercer University Press, 1987), xxiii.

5   For more on this topic, please see the appendix, "A Brief Note on Spiritual Formation, Individualism, and the Church."

growth. In all of it, the emphasis is on how Christian relationships help advance our spiritual formation.

Relational Contexts and the Art of "Conference"

From one perspective, the true Christian can never be truly alone, for he or she is called to be, like Abraham, "a friend of God" (James 2:23). As Richard Sibbes put it, "Christ is our friend in taking our nature to make God and us friends again."[6] Jesus has called us his friends (John 15:15), and as the good shepherd (John 10:14), he will lead us "in paths of righteousness" for his name's sake (Ps. 23:3). To know God in this intimate way is the greatest comfort that a person can have and is the ultimate answer to fear, anxiety, and loneliness:

> My flesh and my heart may fail,
> > but God is the strength of my heart and my portion forever.
> > > (Ps. 73:26)

Having said this, we can also rejoice in the reality that God does not ordinarily ask us to walk apart from other people. Instead, he gives us the good gift of companionship: friends and spouses, pastors and parents, all those who come alongside in the home, the church, and beyond to encourage us in our Christian walk. Let's begin to explore this theme by considering two of the basic contexts in which we meet other Christians—home and church—and then consider how Puritan authors envisioned those relationships as profound sources of spiritual nurture.

Relationships in the Home

For most people, their very first relationships are those forged within the context of the home into which they are born. Few would discount

---

6 Richard Sibbes, *Works of Richard Sibbes*, ed. Alexander B. Grosart (Edinburgh: Banner of Truth, 1973), 7:122.

the lasting significance of one's family of origin, and when we consider spiritual formation specifically, the relationships between husbands and wives, parents and children, and brothers and sisters have long been understood to play a decisive role. This was especially true among Puritan writers, who consistently taught that "fathers and mothers must introduce their children to Scripture and other godly books and, by personal example, prepare them for the pilgrim's life of self-discipline."[7] Though we can only scratch the surface of this theme here, it is worth underscoring some of the ways the household offers unique opportunities for spiritually significant relationships.[8]

At the center of the Puritan family was the relationship between husband and wife, who, as Richard Baxter put it, "must take delight in the love, and company, and converse of each other." This is because "when husband and wife take pleasure in each other, it uniteth them in duty, it helpeth them with care to do their work, and bear their burdens."[9] In addition to such affection, the ideal Puritan marriage was to be a source of spiritual encouragement, something that comes across clearly in a letter from Margaret Winthrop (ca. 1591–1647) to her husband, John (1588–1649):

> I must part with my most dear Husband, which is a very hard tryall for me to undergoe; if the Lord does not support and help me in it, I shall be unable to beare it. I have now received thy kinde letter which I cannot read without shedding a great many teares, but I will resign thee and give thee into the hands of the almighty God who is all sufficient for thee, whome I trust will keep thee and prosper thee; if thou walke before him in truth and uprightnesse of heart, he

---

7   David D. Hall, *The Puritans: A Transatlantic History* (Princeton, NJ: Princeton University Press, 2019), 127.

8   For more on this theme, see J. I. Packer, *A Quest for Godliness: The Puritan Vision of the Christian Life* (Wheaton, IL: Crossway, 1990), 259–73; Leland Ryken, *Worldly Saints: The Puritans as They Really Were* (Grand Rapids, MI: Zondervan, 1990), 39–54; 73–88.

9   Richard Baxter, *The Practical Works of Richard Baxter* (London: Arthur Hall, 1847), 1:432.

will never fail of his promise to thee. Therefore my good Husband, cheer up thy heart in God and in the expectation of his favors and blessings . . . with assurance of his love in Christ Jesus our Lord.[10]

When husband and wife were relating well, the smooth functioning of the family unit would more readily follow. In the opening sentences of his bestselling treatise *A Godlie Forme of Householde Government* (1598), Robert Cleaver declared that households exist so that "God's glorie may be advanced." He then outlined in some detail how this would be accomplished through a set of mutually reinforcing duties between husbands, wives, and their children. For Cleaver and other Puritan authors, the husband and father took on a special role in leading and guiding his wife and children toward godliness. Cleaver described the man as the "Cheefe governour" in the home and said that his first and most important duty was to ensure that his family was sitting under the ministry of God's word. Here he envisioned husbands who both take initiative to open the Bible in the home, reading and leading in family devotions, and take responsibility to ensure that the family is in church on Sunday. This is nonnegotiable, argued Cleaver, because the word "is the meanes to beget a new life, and to nourish them in it." As a result, "a great dutie lieth upon the governours of families, to provide some means that they may have it."[11]

And though husbands and fathers often took the spotlight in such discussions, wives and mothers, of course, were also understood to be key conduits of spiritual advice and counsel. "Stir up your husband," urged the Scottish Presbyterian Samuel Rutherford in a letter written to a noblewoman: "Counsel him to deal mercifully with the poor people of God under him."[12] A remarkable example of a Puritan woman spur-

---

10 Margaret Winthrop to John Winthrop, February 2, 1630, *Winthrop Papers*, vol. 2, *1623–1630* (Boston: Massachusetts Historical Society, 1931), 200.

11 Robert Cleaver, *A Godlie Forme of Householde Government* (London, 1598), 13, 19, 20–21.

12 Samuel Rutherford, *Letters of Samuel Rutherford* (Edinburgh: Oliphants, 1904), 214.

ring her family on toward spiritual maturity comes from the Puritan gentlewoman Lady Brilliana Harley (bap. 1598–1643), who wrote regular letters of Christian encouragement to her husband, Robert, and her eldest son, Edward.[13] In her study of Harley's correspondence with Edward, Jenny-Lyn de Klerk concludes that "most often, her mind was on spiritual things, . . . encouraging him to live for God, sharing her own religious experiences, and connecting him to the community of faith." In one such letter, Harley wrote, "I desire you may have that true health in your soul of a sound mind, that so in these days of wavering and doubting you may hold the truth."[14]

But whether considering the contributions of the husband as "Cheefe governour" or the wife as his "fellow helper,"[15] Puritan advice manuals remained consistent and clear in their overarching theme: the household, by its very God-given nature, *is* a crucial site of formation, whether you like it or not, and so it becomes incumbent on those in charge to make sure that the direction of spiritual travel is consistently upward toward growth and godliness. Richard Baxter put the matter starkly when he described the "ungoverned, ungodly family" as "a powerful means to the damnation of all the members of it" and as a "ship . . . bound for the devouring gulf." By contrast, "a well-governed family is an excellent help to the saving of all the souls who are in it" because such a home provides "continual provocations to a holy life, faith, love, obedience, and heavenly-mindedness."[16] The implication here is that if God has placed you within a family, then you have an obligation to work toward the spiritual formation of your household in a manner appropriate to your role within it. When this happens, wrote Baxter, the family is "blessed with the presence and favor of God," becoming

13 Raymond A. Anselment, "Katherine Paston and Brilliana Harley: Maternal Letters and the Genre of Mother's Advice," *Studies in Philology* 101, no. 4 (2004): 431–53.

14 Jenny-Lyn de Klerk, *5 Puritan Women: Portraits of Faith and Love* (Wheaton, IL: Crossway, 2023), 115, 120.

15 Cleaver, *Godlie Forme*, 19.

16 Richard Baxter, *The Godly Home*, ed. Randall J. Pederson (Wheaton, IL: Crossway, 2010), 106.

"a garden of God . . . beautified with his graces and ordered by his government and fruitful by the showers of his heavenly blessing."[17]

Relationships in the Church

Despite the lofty rhetoric used to describe the significance of the household within God's vision for human flourishing, we should not lose sight of the reality that another family, the church family, actually holds the greatest degree of spiritual significance for Christians. "How refreshing it is for God's children, being hated by the world, to have communion with each other," wrote Wilhelmus à Brakel. In so doing, they "make their needs known to each other, and in love and familiarity may enjoy each other's fellowship."[18] As mentioned in the introduction to this book, the role of the church as God's ordained means for our spiritual formation cannot be overstated and is worthy of its own book—in fact, of many books. And so its relatively brief treatment here should not be taken as a suggestion that it is in any way unimportant.[19] But while we cannot here give a full account of what the church is and does, we can briefly sketch how Puritan authors viewed the church as that which, by its very nature, puts us into spiritually meaningful relationships with other people and thus becomes a powerful locus of spiritual formation. Just as the household places you into relationships with others by virtue of your birth, the household of God automatically relates you to other people by virtue of your new birth in Christ.

The individual Christian is always understood as one who belongs to the larger people of God. Over and against the distortions of an overly romanticized individualism and the manifest evils of an unchecked collectivism, the Bible exhibits a beautiful balance. When an

---

17   Baxter, *Godly Home*, 112.

18   Wilhelmus à Brakel, *The Christian's Reasonable Service*, trans. Bartel Elshout (Morgan, PA: Soli Deo Gloria, 1995), 2:100.

19   See the appendix, "A Brief Note on Spiritual Formation, Individualism, and the Church."

individual is adopted by the Father, he joins a family of brothers and sisters. Though an individual Christian is one "living stone," she is placed alongside others within a "spiritual house" of God's design (1 Pet. 2:4–5). Each individual branch connects to the one true vine and thus, by extension, to all the other branches as well (John 15:5). Throughout its pages, Scripture consistently maintains the reality and integrity of the individual—"Even the hairs of your head are all numbered" (Luke 12:7)—without ever losing sight of the community in which each individual is known and valued—"You are fellow citizens with the saints and members of the household of God" (Eph. 2:19). Paul's body metaphor captures the balance perfectly (Rom. 12:4–5; 1 Cor. 12:12–27). Though the eye is appreciated precisely as an eye, distinct from and contributing something different from the ears, hands, and feet, that same eye can only function—and indeed, only really makes sense—within the larger context of the entire body.

This balance between the individual and the collective is what grounds the necessity and meaning of Christian relationships within the church. Puritan pastors often reflected on this dynamic, insisting that fellowship and worship with other believers conferred special blessings that could not be replicated in private. As David Clarkson expressed it, solitary Christians each enjoy a steady stream of God's presence, but when "these several streams are united and meet in one, . . . the presence of God . . . becomes a river, a river that makes glad the city of God." Similarly, while "the Lord has a dish for every particular soul that truly serves him," there is a special goodness when "a multitude of dishes" come together to create "a spiritual feast."[20] These images communicate a conviction that the body of Christ gathered represents something more than merely the sum of its parts. Though in a sense some of the means for spiritual formation that we pursue in solitude are identical to those undertaken in corporate worship, early modern

---

20 David Clarkson, *The Practical Works of David Clarkson* (Edinburgh: James Nichol, 1865), 3:190–91.

Protestants were convinced that something special is at work when God's people come together.

One of those special things, of course, is the opportunity to observe the lives of other Christians up close. Commenting on Paul's instruction to "keep your eyes on those who walk according to the example you have in us" (Phil. 3:17), D. A. Carson wisely notes that "Christian character is as much caught as taught—that is, it is picked up by constant association with mature Christians."[21] Early modern Reformed writers would have eagerly agreed, and they often extolled the tremendous benefit of watching and learning from others. "Each believer furnishes an example that benefits his neighbor," wrote Campegius Vitringa, and "each one acts to arouse and enliven others, and this greatly fosters the godliness and sanctification of each participant." Why would this be so? Because in God's wisdom "we humans are more quickened and stimulated by example than by instructions and warnings."[22] God has made us to be inherently relational creatures, and when we see excellence in others, it draws us up toward excellence. This would hold true across any field of endeavor, whether carpentry, watercolor painting, or playing the piano. But in the context of living the Christian life, there is a special reason why, as Thomas Manton put it, "examples work more than precepts." It is because "in them we see that the exercise of godlinesse, though difficult, yet is possible." When we observe that men and women who "are subject to like passions, and have the same interests and concernments of flesh and blood that we have, can be thus mortified, self-denying, heavenly, holy," we are encouraged to press on in the Christian life.[23] If they can do it, fallen and frail as they are, we can do it too.

21 D. A. Carson, *Basics for Believers: An Exposition of Philippians* (Grand Rapids, MI: Baker Academic, 1996), 69.

22 Campegius Vitringa, *The Spiritual Life*, trans. Charles K. Telfer (Grand Rapids, MI: Reformation Heritage Books, 2018), 133.

23 Thomas Manton, "To the Reader," in *The Life and Death of Mr. Ignatius Jurdain*, by Ferdinand Nicolls (London, 1655), aV.

The Art of "Conference"

Whether in the context of home or church, one of the primary ways that Christian relationships advance our spiritual formation is through the honest, serious, God-honoring conversations that they make possible. The apostle Paul teaches that when believers are "speaking the truth in love" to one another, they will "grow up in every way into him who is the head, into Christ" (Eph. 4:15). Reformation-minded Christians have always taken this idea seriously; as historian Alec Ryrie notes, "One of early Protestantism's distinctive features was enthusiasm for spending swathes of time simply talking about religion with fellow believers."[24] For Wilhelmus à Brakel, "mutually promoting one another's spiritual growth" through such conversation is one of the key ways that a real "communion of saints is practiced." This can take the form of "helping each other to arise again after having fallen," "encouraging and exhorting one another," "comforting each other in times of discouragement," and "faithfully assisting each other in times of perplexity."[25] This last one is an especially good example of how Christian relationships further spiritual formation in a way that few other things can. Each one of us will face situations in life that are unique, and what we often need isn't so much a set of generic rules but rather wisdom to apply those rules to the complicated situation before us. As Proverbs 11:14 reminds us, "In an abundance of counselors there is safety," and wise Christians will make good use of the other people God brings into their lives.

For the Puritans, this pursuit of relationships that angled deliberately toward spiritual formation went under the name of "conference." Early moderns could use the word "conference" broadly, much in the way we use the word "conversation" today, but often in Puritan devotional writing, one finds a stress on the need for a special kind of "holy conferences" among Christians. Whether they involved "instructing,

---

24 Alec Ryrie, *Being Protestant in Reformation Britain* (Oxford: Oxford University Press, 2013), 390.
25 À Brakel, *Christian's Reasonable Service*, 2:102–3.

exhorting, admonishing, counselling, [or] comforting one another,"
wrote the Puritan pastor John Downame, "we must use the help of
holy conferences . . . that we may be further edified in our holy faith."
Explaining this idea further, Downame likened believers in conference
to sticks in a firepit: when "scattered asunder," they "hardly keep fire,"
but once gathered together, they "quickly grow to a great flame."[26] The
basic conviction underlying such rhetoric is that contact and conversation with godly people can help us become more godly ourselves, and
hence we should always be looking "to stir up one another to love and
good works" (Heb. 10:24).

Sometimes such conference would involve only two believers encouraging each other and holding one another accountable. Richard
Baxter recalled how one "intimate Companion" helped sustain Baxter's
Christian zeal during his time studying at university. For Baxter, this
friend became "the greatest help to my Seriousness in Religion, that
ever I had before," and as the pair regularly walked, prayed, and read
good Christian books together, Baxter recounts that his friend "would
be always stirring me up to Zeal and Diligence."[27] But more often than
not, when Puritans stressed the need for "conference," they imagined
small groups of Christians talking deliberately about spiritual things.
Echoing the language of Ephesians 4, the Scottish theologian Robert
Rollock (ca. 1555–1599) explained,

> They who are Christ's, are ever going about to meet and to holde them-
> selves together, that they may speake, and confer of all thinges, that
> fall out concerning Christ, and the estate of His Church, whether
> they be joyfull, and comfortable, or sad and sorrowfull, that they
> may edifie and further one another, mutually in the course of their

26 John Downame, *The Christian Warfare* (London, 1634), 1165.
27 Richard Baxter, *Reliquiae Baxterianae: Or, Mr Richard Baxter's Narrative of the Most Memorable Passages of His Life and Times*, ed. N. H. Keeble, John Coffey, Tim Cooper, and Tom Charlton (Oxford: Oxford University Press, 2020), 1:215–16.

salvation, that they may be joyned together, and make up, and complete one body.[28]

We note that the above description must have gone beyond the ordinary church service because it explicitly involved everyone present speaking and sharing together, something that would not have ordinarily occurred during Sunday morning worship. Yet Rollock insisted that such "meeting together" held out a particular blessing, bringing "with it an exceeding consolation and joy."[29]

Retrieving this Puritan practice of conference could represent a helpful way to relationally reignite spiritual fervor in our own contexts. That is the conclusion of Joanne Jung, who describes conference as "piety's forgotten discipline" and suggests that its recovery "would serve as a welcomed catalyst for spiritual formation, strengthening the spiritual pulse of community" in evangelical churches and small groups.[30]

But it is fair to ask, What would the idea of Puritan "conference" actually add to an evangelical culture that already prominently features small groups and other opportunities for Christian fellowship? To my mind, the most helpful thing to come from reading the Puritans and other early modern Reformed authors on this subject is the intensity of their insistence that conversation among believers actually matters and that it can function as a spur or hindrance to spiritual formation. When we're standing around with coffee cups on a Sunday morning after church, it's very easy to lose sight of this reality. And while I would not want to belittle the value of ordinary conversation revolving around sports scores, vacation plans, and who is starting up at which school when, we should also not lose sight of the fact that if *all* our conversation takes this shape, then we are not only missing a source of real

---

28 Robert Rollock, *Lectures upon the History of the Passion, Resurrection, and Ascension of Our Lord Jesus Christ* (Edinburgh, 1616), 392–93.

29 Rollock, *Lectures*, 393.

30 Joanne J. Jung, *Godly Conversation: Rediscovering the Puritan Practice of Conference* (Grand Rapids, MI: Reformation Heritage Books, 2011), 1, 179.

blessing but also failing to do our Christian duty to "stir up one another to love and good works" (Heb. 10:24). So the first step in retrieving something on par with the Puritan practice of conference is simply to acknowledge the role that intentional conversation can play, and the second is to look intentionally for ways to pursue it.

Christian Friendship

The home and the local congregation offer significant contexts in which Christian relationships emerge. Yet in both cases, the ongoing vitality and maintenance of these connections often depend heavily on the institutional structures out of which they arise. Young people don't remain at home forever, and just as you might have colleagues at work you get along with fine but don't see much outside the office, you will likely enjoy many healthy relationships with people at church that don't extend far beyond the chapel walls. This observation does not diminish the value of these relationships—on the contrary, especially in the case of the local church, one of its great glories is the way it unites people who would otherwise ignore or even oppose each other. Still, it does recognize the reality that some relationships with other Christians are more meaningful and significant in a person's life than others. Some blossom into real friendships that spill out into coffee shops, playdates, and shared trips to the lake, while others never move beyond the mid-week Bible study. And that is okay: yes, we have a powerful, Spirit-wrought bond with all our brothers and sisters in Christ, but those individual relationships inevitably vary in their intimacy and extent.

In part, this reality reflects an aspect of our finitude. Social psychologists suggest that there is an upper limit on the number of friends and acquaintances an individual can comfortably maintain, one prominent researcher putting the estimate at around 150 acquaintances, only about five of whom might be reasonably described as close friends.[31]

---

31 Rachel Cooke, "*Friends* by Robin Dunbar Review—How Important Are Your Pals?," *Guardian*, February 21, 2021, https://www.theguardian.com/.

But beyond our limited stores of time and emotional energy, it seems self-evident that because the Lord makes us all to differ, we connect with some people better than others. In his discussion of Christian relationships as a spur to our spiritual growth, Campegius Vitringa highlighted what he called "private friendship," distinguishing this from the normal bond of fellowship that should link all Christians together. "No one is required by force of the law of Christ Jesus to develop familiar personal relations with everyone indiscriminately," explained Vitringa. Instead, "what is clearly required is to have similar temperaments, to be like each other in character, to share a common disposition and spirit, and to be in a similar status."[32] Brilliana Harley sounded a similar note when she wrote that two friends must share "the same religion, affection and disposition."[33] Though these observations might make us uncomfortable and should certainly put us on guard against sinful cliques and exclusion, they also seem to point to an inescapable reality: a friend is in large measure worthy of the name precisely because a friend is closer and dearer to you than are other people.

Such friendship was certainly an important theme for Puritan writers, and when one considers the times during which they lived, it's not hard to see why. If adversity highlights the value of friendship like nothing else (Prov. 17:17), then the Puritans would have been especially aware of just how important a good companion can be. Upheaval and hardship featured prominently in their lives. During the 1620s and 1630s, many of them fled religious persecution in England, leaving familiar homes and churches to take up a rugged and uncertain existence on the frontiers of North America. Others stayed home to face civil war and revolution during the 1640s and 1650s. And then during the later Restoration period of the 1660s and 1670s, Puritans in England "witnessed a persecution of Protestants by Protestants without

---

32 Vitringa, *Spiritual Life*, 134–35.
33 Quoted in Jacqueline Eales, *Puritans and Roundheads: The Harleys of Brampton Bryan and the Outbreak of the English Civil War* (Cambridge: Cambridge University Press, 1990), 61.

parallel in seventeenth-century Europe."[34] Read against this backdrop, the vehemence and feeling with which Thomas Brooks denounced what he called "summer friends" can perhaps be better understood. These "counterfeit friends" are happy enough to walk alongside you when the weather is warm and all is well, but as soon as things turn cold, they are nowhere to be found. From such individuals, wrote Brooks, "it is a mercy to be delivered." By contrast, "real friends, faithful friends, active friends, winter friends, bosom friends, fast friends" represent an almost unparalleled blessing, a cherished gift from God and a vital means of spiritual formation.[35] "Puritans were not solitaries," writes J. I. Packer; instead, "they valued their friends, cultivated their friendships, wrote affectionate letters to each other, and held no brief whatever for choosing isolation when one could join with a group of believers."[36] As Brooks put it, "Man is made to be a friend, and apt for friendly offices."[37]

For the Puritans, the paradigmatic biblical friendship was that between David and Jonathan. When they read that "the soul of Jonathan was knit to the soul of David, and Jonathan loved him as his own soul" (1 Sam. 18:1), they found both a description of and a mandate for the sort of close, intimate friendship that would not only endure amid difficulty but actually come out the better for it. As historian Francis Bremer explains, "The scriptural story helped them define what they experienced, just as their experience gave new meaning to their reading of scripture." To illustrate, Bremer cites a letter from John Winthrop, the governor of the Massachusetts Bay Colony, written to his longtime friend back in England, Sir William

---

34 John Coffey, "The Toleration Controversy during the English Revolution," in *Religion in Revolutionary England*, ed. Christopher Durston and Judith D. Maltby (Manchester, UK: Manchester University Press, 2006), 60.

35 Thomas Brooks, *The Works of Thomas Brooks*, ed. Alexander Balloch Grosart (Edinburgh: James Nichol, 1866), 1:289–90.

36 Packer, *Quest for Godliness*, 259.

37 Brooks, *Works*, 1:289.

Spring (1588–1638). Notice how Winthrop naturally reached for David and Jonathan to help express his own affection for and commitment to Spring: "I embrace you and rest in your love, and delight to solace my first thoughts in these sweet affections of so deare a friend. . . . I must needes tell you, my soule is knitt to you, as the soule of Jonathan to David. . . . O what a pinche will it be to me, to parte with such a freinde!"[38]

Reading such correspondence, modern readers are perhaps struck by the intensity of the language, Winthrop employing words and phrases that we would typically reserve for the most intimate communication between a husband and wife. At another point in his letter, Winthrop wrote to his friend, "I loved you truely before I could think that you took any notice of me: but now I embrace you and rest in your love."[39] He not only felt strong affection for his friend, but he was not too embarrassed to express those feelings in written form. In this, Winthrop's letter is typical rather than unusual. Most of us don't communicate in quite this same way today and wouldn't feel comfortable doing so. And as with many points of discontinuity between our perspective and that of people from the past, we shouldn't rush to blindly imitate them. There are all sorts of cultural and social reasons why Winthrop thought it was appropriate to express himself as he did, and I, for one, am certainly not about to copy and paste his precise language into any emails to my friends.

Without following early modern practice to the letter, however, we can still learn from their spirit on this point. We might begin by noting that Winthrop's outpouring of love for his friend does sound a lot more like the language used to describe Jonathan and David's friendship than our rather more muted expressions today (see 1 Sam. 18:1–3;

---

38 Francis J. Bremer, *Congregational Communion: Clerical Friendship in the Anglo-American Puritan Community, 1610–1692* (Boston: Northeastern University Press, 1994), 6–7; John Winthrop to Sir William Spring, February 8, 1630, in *Winthrop Papers*, 2:205.

39 Winthrop to Spring, February 8, 1630, 2:205.

2 Sam. 1:25–26).[40] From this we might be persuaded to celebrate our friends and our friendships more liberally than we typically do, finding culturally appropriate ways to communicate to our friends that we care about them and thank God for them.

And we should thank God for them because Christian friends are used by God to sanctify us and advance our spiritual formation. "Just as bad company is damaging, so good company is edifying," wrote Campegius Vitringa. Investing in friendship with a like-minded believer "results in your growth and progress in sound doctrine and virtue."[41] How do friends help us grow? Many answers could be given, but Vitringa drew out four principles from his reading of Ecclesiastes 4:9–12, a classic biblical passage on friendship.

First, friends coordinate their energies to accomplish common goals, for "two are better than one" (Eccl. 4:9). Whether in the home, at the local church, or around the neighborhood, the fruit of one's labor tastes twice as sweet when shared.

Second, friends hold each other accountable. They do so "by mutual admonition, correction and faithful exhortation to repentance so that a person does not remain in the state of sin into which he has fallen."[42]

Third, friends encourage each other to pursue godliness and run the Christian race with joy. In this connection, Vitringa used the language of "holy jealousy and honest competition" to describe the way that two Christian friends might stir and spur each other on to good works.[43] Though perhaps a provocative way of putting it, Vitringa's expression echoes the apostle Paul's prompt to the Christians in Rome, "Outdo one another in showing honor" (Rom. 12:10), and captures

---

40 It should be noted that attempts to read homoerotic undertones into the story of David and Jonathan have been thoroughly debunked. See Robert A. J. Gagnon, *The Bible and Homosexual Practice: Texts and Hermeneutics* (Nashville: Abingdon, 2001), 146–54.

41 Vitringa, *Spiritual Life*, 135.

42 Vitringa, *Spiritual Life*, 136.

43 Vitringa, *Spiritual Life*, 136.

that energizing spark of mutually upbuilding, God-honoring rivalry that's surely implicit in Proverbs 27:17:

> Iron sharpens iron,
>   and one man sharpens another.

Fourth and finally, friends pray for one another. In this way, they kneel side by side to better "stand against the schemes of the devil" (Eph. 6:11).[44]

In light of all these benefits, it behooves us to intentionally embrace the gift of Christian friendship, pushing ourselves to actively initiate, forge, and maintain godly relationships with other believers. As noted earlier, there are good reasons to suspect that modern life militates against the natural cultivation of relationships that previous generations enjoyed. Indeed, social scientist Daniel Cox claims that America is in the midst of a major "friendship recession."[45] Commenting on the research he conducted in connection with the Survey Center on American Life, Cox writes, "The results were jaw-dropping—Americans reported a massive drop in the number of close friends, with men experiencing the steepest decline."[46] Ironically, one major contributing factor to this trend may well be our addiction to social media—to websites and apps that promise social connection but, as Sherry Turkle argues, actually diminish our appetite and capacity for real relationships. Such technology leaves us in a strange state of being "alone together," expecting "more from technology and less from each other," increasingly "drawn to connections that seem low risk and always at hand."[47]

---

44 Vitringa, *Spiritual Life*, 136.

45 Daniel A. Cox, "American Men Suffer a Friendship Recession," *National Review*, July 6, 2021, https://www.nationalreview.com/.

46 Daniel A. Cox, "America's 'Friendship Recession' Is Weakening Civic Life," August 24, 2023, Survey Center on American Life, https://www.americansurveycenter.org/.

47 Sherry Turkle, *Alone Together: Why We Expect More from Technology and Less from Each Other* (New York: Basic Books, 2011), 295.

But whatever the reasons for our difficulty, if we are interested in running the Christian race with joy and endurance, we should be looking to cultivate new friendships and invest in the ones we already have. And though we'd like to imagine that deep friendships just emerge, many find that the pressures and complexities of adulthood make that wishful thinking. Observing her own life and those around her, the journalist and writer Anne Helen Petersen remarks that "the way our society is organized, we have a prolonged stretch of adulthood that is not conducive to forging or sustaining friendship or community." Fueled by a toxic combination of materialistic individualism and the sort of "all consuming . . . slippery work . . . that becomes the central axis of our lives," Petersen calls this relational midlife rocky patch the "friendship dip," a reality, she argues, that "makes a lot of us miserable."[48] Many people report a sense of relational disillusionment after graduating from high school or college—it's just not so easy to make friends anymore. Combatting this trend requires that we take intentional action.

Some time ago, I became the pastor of a small church in a town where I had no previous connections. After a few months of settling in, I concluded that if I didn't become more intentional in making and sustaining meaningful Christian friendships with other pastors, I simply wasn't going to have any. As Petersen and others observe, the busyness of modern life makes this feel difficult. So I tried something that was very simple yet at the time felt like a revelation: I identified a like-minded minister with whom I seemed to have some rapport and asked if he wanted to grab an early breakfast at the local diner before work. Over bacon, eggs, and coffee, we talked about how things were going in ministry and what books we had been reading. Then about a month later, we had another breakfast, and then each month for many years, we kept up the tradition. What amazed me about this is that apart from these monthly breakfasts, we really didn't see much of each

---

48 Anne Helen Petersen, "The Friendship Dip," Culture Study, November 5, 2023, https://annehelen
    .substack.com/.

other—our families occasionally got together, but the breakfasts were the primary driver. I was astonished at how much relational capital you can build with just one breakfast a month. The key was that the meetings were consistent and concentrated: we met every month, and when we sat down, we talked together about mostly serious subjects, often having to do with ministry, theology, and the Christian life. And yet through just the one breakfast a month, we were able to forge a strong friendship. Though this friend and I have both since moved on to different towns, we are still in touch, still encouraging and praying for each other, largely off the strength of those early morning meetings.

And once you have a Christian friend like this in your life, whether new or old, what do you do next? Campegius Vitringa is a wise guide:

> Beloved, if you find a friend who is good, sincere, faithful, honest, gentle, humble, godly, similar to you in temperament and spirit, sharing with you in Christ's grace, seeking the same goals as you, committed to sharing the same responsibilities, and oriented to the same pursuits as you are, then foster this friendship. Cherish this friend and hold close to him. . . . Attach yourself to that friend with such constancy and propriety that he may never have cause to blame you or doubt your faithfulness. In sum, treat him as Jonathan did David. This will profit you greatly as you run your race in the Lord. It is enormously beneficial both from the pleasure you will have from this kind of honest fellowship as well as from its usefulness, which is not paltry.[49]

This book focuses largely on things done in solitude: quiet prayer, private Bible reading, a walk alone through the woods to meditate on the things of God. Yet in all this we should never lose sight of our

---

49 Vitringa, *Spiritual Life*, 135.

inherent need for other Christians. Here, as in other areas, past saints have much to teach us. If "in natural things man standeth in need of helpe," wrote Richard Greenham, "then how much more in spirituall things he standeth in need of others." For Greenham and other early modern Christians, it was axiomatic that just "as two eyes see more, two eares heare more, and two hands can doe more [than] one," so too Christians joining together enjoy "a special communion of Saints" that an individual could never have on one's own.[50] Whether at home, in church, or through the pages of a book, let us not neglect the gift we have in other Christians, but instead, let's seize hold of one another so that together we might grow in grace.

50 Richard Greenham, *A Profitable Treatise, Containing a Direction for the Reading and Understanding of the Holy Scriptures*, in Kenneth L. Parker and Eric J. Carlson, *Practical Divinity: The Works and Life of Revd Richard Greenham*, St. Andrews Studies in Reformation History (Aldershot, UK: Ashgate, 1998), 343.

PART 4

CHALLENGES

9

What about the Body?

Connecting the Spiritual and the Physical

THROUGHOUT THIS BOOK we have described a Reformed approach to spiritual formation as word centered.[1] By this we mean that the actual practices through which Reformed Christians are expected to grow in grace all involve words: first and foremost, God's word to us in Scripture but then also, derivatively, our words formed as meditations and offered back to God as prayers. Even as we expanded outward to consider self-examination, the natural world, and Christian relationships, words were an inextricable part of the program: self-examination involves coherent, word-based meditation on oneself in light of Scripture; our appreciation of the natural world leads to biblically grounded meditations on the glory of God revealed therein; and our relationships with one another revolve around "speaking the truth in love" so that we might "grow up in every way into him who is the head, into Christ" (Eph. 4:15). Together, these word-based practices constitute the Reformed approach to spiritual formation that we've labored to unpack throughout this book.

---

1 This chapter represents a revised version of my article "Brains, Bodies, and the Task of Discipleship: Re-aligning Anthropology and Ministry," *Themelios* 46, no. 1 (2021): 37–54. I am grateful to *Themelios* editor Brian Tabb for granting permission to adapt this material here.

Such an approach is consistent with what Reformation-minded Protestants have always taught and, more importantly, with the Bible's vision of spiritual formation, in which a Christian "shall not live by bread alone, / but by every word that comes from the mouth of God" (Matt. 4:4). Some, however, find this approach deficient in at least one key respect: it seems to neglect the role of the body in spiritual formation. God created us as embodied creatures, and a growing number of evangelicals worry that the historic word-based piety described in this book inappropriately downplays that fact. Moreover, they argue, by neglecting such a key component of our humanity, an overly word-based approach can actually *harm* rather than *help*, breeding disillusionment and inhibiting Christian growth. Their solution to this perceived deficiency is to encourage evangelicals to incorporate embodied rituals into their program of spiritual formation, a proposal we consider in this chapter.

Such concerns have been raised in various ways by a number of authors,[2] but leading the pack in terms of scholarly productivity, influence, and depth of vision is surely theologian and philosopher James K. A. Smith. Particularly in his *Desiring the Kingdom* (2009) and its more accessible follow-up, *You Are What You Love* (2016),[3] Smith argues that the "approach to discipleship and Christian formation" advanced by most evangelicals today conceals an impoverished anthropology that does not properly align with a more holistic and biblical understanding of the same. Christian anthropology refers to how we understand our humanity: What exactly *is* a human being made in God's image? And on this point, Smith claims that most evangelicals assume "an overly cognitivist picture of the human person" that

2 E.g., Justin Whitmel Earley, *The Common Rule: Habits of Purpose for an Age of Distraction* (Downers Grove, IL: IVP, 2019); Tish Harrison Warren, *Liturgy of the Ordinary: Sacred Practices in Everyday Life* (Downers Grove, IL: IVP Books, 2016); Dru Johnson, *Human Rites: The Power of Rituals, Habits, and Sacraments* (Grand Rapids, MI: Eerdmans, 2019).

3 James K. A. Smith, *Desiring the Kingdom: Worship, Worldview, and Cultural Formation*, Cultural Liturgies 1 (Grand Rapids, MI: Baker Academic, 2009); Smith, *You Are What You Love: The Spiritual Power of Habit* (Grand Rapids, MI: Brazos, 2016).

"tends to foster an overly intellectualist account of what it means to be or become a Christian." This misshapen faith, Smith contends, "is a talking-head version of Christianity that is fixated on doctrines and ideas" but neglects equally important aspects of being human, things like desire, love, and imagination.[4]

This important critique should not be ignored. My own experience of American and British evangelicalism, particularly in its Calvinist and Reformed expressions, suggests that Smith's diagnosis of a "talking-head" Christianity that fails to really engage the hearts of its adherents is often worryingly accurate. Were critics like Smith to review my own past preaching efforts, for example, they would certainly find ample evidence to advance their thesis. I recall one particular attempt to preach 1 Corinthians 15 on Easter Sunday in which I delivered up a 5,300-word treatise that featured technically sound exegetical and theological commentary but offered little that would actually engage the hearts and imaginations of my hearers. Such preaching does indeed seem to betray precisely the sort of misalignment of ministry and anthropology that worries thinkers like Smith, a misalignment that implicitly "reduces human beings to brains-on-a-stick."[5]

And yet while one might affirm this diagnosis of the problem, serious questions can still be raised regarding the solution offered by Smith and company. Of particular interest is the increasingly popular claim that the road back from an overly intellectualized faith runs through the body. Evangelicals are told that the best, or perhaps *only*, way to properly form disciples is to find modes of worship and reverence that engage bodies rather than just minds. At their most forceful, these authors seem to claim that real spiritual growth is difficult, if not impossible, apart from holistic bodily engagement. As Smith has put it, the "way to the heart is through the body."[6]

4 Smith, *Desiring the Kingdom*, 42.
5 Smith, *You Are What You Love*, 3.
6 Smith, *You Are What You Love*, 46.

If such claims could be substantiated, they would represent a major indictment of the Reformed approach to spiritual formation advanced in this book, an approach that is word heavy and body light. These claims regarding the primacy of the body would also lend credibility to many long-standing critiques of the Protestant tradition as leveled by Roman Catholic and Eastern Orthodox Christians. For example, in an essay describing why he left evangelicalism to join the Roman Catholic Church, Douglas Beaumont explains his growing dissatisfaction with an evangelical approach to formation that "limited faith expressions to between-the-ears activity" and his longing for "tactual worship services that respected our nature as embodied beings."[7] In his own account of leaving evangelicalism for Rome, sociologist Christian Smith sounds a similar note when he complains that Protestantism naively equates spiritual formation with "didactic learning."[8] And for Joel and Stephanie Dunn, the Baptist-turned-Orthodox couple we met in the introduction to this book, one attraction of Eastern Orthodoxy was the way it "incorporates your body. You're standing up, sitting down. You're smelling incense. You're singing and hearing bells."[9] Compare these claims with those made by James K. A. Smith himself, who channels the Catholic philosopher Charles Taylor to suggest that "one of the unintended consequences of the Protestant Reformation . . . was a process of excarnation—of disembodying the Christian faith, turning it into a 'heady' affair that could be boiled down to a message and grasped with the mind."[10]

---

7   Douglas M. Beaumont, "Tiber Treading No More," in *Evangelical Exodus: Evangelical Seminarians and Their Paths to Rome*, ed. Douglas M. Beaumont and Francis Beckwith (San Francisco: Ignatius, 2016), 35–36.

8   Christian Smith, *How to Go from Being a Good Evangelical to a Committed Catholic in Ninety-Five Difficult Steps* (Eugene, OR: Cascade Books, 2011), 100. On the appeal of Catholicism and Orthodoxy among evangelicals, see Kenneth J. Stewart, *In Search of Ancient Roots: The Christian Past and the Evangelical Identity Crisis* (London: Apollos, 2017), 253–73.

9   Brandon Showalter, "Why This Evangelical Couple Became Eastern Orthodox (Part 1)," *Christian Post*, October 24, 2020, https://www.christianpost.com/.

10 Smith, *You Are What You Love*, 101. Cf. Brad S. Gregory, *The Unintended Reformation: How a Religious Revolution Secularized Society* (Cambridge, MA: Belknap Press of Harvard University Press, 2012).

These assertions raise a troubling question for Reformation-minded evangelicals whose approach to spiritual formation is decidedly word centric: Does our failure to promote embodied practices in worship and discipleship result in stunted spiritual growth? If the Reformed tradition is indeed operating with an implicit anthropology that is malformed and subbiblical, an anthropology that regards men and women made in God's image as little more than brains on a stick, then we have serious work to do. But if, on the other hand, the charge rests on faulty assumptions and fails to capture the richness of the Protestant tradition, then the rising popularity of such rhetoric among ostensibly Reformation-minded evangelicals is itself a cause for legitimate concern.

In what follows, this chapter interacts with this cluster of issues across four sections. To begin, we glance back to the Protestant Reformation to examine how the Reformers themselves sought to align Christian ministry with a more biblical anthropology. Then we shift our attention from the Reformers' realignment project to the proposals advanced by contemporary critics like Smith. After that, we consider both an analysis and an appreciative critique of this realignment project. And we conclude by briefly exploring how we might capitalize on some of the helpful insights advanced by the aforementioned authors, while also avoiding roads that may lead to unhelpful places.

Past Alignments

The quest to successfully align anthropology and ministry is not new. One might even conceive of the Reformation itself as an attempt to do just that. Though we typically identify the Reformation's raison d'être with the doctrine of justification by faith alone, it is also worth noting that the recovery of that soteriological insight into how a person stands before a holy God was inseparable from the recovery of a vital anthropological insight about the kind of creatures God made us to be. Namely, God made men and women as creatures who acquire that justifying faith through hearing God's word. The Reformers recovered not only the centrality of faith but also an apostolic anthropology that foregrounds the divinely appointed means through which that faith is kindled: "Faith comes from hearing, and hearing through the word of Christ" (Rom. 10:17). The Reformers understood the human person as the kind of creature that is spiritually transformed through hearing, understanding, and appropriating the proclamation of God's word, and thus they "all, without exception, regarded preaching as fundamental to their duty as pastors, and to their evangelical mission."[11]

The Reformers' enthusiasm for preaching is well appreciated, but what is perhaps less appreciated is the way that this privileging of word ministry represented a profound attempt to align anthropology with ministry. Think of what Protestants were rejecting when they did this: they were rejecting a religious world of late medieval Catholicism in which the body was effectively privileged over the mind and heart, an observation best illustrated by considering the medieval Mass. As the Roman Catholic historian Eamon Duffy has documented, "The liturgy lay at the heart of medieval religion, and the Mass lay at the heart of the liturgy."[12] But by what mechanism did the Mass shape the people of God? Medievals certainly did not imagine that transformation happened through hearing the words of life, meditating on them, and being reshaped thereby. The words of the Mass, after all, were recited in a Latin that very few could understand and were delivered with the priest facing *ad orientem*, with his back to the people. Thus the late medieval Mass seemed signally unconcerned with how words and ideas might affect the faithful. Rather, the Mass achieved its desired effects through the proper arrangement of physical bodies.

For the Mass to be efficacious, one required, in the first place, a proper *body* to officiate—that is, a priest's body, a rightly ordained

---

11 Andrew Pettegree, *Reformation and the Culture of Persuasion* (Cambridge: Cambridge University Press, 2005), 10.

12 Eamon Duffy, *The Stripping of the Altars: Traditional Religion in England, 1400–1580* (New Haven, CT: Yale University Press, 1992), 91.

body, a body that through the sacrament of holy orders had been impressed with a special metaphysical character differentiating it from nonordained bodies. One sixteenth-century Catholic source states that even if a man were "as holy as our Lady, the mother of God," he could in no way say the Mass unless he were first ordained.[13] Then one needed this proper body to be physically located in the proper place: in the church, at the altar, facing east. And then while there, this particular body in this particular physical location needed to coordinate his lips and arms in a series of carefully prescribed movements, uttering the words of institution and elevating the consecrated host above his head—a choreographed liturgical dance that, if done correctly, effected necessarily the miracle of transubstantiation and the concomitant flow of divine grace.

At each step, this liturgy represented a privileging of the physical over the cognitive and the affective—right bodies, in right places, doing right things, and repeating right words. If the priest happened to be reflecting deeply on sacred mysteries while raising the host above his head, that would be wonderful, but if instead he rushed, if he mumbled, if his thoughts wandered and were largely elsewhere, it did not compromise the efficacy of the Mass performed because ultimately what mattered was that the proper physical things were rightly coordinated in time and space. This basic logic was intrinsic to the system, and it generated "a sort of 'arithmetical piety' that gave 'almost a magical value to mere repetition of formulae.'" It was just this sort of "arithmetical piety" that induced the wealthy to hire "Mass priests," clerics paid to perform these embodied actions over and over again for the exclusive benefit of their patrons. King Henry VII (r. 1485–1509) is said to have ensured that no fewer than ten thousand Masses would be said on his behalf, and according to historian Francis Oakley, even an "ordinary merchant" might manage to finance

13 Peter Marshall, *The Catholic Priesthood and the English Reformation*, Oxford Historical Monographs (Oxford: Oxford University Press, 1994), 45.

several hundred.[14] And while the priest enacted his ritualized movements, the people's successful engagement with the Mass was likewise predicated on the proper configuration of their bodies. For the Mass to achieve its intended spiritual effect, the people needed to be in the right place, at the right time, and looking in the right direction.

Thus, for priest and layperson alike, the ministry of medieval Christendom was a ministry finely attuned to the proper coordination of bodies—bodies located in particular physical spaces and rightly coordinated in their movements. If you were in the same physical space as the host properly consecrated and elevated and if you lifted up your gaze at the right moment, blessings would be yours. But if the right bodies were not arranged in the right ways in the right places at the right times, then those blessings would be missed. Now obviously, there was much more to late medieval piety than this, but while there was more to it, there was not less. And this emphasis on people as physical bodies in need of physically mediated remedies loomed large as the irreducible baseline. If James K. A. Smith and others are worried that evangelicals often reduce people to brains on a stick, then here was a nexus of ministry and anthropology that often treated people as nothing but sticks—sticks to be stacked and arranged in configurations designed to produce maximum spiritual effect.

This was the world out of which the Reformers emerged and into which they introduced a new approach to spiritual formation that represented an incredible realignment of anthropology and ministry. The Reformers reemphasized with fresh clarity that a human is not just a body needing to be physically manipulated in just the right manner. The Reformers foregrounded the idea that a human being made in God's image was deeply and profoundly a creature who listens for the word of God, who hears, who understands, who believes, and who is spiritually transformed thereby. If "faith comes from hearing, and hear-

14   Francis Oakley, *The Western Church in the Later Middle Ages* (Ithaca, NY: Cornell University Press, 1979), 118.

ing through the word of Christ" (Rom. 10:17), then when the church looks to Christ, she sees the one who "loved her and gave himself for her" so "that he might sanctify her, having cleansed her by the washing of water *with the word*" (Eph. 5:25–27). In this way, the Reformation was an attempt to realign anthropology and ministry by recognizing that people have minds and hearts, minds that need to be taught so that hearts might be moved to love and service.

We see this new Protestant culture of prioritizing mind and heart in the renewed enthusiasm for and priority given to preaching among the Reformers. The Hungarian Lutheran scholar Vilmos Vajta has written on the incredible degree to which Martin Luther equated right worship with the hearing and understanding of God's word so that one might be transformed by it. One of Luther's favorite stories from the life of Jesus was that of Mary and Martha, a story in which the Reformer saw the Lord commending not Martha and her whirlwind of activity, action, and service but Mary, who "sat at the Lord's feet and listened to his teaching" (Luke 10:39). So it is for Christ's people, said Luther and the Reformers; only "one thing is necessary" (Luke 10:42): they too must sit at the feet of their Lord and *listen* to him. Vajta concludes that for the Reformers—and Luther in particular—"to hear God's Word and to believe it is worship at its highest."[15]

Thus, in their attempt to realign ministry and anthropology, the Reformers prioritized the mind and heart over the body, the interior over the exterior, the word over any enacted practice. And though this realignment project announced itself first and most boldly in the Reformation emphasis on preaching, as the Protestant tradition continued to develop, the same basic logic emerged through a renewed emphasis on personal piety as cultivated through reading and prayer—not memorized Latin prayers the speaker might have little sense of but prayers, whether

15 Vilmos Vajta, quoted in Hughes Oliphant Old, *The Reading and Preaching of the Scriptures in the Worship of the Christian Church*, vol. 4, *The Age of the Reformation* (Grand Rapids, MI: Eerdmans, 2002), 39–40.

set or extempore, that were composed in the vernacular language and fully understood by the one offering them to the Lord. Such tendencies were pronounced among English Protestants and the Puritans in particular. As historian Alec Ryrie has put it, the "intellectualism of early Protestantism is hard to overestimate."[16] By "intellectualism," he means not a sense of elitism but a priority given to the mind and to learning that embraced the entire worshiping community.

The priority given to the mind by early modern Protestants is encapsulated nicely by the Puritan Jeremiah Dyke (1584–1639), who explained Christian growth as a movement from right knowing to right doing: "They must be first full of knowledge, that will be full of goodnesse. Full of knowledge, full of goodnesse, voyde of knowledge, voyde of goodness."[17] According to this logic, spiritual growth was initiated by stimulating the mind rather than manipulating the body. And by shifting emphasis away from bodies coordinated according to the rhythms of the Mass and toward a worship that prioritized hearing, thinking, meditating, feeling, and knowing, the Protestant project realigned ministry and anthropology in an extraordinarily fruitful way.

Proposed Realignments

Yet whatever successes the traditional Protestant alignment of ministry and anthropology may have had in the past, influential voices within evangelical circles today are wondering whether the model has finally outlived its usefulness. As we have already observed, many are deliberately moving away from the word-centered piety that long characterized a Protestant approach to spiritual formation and toward a renewed interest in the role of the body. Focusing especially on the work of James K. A. Smith, we now examine more closely this new proposed realignment of ministry and anthropology, and I offer what I am calling an appreciative critique. Much that these authors have said

16   Alec Ryrie, *Being Protestant in Reformation Britain* (Oxford: Oxford University Press, 2013), 261.
17   Jeremiah Dyke, *A Worthy Communicant* (London, 1636), 111.

is good, fresh, and helpful. At the same time, I worry that on the back of these salutary insights, this literature also smuggles in some ideas that are decidedly less beneficial.

We begin by recalling that Smith frames his argument in terms of the need to carefully align one's approach to formation with one's anthropological conviction: "Every approach to discipleship and Christian formation assumes an implicit model of what human beings are [i.e., anthropology]."[18] Smith's project speaks to both aspects of that alignment and advances two major premises. First, he puts forward the anthropological premise that human beings are primarily "lovers" rather than "thinkers"—what we will call "big premise 1" (BP1). And second, he builds on BP1 to press home what we will call "big premise 2" (BP2): we can learn to love rightly through embodied ritualistic practices. In what follows, we consider BP1 and BP2 in turn, and I attempt to explain why I gladly embrace BP1 while raising serious concerns about BP2.

Smith's BP1 offers an anthropological vision: a theological account of what a human being is. Namely, Smith states that "human persons are not primarily or for the most part thinkers. . . . Instead, human persons are—fundamentally and primordially—lovers."[19] A human being, we are told, can be defined by what he or she *loves best*. The primary alternative to the model of human as lover has historically been, at least in the West, the model of human as thinker. This model of the human person as essentially a "thinking thing"—or, as Smith has more memorably put it, a "brain-on-a-stick"—is "as old as Plato but was rebirthed by Descartes and cultivated throughout modernity." It is a model that imagines people as needing above all else "a steady diet of ideas, fed somewhat intravenously into the mind through the lines of proposition and information."[20]

18 Smith, *You Are What You Love*, 3.
19 Smith, *Desiring the Kingdom*, 41.
20 Smith, *You Are What You Love*, 3.

But, Smith warns, when Christians absorb this sort of anthropology, they unwittingly produce a "talking-head version of Christianity that is fixated on doctrines and ideas" rather than on things like desire, love, and imagination.[21] Smith contends that precisely such an "intellectualist model of the human person" has dominated evangelical Christian ministry, reducing people to "mere intellect" and naively assuming that discipleship is "primarily a matter of depositing ideas and beliefs into mind-containers."[22] Dru Johnson raises a similar point when he observes that in Matthew 16, "Jesus didn't call people to take up their *minds* and follow him."[23] Likewise, Tish Harrison Warren has warned against "imagin[ing] the Christian life primarily as a quest to get the right ideas in [one's] head." She recalls with regret a time in her own life when she "began to feel like the sort of Christianity that I gravitated toward only required my brain."[24]

What then is to be done? Rather than reducing the richness of human identity to something more like a fleshy supercomputer, Smith, inspired by Augustine, insists that we must "attend to our loves." A strong sense of this thesis is neatly communicated through the titles of his books. The title *You Are What You Love*—as opposed to, say, *You Are What You Think*—suggests a fundamental continuity between one's core identity and what one desires most deeply. Smith's more academic treatment of these themes is titled *Desiring the Kingdom*, as opposed to, perhaps, *Learning about the Kingdom* or *Analyzing the Kingdom*. "To be human," Smith explains, "is to be animated and oriented by some vision of the good life. . . . And we *want* that. We crave it. We desire it. This is why our most fundamental mode of orientation to the world is love."[25]

If that is what a human person is, then our goal in ministry and discipleship should not be so much to fill the head as to train the

---

21 Smith, *Desiring the Kingdom*, 42.
22 Smith, *You Are What You Love*, 3.
23 Johnson, *Human Rites*, 26.
24 Warren, *Liturgy of the Ordinary*, 41–42.
25 Smith, *You Are What You Love*, 11.

heart, fire the imagination, and kindle desire for God and his glory. What is most important, on this account, is not ultimately whether you have your propositional ducks all in a tidy row but whether your heart beats in time with the rhythms of Christ and his kingdom. As Smith summarizes, "Being a disciple of Jesus is not primarily a matter of getting the right ideas and doctrines and beliefs into your head in order to guarantee proper behavior; rather, it's a matter of being the kind of person who *loves* rightly—who loves God and neighbor and is oriented to the world by the primacy of that love."[26]

This is what I am calling big premise 1. It strikes me as an undeniably attractive premise, one that, on balance, accords with the Reformed approach to spiritual formation we've been commending throughout this book. The kind of brains-on-a-stick anthropology that Smith is surely right to criticize is one in which we assume, implicitly or explicitly, that if we can just learn all the right things, then our Christian work is largely done. Instead, as Smith suggests, spiritual formation involves more than merely acquiring knowledge and is intended to shape us into people who love God and love neighbor, people who want what God wants and who long to see his will be done on earth as it is in heaven. This is why, throughout the Bible, the blessed man or woman is one who does not merely *know* what God's law says but with the psalmist proclaims,

> Oh how I *love* your law!
>   It is my meditation all the day! (Ps. 119:97)

Indeed, as we have seen throughout these pages, a great deal of post-Reformation Protestantism, especially in its Puritan manifestation, has been preoccupied with this very point, pressing home the reality that while salvation certainly entails coming "to the knowledge

---

26 Smith, *Desiring the Kingdom*, 32–33.

of the truth" (1 Tim. 2:4), for that knowledge to be saving knowledge and not *mere* knowledge, the heart must be fundamentally reoriented toward God. The English Puritans were indeed enthusiastic advocates of right *knowing*, but they also always insisted that such knowledge was ultimately the God-appointed means to stir up godly affections and God-honoring loves. One thinks of how Richard Baxter, for example, could recall his younger years in just such categories:

> I wondered at the senseless hardness of my heart, that could think and talk of Sin and Hell, and Christ and Grace, of God and Heaven, with no more feeling: I cried out from day to day to God for grace against this senseless deadness: I called myself the most hard hearted Sinner, that could feel nothing of all that I knew and talkt of.[27]

Clearly, for Baxter, right *knowing* without right *feeling* was insufficient.

Similarly, for Thomas Watson, the key question to put before his hearers was not so much about what they knew or what they did but about whether they were truly "lovers" of God. "It is not how much we do," Watson insisted, "but how much we love."[28] Campegius Vitringa nicely summarized the tradition when he wrote that the "source of the spiritual life is precisely this love for God. Where it reigns in a human heart, it absorbs and subordinates to itself all feelings and desires."[29] Such examples could be endlessly multiplied, for even a cursory examination of Protestant piety demonstrates that thinkers from Jonathan Edwards and Thomas Chalmers to J. I. Packer and John Piper have taught that Christian maturity entails renewed hearts that

---

27 Richard Baxter, *Reliquiae Baxterianae: Or, Mr Richard Baxter's Narrative of the Most Memorable Passages of His Life and Times*, ed. N. H. Keeble, John Coffey, Tim Cooper, and Tom Charlton (Oxford: Oxford University Press, 2020), 1:217.

28 Thomas Watson, *Heaven Taken by Storm: Showing the Holy Violence a Christian Is to Put Forth in the Pursuit after Glory*, ed. Joel R. Beeke (Grand Rapids, MI: Soli Deo Gloria, 2019), 64.

29 Campegius Vitringa, *The Spiritual Life*, trans. Charles K. Telfer (Grand Rapids, MI: Reformation Heritage Books, 2018), 17.

are ever more inclined to delight in godly things and feel repulsed by sinful things.

Thus it seems that if we would heed the call from Smith to avoid a brains-on-a-stick Christianity, our personal piety and public ministries would be the better for it. Many recent authors pressing this point, however, do not stop there. Having established this first premise, they quickly move to a second one, namely, that God-honoring affections are best cultivated through embodied ritualistic practices. Big premise 2 is put most concisely by Smith when he writes that the "way to the heart is through the body."[30] But what exactly does he mean by this?

The basic idea is that if love and desire are far more fundamental to a person's identity than is their accumulated collection of facts and figures, then any attempt to shape or reshape that love and desire through an appeal to more facts and figures is clearly wrongheaded and doomed to fail. The preacher expounding Matthew 6:33—"Seek first the kingdom of God and his righteousness"—typically addresses men and women who already know intellectually that God should be their first priority, but this does not mean that those same well-informed folks will actually *feel* the weight of that and desire to live it out. What is a pastor to do?

The answer that Smith and others provide is that we need to train people's hearts by engaging their bodies:

> We learn to love . . . not primarily by acquiring information about *what* we should love but rather through practices that form the habits of *how* we love. These sorts of practices are "pedagogies" of desire, not because they are like lectures that inform us, but because they are rituals that form and direct our affections.[31]

Embodied rituals, liturgies, and habits are "'pedagogies' of desire" that can, we are told, reach and redirect the wayward heart in ways that

30 Smith, *You Are What You Love*, 46.
31 Smith, *You Are What You Love*, 21 (emphasis original).

sermons, lectures, essays, and the like simply cannot. Smith explains that "disoriented heart-compasses requir[e] recalibration" and that "our loves need to be reordered (recalibrated) by . . . embodied, communal practices that are 'loaded' with the gospel and indexed to God and his kingdom."[32]

It is especially important to employ such embodied "liturgies," Smith says, because the world is full of its own "liturgies"—secular liturgies that are also operating on the heart level to turn people toward idolatrous loves. Christian formation means turning people back through our own embodied ritualistic counterliturgies. As Smith puts it,

> You won't be liberated from deformation by new information. God doesn't deliver us from the deformative habit-forming power of tactile rival liturgies by merely giving us a book. Instead, he invites us into a different embodied liturgy that not only is suffused by the biblical story but also, via those practices, inscribes the story into our hearts.[33]

An obvious example that nearly anyone who advocates this position seems to bring up early and often is kneeling to pray. And indeed, kneeling to pray is a widespread Christian practice in which the logic of a positive feedback loop between embodied practice and heart affection seems to make good sense. For example, in his book *The Common Rule*, in which he openly acknowledges his intellectual debt to Smith, author Justin Whitmel Earley talks about enhancing his prayer life through the embodied ritual of kneeling to pray: "Often one of the only ways to take hold of the mind is to take hold of the body." He goes on to note that if kneeling is impracticable in a given context, he will substitute some other physical posture or gesture because, as he says, "I need something physical to mark the moment for my slippery mind."[34]

---

32 Smith, *You Are What You Love*, 57–58.
33 Smith, *You Are What You Love*, 83–84.
34 Earley, *Common Rule*, 37, 41.

Now, of course, on one level, who could disagree with such comments? Might kneeling to pray bring about a pleasing congruity between one's actual bodily posture and one's intended spiritual posture, the outer and inner life coalescing as the forgiven sinner approaches a gracious God? Of course it could, and we would note in passing that Reformed Protestants, far from objecting to kneeling in prayer, often suggested that this was the ideal way to pray.[35] And thus, if Smith and others were simply trying to draw attention to our embodied nature and offer a gentle reminder that our conception of the Christian life should not wholly ignore this fact, it would be difficult to find fault with them.

But actually, Smith and company are not just saying that. Rather, they are saying quite a bit more. When Smith repeatedly stresses that "the way to the heart is through the body," he clearly implies that if you are not reaching the body, then you are *not* reaching the heart. This amounts to a sweeping indictment of word-centered Reformation piety and goes well beyond the suggestion that kneeling in prayer might be a helpful thing. If taken at face value, this logic suggests that Protestant parents and church leaders are guilty of serious spiritual negligence when they continue to emphasize things like catechesis and Scripture memory while excluding the sort of sensory, embodied liturgical experiences more characteristic of worship in the Roman Catholic and Eastern Orthodox traditions. Such an argument raises the temperature of the discussion considerably and forces the Reformation-minded evangelical to ask with some urgency, Should I accept Smith's big premises 1 and 2?

Proposed Realignments Reconsidered

Big premise 1, as I have already suggested, seems a helpful corrective. Seeking to distance oneself from a brains-on-a-stick Christianity accords with Scripture, the Reformed tradition, and common sense. But what about big premise 2? What about the idea that the best, or perhaps only,

---

35 E.g., William Gouge, *The Whole-Armour of God* (London, 1616), 341.

means to truly train the heart is through embodied ritual and sensory experience, the idea that "the way to the heart is through the body?"

Smith and other authors often suggest that accepting BP1 necessarily entails accepting BP2. BP1 is regularly conflated with BP2, and as these authors move seamlessly from one to the other, the clear implication is that if you are nodding along with BP1, then you must inevitably also nod along with BP2. Unfortunately, this implication is rarely made explicit; instead, these authors assert rather than demonstrate a logical connection between BP1 and BP2. Consider, for example, the following passage from Smith:

> To be conformed to the image of his Son is not only to think God's thoughts after him but to desire what God desires. That requires the recalibration of our heart-habits and the recapturing of our imagination, which happens when God's Word becomes the orienting center of our social imaginary, shaping our very perception of things before we even *think* about them.[36]

This is an eloquent statement of BP1, to which I can only say, Amen. But notice what happens next:

> So, like the secular liturgies of the mall or the stadium or the frat house, Christian liturgies can't just target the intellect: they also work on the body, conscripting our desires through the senses. Christian worship that will be counterformative needs to be embodied, tangible, and visceral. The way to the heart is through the body.[37]

This is all BP2, but it is presented seamlessly as though it were an obvious and necessary implication of the preceding elucidation of BP1. Immediately after the paragraph cited above, Smith pivots back to

---

36 Smith, *You Are What You Love*, 85.
37 Smith, *You Are What You Love*, 85.

BP1 to draw his conclusion: "That's why counterformative Christian worship doesn't just teach us how to think; it teaches us how to love, and it does so by inviting us into the biblical story and implanting that story into our bones."[38] This concluding sentence intermingles BP1 and BP2 as though the two propositions were self-evidently inseparable and mutually reinforcing.

This conflating of BP1 and BP2 is typical of the way these arguments proceed. Rhetorically, the effect is to use the obvious strength of BP1 to carry BP2 along in its wake. And yet upon closer examination, it is not at all obvious to me that BP2 flows from BP1, nor does it seem evident, whatever the relationship between the two premises, that BP2 is actually true. What reasons are we given to accept the truth of BP2?

The case Smith makes for why one should accept the claim that "the way to the heart is through the body" takes the form of argument by analogy. According to philosopher Paul Bartha, to advance one's argument through analogy involves taking "accepted similarities between two systems to support the conclusion that some further similarity exists." In Smith's work, the case for BP2 often employs such analogical reasoning: training the heart and cultivating godly affections is compared to some other kind of training—learning to play the piano, for instance—and the reader is invited to accept by the force of the analogy that certain principles governing, say, piano lessons would also apply to heart lessons. But is this argument by analogy valid? As Bartha goes on to indicate, conclusions drawn from analogical arguments "do not follow with certainty but are only supported with varying degrees of strength."[39] In other words, an analogical argument is only valid to the extent that the two things brought into analogical relationship actually share the similarities suggested. And I would argue that the analogies invoked to establish BP2 are not particularly convincing.

---

38 Smith, *You Are What You Love*, 85.
39 Paul Bartha, "Analogy and Analogical Reasoning," in *The Stanford Encyclopedia of Philosophy*, ed. Edward N. Zalta, spring 2019 ed., rev. January 25, 2019, https://plato.stanford.edu/.

One notices rather quickly that when analogies are used to establish that "the way to the heart is through the body," they invariably draw on examples of people trying to learn some sort of physical movement. In *Desiring the Kingdom*, for example, Smith explains the body-heart connection as follows:

> Habits are inscribed in our heart through bodily practices and rituals that train the heart, as it were, to desire certain ends. This is a non-cognitive sort of training. . . . Different kinds of material practices infuse noncognitive dispositions and skills in us through ritual and repetition precisely because our hearts (site of habits) are so closely tethered to our bodies. The senses are portals to the heart, and thus the body is a channel to our core dispositions and identity.[40]

What is being proposed is straightforward enough, but it gives us very little reason to believe that the proposal advanced is, in fact, true. Why should I accept the assertion that "the body is a channel to [my] core dispositions and identity"?

To establish his point, Smith turns to analogy. First, he compares training the heart to learning to type: "How did your hands get to 'know'" where the correct keys on the keyboard were? Smith's answer is that your hands "learned" all this "through rituals, routines, and exercises that trained your adaptive unconscious."[41] He then provides a second example: learning to play baseball. As baseball players field endless grounders, "the bodily practices (drills) . . . train the body (including the brain) to develop habits or dispositions to respond automatically in certain situations and environments. Our desire is trained in the same way."[42] The analogy is clear enough, and there is certainly an inner logic

---

40 Smith, *Desiring the Kingdom*, 58–59.

41 Smith, *Desiring the Kingdom*, 59.

42 Smith, *Desiring the Kingdom*, 60. For an example of a similar use of analogical reasoning to make essentially the same point, though this time using basketball rather than baseball practice, see Mat-

to it, but the real question is not whether the analogy makes sense on its own terms but whether the proposed congruities between the two essentially different worlds of discourse actually hold up to scrutiny. In this case, do the suggested correspondences between physical training and heart training actually correspond? Are the things drawn together into analogical relationship actually congruent at the points the author imagines them to be?

If no such congruity can actually be demonstrated, then the entire case for BP2 begins to look rather suspect. This is because such analogical moves are so heavily emphasized in the literature. In *You Are What You Love*, for example, Smith likens training the heart to learning, among other things, to play the piano, master a great golf swing, drive a car, type, acquire tastes for certain foods, enjoy exercise, ride a bicycle, play tennis, and physically navigate a town.[43]

All these proposed analogies are readily understood and internally coherent, but I do not believe they are actually good analogies. The chief defect stems from the fact that in all these scenarios, both the means of acquiring skills and the ultimate activity performed are physical. Typically, the means of acquiring skills involve breaking down some complex physical movement into its constituent parts and then working on each discrete part over and over again until the entire operation can be performed smoothly—think of perfecting one's golf swing by first working on one's stance, then addressing the movement of one's hips, then mastering one's elbow placement, and so forth. And thus, in all the analogies offered, the physical *means* of acquiring skills correspond perfectly to the very physical *end* in view: rapid, consistent, smooth, physical execution. So something like learning to play the piano—a physical end—requires a physical means—repeatedly firing one's fingers according to specific drills, muscle movement leading to muscle memory.

---

thew Lee Anderson, *Earthen Vessels: Why Our Bodies Matter to Our Faith* (Minneapolis: Bethany, 2011), 210–11.

43 Smith, *You Are What You Love*, 18, 19, 35, 36, 58–59, 62, 64, 107–8, 137–38.

But a serious problem arises when Smith and others then carry these physical means of acquiring skills into realms in which the ends in view are not physical but mental, emotional, and cognitive. When we are told that learning to love God is like learning to swing a golf club, the unstated premise is that because the latter is amenable to embodied, repeated practice, the former must be too. But what is never actually proved is why anyone would ever think that this was actually the case. By repeatedly likening the cultivation of godly affections to the acquisition of various physical skills, these authors smuggle in the idea that the same physical means of acquiring skills applicable to things like riding a bicycle will also apply to spheres in which the end result is not physical at all. But this is problematic. Analogies used in this way can clarify a relationship the author wishes to posit, but they cannot establish that the posited relationship actually exists. And thus, because the analogies used by Smith and company inappropriately confuse very different arenas, they cannot carry the persuasive weight these authors would like them to.

Furthermore, as one begins to evaluate the assertion that "the way to the heart is through the body," life seems to be brimming with very obvious counterexamples, examples of situations in which the body is not recruited in any way and yet the affections are stirred and shaped. One imagines, for example, a movie theater full of people watching the film adaptation of J. R. R. Tolkien's *Return of the King* and being moved right across the emotional spectrum, all while their bodies are utterly motionless and inert. If people reply that the 2004 winner of the Academy Award for Best Picture is a sensory feast for the ears and eyes, I would remind them that the claim Smith and company make again and again is that embodied practices, rituals that physically move and position the body, offer the essential key to unlocking heart change. But in the movie theater, whatever sounds and sights are on offer, the bodies are not moving—and still the film can deeply affect its viewers. Similarly, anyone who has read a novel, listened to a piece of music, or sat silently before a painting understands that affections are stirred, imaginations are kindled, and hearts are trained more often than not by the relatively *disembodied* appreciation of ideas, words, and images.

Experience also proves that the converse holds true: embodied rituals often fail to ignite the hearts of those involved. One thinks, for example, of the many people raised in highly liturgical, embodied traditions like Orthodoxy and Catholicism whose hearts were left cold and unmoved by what they came to regard, fairly or unfairly, as "mindless repetition." Alex Morbelli left Roman Catholicism for evangelicalism as she came to realize that "all of the rituals and the religion I had used to relate to God . . . were as hollow as the icons on the walls."[44] Or consider Gerard O'Brien, who grew up in the Roman Catholic Church and served as an altar boy at Mass and yet recalls how the experience did nothing to shape and form his heart: "It wasn't that I hated mass; it just didn't interest me. It was a suite of ceremonies that, in hindsight, I can say I didn't really understand. It was boring and it didn't seem to have any relevance to my life."[45]

In light of such stories, of which there are many,[46] a question arises: If "embodied rituals" are such powerful agents of real heart change, why are there so many nominal Catholic and Orthodox parishioners? When such obvious counterexamples are combined with the confused quality of the analogical argumentation on offer, one is left wondering what reasons there might be to accept the premise that "the way to the heart is through the body." Absent such cogent, compelling reasons to accept this premise, it does not seem at all obvious that Christians steeped in a logocentric Protestant religious culture should be urged to adopt a new approach to spiritual formation.

---

44 Alex Morbelli, "When Everything Else Is Gone," in *Stepping Out in Faith: Former Catholics Tell Their Story*, ed. Mark Gilbert (Kingsford, AU: Matthias Media, 2012), 17.

45 Gerard O'Brien, "Confident in God's Love," in Gilbert, *Stepping Out in Faith*, 23.

46 "The information we have indicates that since at least 1950, the 'traffic' of those leaving Roman Catholicism for forms of Protestantism far exceeds the traffic of those moving in the opposite direction." Stewart, *In Search of Ancient Roots*, 256.

A Settled Alignment

If, like me, you find yourself attracted to what I've described here as big premise 1 yet remain skeptical of big premise 2, then the foregoing reflections perhaps leave you wondering where we might go from here. If, like me, you are convinced that the Reformers' emphasis on word ministry and their resistance to the use of extrabiblical rituals and forms in worship were, in the main, wise and congruent with the spirit of the New Testament, then you are left to puzzle through how your own approach to spiritual formation can both preserve those biblical insights and avoid falling into the trap of imagining God's image bearers as mere brains on a stick. Let's conclude with two suggestions for how we can appropriate some of the best insights from authors like James K. A. Smith without sacrificing the word-based piety that both the Reformation and Scripture commend.

First, without necessarily agreeing with the idea that the "way to the heart is through the body"—or, as I have been calling it, big premise 2—we can still accept the reminder that God has indeed created us with bodies. Our embodiment is not an accident or a mistake or a mere concession to our finitude but something that reflects the will of an infinitely wise, wonderfully good, and unimaginably creative God. Thus, the reality of embodiment can and should shape the way we think about what it means to live in a God-honoring way.

Giving more weight to embodiment could take any number of forms. For example, rather than trying to invent new extrabiblical "embodied rituals," we could more carefully consider how we approach those "embodied rituals" that Scripture already gives us: the Lord's Supper and baptism. Do we treat these like optional add-ons to be rushed through every so often, or do we approach them as key components in the life of the church? We could also attend more carefully to the ways our physical worship spaces affect our worship experience. How do the spaces we create either facilitate or militate against reverent worship? It seems to me that one can be fully committed to the second commandment's perpetual relevance without supposing that a lack of aesthetic sense is thereby something virtuous. How then might we creatively add beauty to our churches and homes?[47] And of course, we could also pay more attention to the various ways meeting or failing to meet our need for exercise, healthy food, and restful sleep might affect the trajectory of our spiritual formation.[48] This last topic is one we return to in the next chapter.

Second, we can more intentionally embrace what I have called big premise 1, the idea that human beings are not primarily knowledge receptacles but rather image bearers with imaginations that need to be fired and desires that need to be creatively led toward God-glorifying ends. By casting a vision for this sort of holistic ministry, authors like James K. A. Smith have done us all a tremendous service. But for those of us committed to a Reformation, word-centered approach to spiritual formation, the answer is not to sideline Bible reading and prayer in favor of new embodied rituals but rather to recognize that a word-centered piety is more than able to fulfill Smith's wise call in BP1 to speak to the *whole* person. If we are not doing that, and if our churches *do* sometimes resemble dry information distribution centers, then shame on us. But where I would depart from some recent authors is to strongly affirm that the answer to a dry, unimaginative spiritual life is not less word and more ritual but, with our Reformed forebears, more emphasis on a word-centered piety that actively stirs up the heart.

One key help in this regard is the discipline of meditation. In chapter 4, we discussed the way that early modern Protestants underscored meditation as the key means for moving the truth of God's word from

---

47 See, e.g., Abraham Kuyper, *Our Worship*, ed. Harry Boonstra (Grand Rapids, MI: Eerdmans, 2009), 47–57; Edith Schaeffer, *Hidden Art* (London: Norfolk, 1971).

48 See, e.g., Christopher Ash, *Zeal without Burnout: Seven Keys to a Lifelong Ministry of Sustainable Sacrifice* (Epsom, UK: Good Book, 2016); David P. Murray, *Reset: Living a Grace-Paced Life in a Burnout Culture* (Wheaton, IL: Crossway, 2017); Shona Murray, *Refresh: Embracing a Grace-Paced Life in a World of Endless Demands* (Wheaton, IL: Crossway, 2017); Kelly M. Kapic, *You're Only Human: How Your Limits Reflect God's Design and Why That's Good News* (Grand Rapids, MI: Brazos, 2022).

the head into the heart. For the Puritans, the answer to an arid, overly intellectualized head religion was usually to place a greater emphasis on this neglected means of grace. It's through meditation that the biblical stories come alive and the promises of God intersect with the concrete realities of our lives. Embracing that practice does not require any particular bodily movement, but it may require us to better cultivate our own imaginations. As Richard Winter argues, "Imagination, creativity and interest in life . . . can either be cultivated, strengthened and developed or ignored, suppressed and allowed to wither and even die."[49] I do wonder whether much of the dissatisfaction with evangelical spirituality flows from imaginations that have been too long neglected. In pursuit of a corrective, what might we do?

We might try to deliberately spend less time looking at screens and more time reading, praying, and thinking deeply. We might also try going for a walk and intentionally leaving the phone behind. In recent years, both Christian and non-Christian authors have done fine work documenting the degree to which a more-or-less continuous engagement with screens can disrupt our capacity for serious reflection.[50] When used uncritically, our phones, laptops, and tablets create an environment that is inhospitable to deep thoughts on God and the things of God. Imaginative, faithful, and fresh connections between God's word and God's world abound, but such links are drawn only by those who regularly give themselves the gifts of solitude, quietness, and deep reading, gifts that, upon reflection, don't actually require much movement at all.

---

49 Richard Winter, *Still Bored in a Culture of Entertainment: Rediscovering Passion and Wonder* (Downers Grove, IL: InterVarsity Press, 2002), 82.

50 E.g., Neil Postman, *Amusing Ourselves to Death: Public Discourse in the Age of Show Business* (New York: Penguin, 1985); Sven Birkerts, *The Gutenberg Elegies: The Fate of Reading in an Electronic Age* (New York: Faber and Faber, 2006); T. David Gordon, *Why Johnny Can't Preach: The Media Have Shaped the Messengers* (Phillipsburg, NJ: P&R, 2009); Nicholas G. Carr, *The Shallows: What the Internet Is Doing to Our Brains* (New York: Norton, 2010); Tony Reinke, *12 Ways Your Phone Is Changing You* (Wheaton, IL: Crossway, 2017); Cal Newport, *Digital Minimalism: Choosing a Focused Life in a Noisy World* (New York: Portfolio/Penguin, 2019); Brett McCracken, *The Wisdom Pyramid: Feeding Your Soul in a Post-Truth World* (Wheaton, IL: Crossway, 2021).

10

When Things Go Wrong

Wrestling with Spiritual Weakness

AROUND THE YEAR 1682, the London Presbyterian minister Timothy Rogers (1658–1728) experienced something that would profoundly change the course of his life and ministry. Rather suddenly and without warning, he was thrown into a period of acute spiritual crisis. It was a "long affliction, and great distress of Conscience," a time when Rogers experienced "a deep, and a rooted Melancholly." The experience was, in many ways, inexplicable to him, and he described his "inward Terrors" as "things that may be sadly felt; but . . . cannot be fully express'd." During this time, Rogers was blanketed with a general feeling of sadness, but what made the experience especially difficult was the way his mental anguish was intertwined with his spiritual life. He felt far from God, recording a sense of "God's Displeasure, and the fear of being cast out of his Glorious Presence forever."[1]

The threat of unending spiritual gloom loomed large in Rogers's mind, but in time he saw improvement. Many Christian friends prayed for him, talked with him, and sat with him as he wrestled with an

---

1 Timothy Rogers, *A Discourse concerning Trouble of Mind* (London, 1691), i, A4v.

invisible enemy that he scarcely understood. Eventually, after about two years, the storm passed: "After the many waves and billows that went over me, through the great goodness of God I now enjoy a calm." But the experience so marked him that he directed much of his remaining intellectual and pastoral energy toward "help[ing] those who are yet labouring in the deep," an effort that resulted in the publication of multiple books exploring the spiritual discouragement that can disquiet the Christian soul.[2]

Throughout the preceding pages, our discussion of spiritual formation has been largely positive. We have put forward a positive proposal concerning the things one ought to do in pursuing Christian growth, and we have cast a largely positive vision of what it might look like when things go right. And yet as the story of Timothy Rogers attests and as our own painful experience confirms, things do not always go right. Consider Charles Spurgeon, who experienced unprecedented fruitfulness in his ministry and yet throughout his life battled with sadness and discouragement. "I am sometimes lifted to the very heavens," wrote Spurgeon, "and then I go down to the deep: I am at one time bright with joy and confidence and at another time dark as midnight with doubts and fears."[3] The spiritual sufferings of Timothy Rogers and Charles Spurgeon were especially severe, but even those who have been spared the sort of acute episodes they described surely know what it's like to feel spiritually discouraged.

I will not always want to read my Bible in the morning. At times my prayers will feel perfunctory and my meditations sluggish. Though I might imagine it as a rapturous opportunity to delight in God's creation, when I actually take my walk through the woods, it might well feel like a cold, muddy chore. And sometimes my relationships with

2   Rogers, *Trouble of Mind*, 4. See also Stephen Wright, "Rogers, Timothy (1658–1728), Presbyterian Minister," *Oxford Dictionary of National Biography*, September 23, 2004; https://doi.org/10.1093/ref:odnb/24002.

3   Quoted in Ray Rhodes, *Susie: The Life and Legacy of Susannah Spurgeon, Wife of Charles H. Spurgeon* (Chicago: Moody Publishers, 2018), 171.

other believers will seem more awkward than encouraging, more irritating than edifying. Not only will I often feel as though I'm making little or no spiritual progress, I will sometimes perceive myself to be actually going backward. We are frail, fallen, and finite creatures, and thus trouble is to be expected. In chapter 1, we defined spiritual formation in terms of the conscious process by which we seek to heighten and satisfy our Spirit-given thirst for God (Ps. 42:1–2). Now in this chapter, we are thinking about what happens when that "Spirit-given thirst for God" feels weak or even absent, and here we consider the nature of our spiritual struggles, the causes of our difficulties, and how we might walk faithfully when they arise.

The Reality of Spiritual Struggle

The starting point for any discussion of spiritual difficulty is to underscore the phenomenon's reality and ubiquity: spiritual struggle is a normal part of the Christian life, and no one is exempt. This is exactly what we would expect from reading the Bible, a book that testifies to human suffering on almost every page and never suggests that Christians are immune. Moreover, Scripture does not portray the suffering of God's people as something that is limited to external afflictions, like war, disease, and natural disaster. Instead, the Bible unashamedly indicates that real believers suffer an inner spiritual turmoil that cannot be reduced to enemies outside ourselves but must, at least in part, be attributed to the lingering enemy within. Although the apostle Paul takes "delight in the law of God" in his "inner being," at the same time he confesses, "I see in my members another law waging war against the law of my mind and making me captive to the law of sin that dwells in my members" (Rom. 7:22–23).[4] This is how the Bible portrays the

---

4   Though opinions have differed, the majority report within the Reformed tradition has understood Rom. 7:14–25 to describe the inner conflict that regenerate Christians face. See Willem van Vlastuin, *Be Renewed: A Theology of Personal Renewal* (Göttingen: Vandenhoeck & Ruprecht, 2014), 157–66.

Christian life: as a journey marked by both triumphs and defeats, a fight for faith best summarized by the enigmatic confession of Mark 9:24: "I believe; help my unbelief." The Psalms are especially powerful in this regard, replete as they are with testimony to the spiritual afflictions that can and will weigh us down:

> Why are you cast down, O my soul,
>> and why are you in turmoil within me? (Ps. 42:5)

For John Calvin, one of the chief attractions of the Psalter was precisely this capacity to give voice and legitimacy to "all the griefs, sorrows, fears, doubts, hopes, cares, perplexities, in short, all the distracting emotions with which the minds of men are wont to be agitated."[5]

In this chapter, we are not concerned with suffering per se but with one particular type of suffering—namely, that inner struggle in which believers feel distant from God, lack religious fervor, and generally perceive themselves to be stagnant in their spiritual formation.[6] This condition was a prominent theme among early modern Reformed authors. Indeed, historian Alec Ryrie has identified concern over spiritual struggle as a distinctive mark of Reformation piety, characterizing early modern Protestants as people engaged in a "never-ending battle against this listless, chilling enemy":

> The bane of the earnest Protestant's spiritual life was a condition variously described as dullness, hardness, heaviness, dryness, coldness, drowsiness, or deadness. This insidious malaise could creep into your heart unnoticed; its symptom was numbness, not pain.

---

5   John Calvin, *Commentary on the Book of Psalms*, trans. James Anderson, vol. 1 (Edinburgh: Calvin Translation Society, 1845), xxxvii.

6   There are many excellent Christian treatments of suffering more generally, but the one I've found most helpful is D. A. Carson, *How Long, O Lord? Reflections on Suffering and Evil*, 2nd ed. (Grand Rapids, MI: Baker Academic, 2006).

Alert Protestants learned to keep a careful watch for it, not least because—by common consent—the problem grew more acute, not less, as you matured in your faith.[7]

And though Reformed authors have described this condition using a variety of terms, they all agree that real saints really suffer in this way. The Dutch theologian Wilhelmus à Brakel is representative when he clearly affirms that "it is God's common way to cause His children to occasionally experience desertions. . . . Nothing strange is befalling you, for God does not deal with you any differently from His other children."[8] Another Dutch theologian, Campegius Vitringa, accepted as "a foundational principle for [his] views on the spiritual life" that "no attainments in the spiritual life ever free us from the experience of spiritual diseases and afflictions." As he unfolded what these afflictions might entail, he spoke of a "faith, which, though it survives, becomes so weak that it is near to spiritual death."[9] The authors of the Westminster Confession insisted that "even such as fear" God may be allowed for a time "to walk in darkness and to have no light."[10] And in his *Treatise on Divine Meditation*, John Ball included a section titled "What wee must do if our heart bee so barren that wee cannot call to mind anything that hath been taught us."[11] For Richard Sibbes, it was axiomatic that "God's dearest children are exercised with sharp conflicts in the faith." But rather than become discouraged by this, Sibbes used the ubiquity of spiritual struggle as a way to encourage suffering Christians: "It is the common case of God's dearest children, yea, of the prophets of

---

7   Alec Ryrie, *Being Protestant in Reformation Britain* (Oxford: Oxford University Press, 2013), 20.
8   Wilhelmus à Brakel, *The Christian's Reasonable Service*, trans. Bartel Elshout (Morgan, PA: Soli Deo Gloria, 1995), 4:187.
9   Campegius Vitringa, *The Spiritual Life*, trans. Charles K. Telfer (Grand Rapids, MI: Reformation Heritage Books, 2018), 77–79.
10 "Westminster Confession of Faith," in *Creeds, Confessions, and Catechisms: A Reader's Edition*, ed. Chad Van Dixhoorn (Wheaton, IL: Crossway, 2022), 212 (18.4).
11 John Ball, *A Treatise of Divine Meditation* (London, 1660), 93.

God, David, Jeremiah, and Habakkuk, and therefore we ought not to be dejected too much."[12]

The key thing to recognize here is that these struggles were understood to be those experienced by real, authentic, regenerate Christians. Time spent in the spiritual doldrums was a normal part of one's journey, not to be taken as proof that one lacked a real and living faith. As Thomas Watson put it, "Although true believers do not fall away actually, and lose all their grace, yet their grace may fail in degree, and they may make a great breach upon their sanctification." Using a metaphor we have seen before in this book, he compared the state of such believers to a fireplace that was "dying, but not dead": "Grace may be like fire in the embers; though not quenched, yet the flame is gone out." Such a situation was a common one, and Watson named three telltale marks by which it could be identified: we lose our appetite for spiritual things, we become worldly minded, and we are no longer troubled by sin. Watson's three marks are similar to those repeated across the Reformed tradition and are portrayed as constant temptations for even the strongest Christians.[13]

If we hope to learn from previous generations of Reformed writers and follow their lead in spiritual matters, it is vital that we hear them talking like this. For if we don't, we might come away with the impression that these authors are unrealistic in their expectations. The Puritans often present a special problem on this score, for they regularly attempted to sketch the ideals toward which Christians should aspire; thus Thomas Watson wrote a book titled *The Godly Man's Picture, Drawn with a Scriptural Pencil.*[14] A Christian cannot come nearer to hitting the mark if she doesn't know where to aim, and it is in this spirit that one often finds exhortations like this one from Richard Baxter:

12   Richard Sibbes, *Works of Richard Sibbes*, ed. Alexander B. Grosart (Edinburgh: Banner of Truth, 1973), 7:67.

13   Thomas Watson, *A Body of Divinity* (Edinburgh: Banner of Truth, 1983), 276–77.

14   Thomas Watson, *The Godly Man's Picture, Drawn with a Scripture Pencil* (Edinburgh: Banner of Truth, 1992).

"Diligently labor that God and holiness may be thy chief delight." The aim of such labor, said Baxter, is so that "this holy delight may be the ordinary temperament of thy religion."[15] That is a good and worthy goal, but we will have a distorted understanding of both Puritan devotional literature and the Christian life if we imagine that this ideal will always be our subjective experience. Certainly, Baxter himself harbored no illusions on this score, for when you read on from the lines just quoted, you find page after page in which he documents various obstacles that make it hard, in practice, to maintain the "holy delight" he commends.

And indeed, throughout Puritan sermons, devotional manuals, and diaries, one finds a consistent recognition that the Christian life is not one glorious experience of spiritual bliss. Instead, authors such as John Flavel described seasons "of spiritual darkness and doubting, when it is with the soul as it was with Paul in his dangerous voyage, neither sun, nor moon, nor star appears for many days." During such times, "the soul is even ready to give up all its hopes and comforts for lost; to draw sad and desperate conclusions upon itself; to call its former comforts vain delusions; its grace hypocrisy." There is a gritty realism here that belies any suggestion that Puritan authors were out of touch with what ordinary Christians experienced. Flavel speaks for the tradition when he frankly admits that "to keep the heart from sinking in such a day as this, to enable it to maintain its own sincerity, is a matter of great difficulty."[16]

Beyond the Puritans, other representative Reformed writers have communicated a similar sense that progress in the spiritual life does not come easily. For example, Archibald Alexander discussed this subject at length in his fascinating book *Thoughts on Religious Experience* (1844). There he taught that all Christians "experience short seasons of comparative coldness and insensibility, and they who live near to God have not always equal light and life and comfort in the divine

---

15 Richard Baxter, *The Practical Works of Richard Baxter* (London: James Duncan, 1830), 2:408.
16 John Flavel, *The Works of John Flavel* (London: Banner of Truth, 1968), 5:480.

life."[17] Sometimes these "short seasons" are extended in their duration or deepened in their intensity. For these more pronounced spiritual maladies, Alexander could use the language of "religious melancholy," a condition that "may be reckoned among the heaviest calamities to which our suffering nature is subject."[18] When the difficulty in view was less about the presence of acute suffering and more about the absence of godly affection, he spoke of "backsliding," a condition in which "the Christian is gradually led off from close walking with God, loses the lively sense of divine things, becomes too much attached to the world and too much occupied with secular concerns." Allowed to persist unchecked, this condition can worsen "until at length the keeping of the heart is neglected, prayer and the seeking of the Lord in private are omitted or slightly performed, zeal for the advancement of religion is quenched, and many things once rejected by a sensitive conscience are now indulged and defended."[19] If this book has sketched what it means to *keep your heart* for God, what Alexander described in his book is its opposite: a heart no longer kept and cared for but encircled by idolatrous loves, its spiritual vigor slowly choked away.

Diagnosing Our Difficulties

The indicative marks of spiritual decay identified by Archibald Alexander, Thomas Watson, and other representative writers help form something of a consensus regarding both the reality of this inner struggle and its characteristic shape. But even once we have affirmed the fact that Christians are troubled in this way, there is still space to explore the causes of our difficulties. Are there particular reasons why a believer finds himself or herself feeling dry and cold toward God and the things of God? Many thoughtful Christians have suggested that there are, and we now explore five of the most common of them.

---

17 Archibald Alexander, *Thoughts on Religious Experience* (Edinburgh: Banner of Truth, 2020), 189.
18 Alexander, *Religious Experience*, 38.
19 Alexander, *Religious Experience*, 189.

Sin in the Life of the Christian

There is no more basic reason for our spiritual disconnect from God than the ongoing presence of sin in our lives. In one sense, *all* spiritual malady flows from the reality of our fallen and sinful state, and in glory the particular tears of spiritual malaise will be wiped away along with all other tears (Rev. 21:4). Yet here we mean something more specific: to the extent that I am deliberately indulging in unrepentant sin, I will find it hard to enjoy communion with God and effectively take up the means of grace. If we define sin with the Westminster Shorter Catechism as "any want of conformity unto, or transgression of, the law of God," then it makes perfect sense that this would be so.[20] Sin is, by its very nature, contrary to God. "God is light, and in him is no darkness at all" (1 John 1:5). Sin is against him, utterly unlike him, and opposed to all his ways. So if I am running toward it, I must of necessity be running away from him.

This point is one that older Reformed writers were far more frank and direct about than we tend to be today. Where we are often concerned—not unreasonably—to avoid laying further burdens on a person who is already hurting spiritually and thus sometimes hesitate to link spiritual struggle with personal sin, early modern writers did not shy away from making this connection. And here, as with other points of discontinuity with those who went before, we can learn from their approach and make course corrections to our own without necessarily blindly copying every aspect of their practice and tone. For better or worse, their comments on the connection between personal sin and zeal typically did not mince words.

Campegius Vitringa, for example, stated that "the majority of spiritual illnesses have been contracted by a person's own failure in his course of living."[21] Thomas Watson was equally blunt when he wrote that "sin lived

---

20 "Westminster Shorter Catechism," in Van Dixhoorn, *Creeds, Confessions, and Catechisms*, 413 (q. 14).

21 Vitringa, *Spiritual Life*, 92.

in will spoil all violence [i.e., zeal] for heaven." Notice that he spoke here of "sin lived in"—he was not denying that all believers battle daily with indwelling sin. Rather, he was talking about the sort of wrongheaded, willful pursuit of that which is contrary to God's will and God's ways, a condition that he said "enfeebles" or weakens the Christian's desire for spiritual formation: "It is like the cutting of Samson's hair, and then the strength departs." Such pursuit of sin is "the soul's sickness," and "a sick man cannot run a race. Sin lived in takes a man quite off from duty or makes him dead in it. The more lively the heart is in sin, the more dead it is in prayer."[22] Or consider Richard Baxter, who warned Christians, "If you grieve your Comforter, he will grieve you, or leave you to grieve yourselves." Here Baxter, like Watson, primarily had in view those sins that are known to us and that we persist in: "In that measure that any known sin is cherished, delight in God will certainly decay."[23]

If you don't "flee from sexual immorality" (1 Cor. 6:18) but instead are habitually looking at pornography, then you shouldn't be surprised when your prayer life runs dry. Because Jesus says that "you cannot serve God and money" (Matt. 6:24), we shouldn't be shocked when an idolatrous obsession with wealth causes our joy in the Lord to evaporate. And if my contribution to my workplace includes a steady stream of gossip and whispers about colleagues when they're not around, then it stands to reason that my sense of close walking with God will suffer. Why? The Lord has told me in his word that he stands opposed to "one who sows discord among brothers" (Prov. 6:19), and insofar as I am "cherishing" or willfully "living in" that particular sin, I am *not* walking closely with him. As I outline below, it's very clear that not all spiritual difficulty is linked directly with "cherished" or "lived in" sin in our lives. But when diagnosing the state of our hearts, biblical realism requires that this be our first port of call.

22 Thomas Watson, *Heaven Taken by Storm: Showing the Holy Violence a Christian Is to Put Forth in the Pursuit after Glory*, ed. Joel R. Beeke (Grand Rapids, MI: Soli Deo Gloria, 2019), 90.

23 Baxter, *Practical Works*, 2:420.

Temperament and Biology

When considering spiritual formation, some of the most perplexing questions emerge from the intersection of one's God-given temperament and one's experience of the Christian life. Paul commands all believers to "rejoice in the Lord" and to "not be anxious about anything" (Phil. 4:4, 6). And yet experience plainly teaches that some people, whether Christians or not, seem naturally more optimistic and buoyant then others. How does Paul's command, which he gives to everyone without exception, relate to the diversity of personalities that characterize God's image bearers? And pressing more directly into the theme of this chapter, is it not evident that some Christians are temperamentally more likely than others to feel "cast down" in soul and "in turmoil within" (Ps. 42:5)?

Moreover, this issue is further complicated by questions of biology and mental illness. To what extent do my spiritual problems have biological roots? And to the extent that my spiritual lethargy is actually a product of my brain chemistry, my hormones, or my blood sugar, is it still even appropriate to describe it as "spiritual" trouble at all? From one angle, such labeling would appear both incorrect and unkind: incorrect because it wrongly interprets the facts and unkind because it ascribes blame to someone who is suffering from something beyond his or her control.

These questions do not admit easy answers, and they take us well beyond the scope of this book.[24] We can note here, however, that Reformation-minded Christians have long been aware of the complexities such issues create, and anyone who is spiritually struggling must

---

24 In thinking about psychiatric treatment from a Christian perspective, one helpful book that seeks a balanced approach is Michael R. Emlet, *Descriptions and Prescriptions: A Biblical Perspective on Psychiatric Diagnoses and Medications* (Greensboro, NC: New Growth, 2017). And yet as an illustration of the issue's complexity, note the helpful questions and caveats that appear in Nate Brooks's otherwise positive review of Emlet's book: "Book Review of *Descriptions and Prescriptions: A Biblical Perspective on Psychiatric Diagnoses and Medications* by Mike Emlet," Biblical Counseling Coalition, November 17, 2017, https://www.biblicalcounselingcoalition.org/.

take those complexities seriously. If we fail to do so, we may end up doing more harm than good, offering incorrect, or at least incomplete, diagnoses, which in turn lead us to unsatisfactory treatments.

Regarding the intersection of sanctification and personality, older writers frequently observed that it is not always easy to distinguish between what is imparted by the Holy Spirit and what is inherited from our human parents. For instance, after he explained that Christians must be characterized by spiritual zeal and "fervencie," the Puritan Robert Bolton (1572–1631) went on to distinguish carefully between a "natural fervencie" that results from one's inborn temperament—some people are just more fiery than others—and a true Christian spiritual fervor that is the fruit of sanctification.[25] And whatever one makes of Bolton's precise formulation, his comments highlight the reality that God has made us to differ in key respects and that these natural differences must affect how we understand our spiritual ups and downs.

If I am naturally inclined toward "fervencie," finding myself easily excited by whatever new hobby or activity I've taken on, then I should be wary of imagining myself to be more godly than others when that same penchant for passion is directed toward the latest initiative at my local church. On the other hand, if my temperament is characteristically muted, then I should avoid reflexively chastising myself for not responding to the things of God in exactly the same way as my more easily excitable friend. Rather, I should trust that the Holy Spirit will form God-honoring affections in me that are in keeping with the personality and character traits he gave me. Christian psychiatrist Gaius Davies wisely observes that "grace does not change us as personalities." By "personalities," he has a limited scope in view: "The bodies, intelligence and natural aptitudes remain the same. Grace does not change temperament." Lest we misunderstand, as he goes on to explain, following Christ and being sanctified by the Spirit do, of course, radically

---

25 Ryrie, *Reformation Britain*, 73.

transform us. Our behavior, attitudes, motivations, and interests, by God's grace, are changed, but in key respects, "the new life, the new creation, expresses itself through the same old personalities."[26]

The question of the extent to which biology and brain chemistry affect our spiritual life is even more vexed. This is because the issues raised are highly personal, emotionally charged, and intrinsically related to medical and scientific questions that seem to lie outside the range of subjects the Bible explicitly interacts with. While we cannot treat these subjects here, we can note that older Reformed writers did acknowledge the possibility of a biological component to common spiritual problems and often explored the phenomenon of "melancholy," or depression, at length in both their treatises and their spiritual autobiographies.[27] And though their understanding of the medical issues at play left much to be desired from a twenty-first-century standpoint, that does not take away from the reality that they were attempting to understand Christian spiritual life as a psychosomatic unity. "There is cause oft in the body of those in whom a melancholy temper prevaileth," wrote Richard Sibbes. Explicitly connecting bodily dysfunction with spiritual dysfunction, Sibbes explained that "the soul . . . by reason of its sympathy with the body, is subject to be misled." He compared the melancholic person's assessment of his or her spiritual life to a person viewing the world through colored glass: "So whatsoever is presented to a melancholy person, comes in a dark way to the soul."[28]

When we feel low in our spiritual lives, we should thoughtfully consider ways that bodily ills may be giving rise to spiritual struggles. How far and in precisely what direction we take that inquiry varies among otherwise like-minded Christians. But the baseline reality that the state

---

26 Gaius Davies, *Genius, Grief and Grace: A Doctor Looks at Suffering and Success* (Fearn, UK: Christian Focus, 2008), 20–21.

27 David Walker, "Piety and the Politics of Anxiety in Nonconformist Writing of the Later Stuart Period," in *Puritanism and Emotion in the Early Modern World*, ed. Alec Ryrie and Tom Schwanda (New York: Palgrave Macmillan, 2016), 144–65.

28 Sibbes, *Works*, 1:136.

of our bodies and the state of our spiritual formation are linked should be something we can all agree on.

Creeping Worldliness

"Dead fish swim down the stream, living fish swim against it," wrote Thomas Watson.[29] If you are experiencing a season of spiritual drought, ask yourself honestly whether you are fighting against the cultural current or simply allowing yourself to be carried along by it. To resist becoming "conformed to this world" (Rom. 12:2) requires that we understand the characteristic drift of our particular cultural moment and then guard against its sinful excesses. The Puritans were excellent on this score, a fact the name Puritan itself attests to. Originally used as an insult by their opponents, the label Puritan was intended to suggest an inhibited, uptight, and perhaps hypocritical individual who had been rendered incapable of joy through his constant need to "purify" everything he encountered of anything that might be remotely pleasurable or fun.

This caricature, of course, was wildly unfair.[30] It did, however, contain this element of truth: more than many of their neighbors, the Puritans were alert to the allure of creeping worldliness, and they took measures to guard against it. They were acutely aware that the spirit of the age permeates one's consciousness by degrees and that Christians must be correspondingly vigilant. Do we actually think about and evaluate new trends, products, and programs before allowing them to take up positions on our mental landscape? Or do we naively accept whatever happens to be floating down the river of pop culture today? Engaging with popular websites, TV shows, and social media is not inherently wrong, and to some extent, doing so represents a healthy impulse to live and work and think where God has placed you. But to accept

---

29 Thomas Watson, *The Great Gain of Godliness* (Edinburgh: Banner of Truth, 2006), 6.
30 For a thorough debunking of the many stereotypes associated with Puritans and Puritanism, see Leland Ryken, *Worldly Saints: The Puritans as They Really Were* (Grand Rapids, MI: Zondervan, 1990).

them uncritically and without discernment opens one up to a mind and heart increasingly distorted by the collection of idolatrous loves that John categorizes as belonging to "the world"—"the desires of the flesh and the desires of the eyes and pride of life" that Christians are called to guard their hearts against (1 John 2:15–16).

Here is where Watson and other Puritan writers can help us, for they saw with crystal clarity that there are "many who have escaped the rock of scandalous sins, yet have sunk in the world's golden quicksands."[31] By contrast, one mark of a healthy, growing Christian life is a growing love for the things that God loves, even when they stand completely out of step with mainstream opinion: "To own the ways of God when they are decried and maligned, to love a persecuted truth, this evidences a vital principle of goodness."[32] This is the renewed mind of Romans 12:2, but if we are not actively pursuing it, we risk being carried in the opposite direction unawares. If it just so happens that all our favorite things align with what's trending at present, and if the only biblical themes on which we opine openly just happen to be precisely those places where the Bible happens to converge with the current pop-cultural consensus, then these might not actually be coincidences at all, and this is likely not a sign of spiritual health. Instead, we must see as clearly as the Puritans did that, as Samuel Clarke put it, "the world useth a man, as the Ivie doth an Oake, the closer it gets to the heart, the more it clings and twists about the affections," seeming "to promise & flatter much, yet it indeed doth but eate out his reall substance, and choake him in the embraces."[33]

Life Circumstances

Life in a fallen world is hard, and all of us are called to walk through burdensome, disappointing, even tragic circumstances. And though the

---

31 Watson, *Heaven Taken by Storm*, 43.
32 Watson, *Great Gain of Godliness*, 6.
33 Samuel Clarke, *The Saints Nosegay, or, A Posie of 741 Spirituall Flowers Both Fragrant and Fruitfull, Pleasant and Profitable* (London, 1642), 105.

Bible promises that God ultimately uses such suffering in the lives of his children to produce endurance, character, and hope (Rom. 5:3–4), a painful turn of events can prove profoundly discouraging in the short term and can deflate our sense of spiritual growth.

After his wife was struck with a serious illness in 1669, the New England farmer Joseph Tompson (1640–1732) took to his diary to record his spiritual struggles: "I took notis in mine owne hart that my spirit was secretly disquieted under the disposeing hand of God." Throughout this ordeal, Tompson found meditation "verye hard," and though he sometimes "found sweet refreshing from the word," even this "did not long continue."[34] It's not hard to understand Tompson's feelings—in the face of difficult, inexplicable providences, trusting God's goodness can feel like an insurmountable challenge, and such circumstances represent one of the most common causes of spiritual malaise.

Note as well that though we don't often think about it as such, prosperity and ease can also create tremendous obstacles for us in our Christian journey. Indeed, after surveying all the various hardships and tragedies that believers face—a list that included war, famine, natural disasters, and plague—Campegius Vitringa concluded that "among all the causes of spiritual feebleness there is none more serious than long-term prosperity in one's temporal or spiritual condition."[35] Though counterintuitive, Vitringa recognized that unbroken ease can interrupt our thirst for God and the satisfaction that he alone provides. Similarly, John Flavel taught that it is precisely "when providence smiles upon us and dandles us upon its knee" that the Christian heart "will be exceeding apt to grow secure, proud, and earthly."[36]

The key point, then, is that whether we perceive things to be going well or poorly, the circumstances in which we find ourselves can af-

---

34 Quoted in Adrian Chastain Weimer, "Affliction and the Stony Heart in Early New England," in Ryrie and Schwanda, *Puritanism and Emotion in the Early Modern World*, 121.

35 Vitringa, *Spiritual Life*, 87.

36 Flavel, *Works*, 5:437.

fect and shape our spiritual formation, and we must be attentive and responsive to that inescapable fact.

Snares of Satan

As with the topics of eschatology, speaking in tongues, and the relationship between church and state, the question of demonic power in the world today tends to be either endlessly investigated or altogether ignored.[37] Some evangelicals cannot seem to stop talking about spiritual warfare and the unseen realm, while others seem mildly embarrassed when the subject is even raised. I observed a bit of both growing up, though as I've gotten older, the churches to which I've belonged have tended to steer closer toward silence on the matter. In twenty-first-century mainstream Western settings, it's often awkward enough to admit to being a Christian at all—far more so when one adds a belief in Satan and demons into the conversation.[38]

And yet to the extent that we ignore the reality of demonic powers, we are out of step with both the Bible and Reformation-minded Christians who went before us. The apostle Paul was so convinced on this point that he could frame the entirety of the Christian life as a battle "against the spiritual forces of evil in the heavenly places," urging believers to "put on the whole armor of God" so that they might "be able to stand against the schemes of the devil" (Eph. 6:11–12). When he wrote to the Corinthians, Paul's concern was that they "would not be outwitted by Satan," a threat requiring that they be "not ignorant of his designs" (2 Cor. 2:11). Early modern Reformed authors were more

37 Cf. the famous opening lines of C. S. Lewis, *The Screwtape Letters: Letters from a Senior to a Junior Devil* (London: HarperCollins, 2016), ix: "There are two equal and opposite errors into which our race can fall about the devils. One is to disbelieve in their existence. The other is to believe, and to feel an excessive and unhealthy interest in them. They themselves are equally pleased by both errors."

38 Though not exactly encouraging news, this reflexive disbelief in supernatural evil may be changing, especially among secular younger people, who, as a group, seem far more interested in the occult than did previous generations. See Tara Isabella Burton, *Strange Rites: New Religions for a Godless World* (New York: PublicAffairs, 2020), esp. 115–39.

sensitive to this reality than we often are, and indeed, it was sensitivity to the passage just quoted from 2 Corinthians that prompted Thomas Brooks to write up a collection titled *Precious Remedies against Satan's Devices* (1652). In this work, Brooks identified dozens of the "devices" or "plots, darts, depths, whereby he outwitted our first parents" and seeks still to "deceive, entangle, and undo the souls of men." Like virtually all his contemporaries, Brooks was absolutely convinced that "Satan watches all opportunities to break our peace, to wound our consciences, to lessen our comforts, to impair our graces, to slur our evidences, and to damp our assurances."[39]

Given our fallen condition, authors like Brooks were somewhat less clear on exactly how the workings of demonic powers interact with our own inclinations toward sin. Indeed, in his survey of how the Reformed tradition has treated this issue, Herman Bavinck noted that "we cannot distinguish absolutely what comes from Satan and what comes out of our own heart."[40] But whatever ambiguities might surround the details, both the Bible itself and a long line of Reformed theologians are absolutely clear on the central point: Satan is a real and personal being who stands opposed to God and the people of God, a reality that should prompt us to be aware and on guard. "Sober-minded" and "watchful," we must pursue our spiritual formation knowing that our "adversary the devil prowls around like a roaring lion, seeking someone to devour" (1 Pet. 5:8).

Dealing with Our Difficulties

As we have now seen, seasons of spiritual difficulty when we feel distant from God and stagnant in our Christian life are common among God's people and admit of many different causes. Sometimes there might not even be any discernible cause at all; as Richard Sibbes noted, there are

---

39 Thomas Brooks, *Precious Remedies against Satan's Devices* (Edinburgh: Banner of Truth, 2019), 3, 280.

40 Herman Bavinck, *Reformed Ethics*, vol. 1, *Created, Fallen, and Converted Humanity*, ed. John Bolt (Grand Rapids, MI: Baker Academic, 2019), 457.

times "when God appears unto us as an enemy, without any special guilt of any particular sin, as in Job's case."[41] But whatever the reason, what can the Christian do? Let's consider three possible cures for our spiritual illnesses.

Remember Your Embodiment

In the previous chapter, we discussed recent evangelical proposals that seem to overemphasize the importance of bodily movement as a vehicle for spiritual formation. To question the validity of some of these specific claims, however, is not in any way to deny the reality and significance of our embodiment. Our bodies are given by our Creator as an inescapable part of what makes us who we are, and as a result, they play a role in every aspect of our lives. So if we want to lift our spirits, we can't neglect our bodies along the way.

"Our physical existence is tied to our spiritual well-being," writes D. A. Carson, and so "sometimes the godliest thing you can do in the universe is get a good night's sleep—not pray all night, but sleep."[42] Previous generations of thoughtful Reformation-minded Christians have articulated precisely the same sentiment. When Archibald Alexander reflected on the experience of Christians he knew who had experienced and then recovered from "religious melancholy," he noted that many of them attributed their sufferings, at least in part, to physical causes, and hence, "they lay particular stress on the regular, healthy state of the body."[43] This embodied approach to soul care was illustrated in the life of Charles Spurgeon, a man who walked through deep spiritual valleys throughout his life and, as a result, highly prized regular winter retreats to the French seaside town of Menton. In his classic treatment of depression in the life of the minister, Spurgeon drew attention

---

41 Sibbes, *Works*, 1:133. For a contemporary and insightful take on this perplexing reality, see Eric Ortlund, *Suffering Wisely and Well: The Grief of Job and the Grace of God* (Wheaton, IL: Crossway, 2022).

42 D. A. Carson, *Scandalous: The Cross and Resurrection of Jesus* (Wheaton, IL: Crossway, 2010), 147.

43 Alexander, *Religious Experience*, 39.

to the way that sitting behind a desk all day tends to diminish one's spiritual vigor:

> To sit long in one posture, poring over a book, or driving a quill, is in itself a taxing of nature; but add to this a badly ventilated chamber, a body which has long been without muscular exercise, a heart burdened with many cares, and we have all the elements for preparing a seething cauldron of despair. . . . A day's breathing of fresh air upon the hills, or a few hours' ramble in the beech woods' umbrageous calm, would sweep the cobwebs out of the brain of scores of our toiling ministers who are now but half alive.[44]

Relative to Spurgeon's nineteenth-century context, ours is a world in which far more of us sit for hours at a time looking at computer screens. In light of this, we would be wise to remember his prescription for spiritual ill health: "A mouthful of sea air, or a stiff walk in the wind's face, would not give grace to the soul, but it would yield oxygen to the body, which is next best."[45]

Make Use of the Means of Grace

If the means of grace considered in this book are indeed the very *means* or instruments through which we enjoy communion with God and "grow in the grace and knowledge of our Lord and Savior Jesus Christ" (2 Pet. 3:18), then it should come as no surprise that to neglect them is to invite spiritual trouble. Thus, when we turn to older devotional manuals, we often find that the basic remedy prescribed for sickness of soul is to go back to the Reformation triangle of Scripture, meditation, and prayer.

Campegius Vitringa, for example, stated that an important "remedy for spiritual illness is the reading of the Holy Scripture, truly a special

---

44   C. H. Spurgeon, *Lectures to My Students* (Fearn, UK: Christian Focus, 1998), 181.
45   Spurgeon, *Lectures to My Students*, 182.

balm which by itself may heal a soul that is languishing, sick, and near death." Unfolding this principle, Vitringa took Psalm 119 as "a rule for the spiritual life," for in and through the psalm's prolonged meditation on God's word, one discovers the "true remedy for a sickly soul."[46]

This is surely good advice. Unfortunately, it is sometimes easier said than done, for in the case of spiritual dryness, the very problem for which we seek a solution is a lack of interest in God and the things of God. Listen to how Wilhelmus à Brakel described the problems faced when a spiritually struggling person attempts to turn to Scripture:

> When she takes refuge to the Word of God in order to derive some comfort from it, it is a closed Book for her. She finds nothing there for herself. Her eyes may indeed fall upon a passage of Scripture, but it disturbs her, and that which should lift her up has the opposite effect, casting her down. The Word of God is nothing more to her than a fire and a two-edged sword. It neither makes an impression nor does it have an effect upon her, for the Spirit neither joins Himself to it, nor works by means of it, and therefore it is not efficacious.[47]

What does one do in such a case?

In a similar way, if we neglect prayer, we should not ordinarily expect a good result. As the nineteenth-century preacher Gardiner Spring (1785–1873) put it, "If you will review your own history, I think you will not fail to see that those periods of it have been most distinguished for usefulness, that have been most distinguished for prayer."[48] The Christian response to trouble of whatever kind is to pray, to "cast [his] burden on the Lord," confident that "he will sustain [him]" (Ps. 55:22).

46 Vitringa, *Spiritual Life*, 92.
47 À Brakel, *Christian's Reasonable Service*, 4:177.
48 Gardiner Spring, "An Address to the Students," in *Princeton and the Work of the Christian Ministry*, ed. James M. Garretson (Edinburgh: Banner of Truth, 2012), 2:46.

But whereas this reality might seem obvious and urgent in response to burdens like illness or financial trouble, what does one do when the presenting problem is prayerlessness itself?

Whether the question is a lack of prayer or a lack of Bible intake, the answer that many wise pastors have offered is as simple as it is frustrating for those looking to find more creative ways out of their spiritual malaise: you must press on and not give up. In response to the complaint that taking up the means of grace felt too hard, Thomas Watson gave a startlingly direct reply:

> Admit it to be hard, yet it is a duty, and there is no disputing duty. God has made the way to heaven hard to try our obedience. A child obeys his father, though he commands him hard things. Peter's obedience and love were tried when Christ bade him come to Him upon the water. God makes the way hard that He might raise the price of heavenly things. Were the kingdom of glory easily obtained, we would not value its worth.[49]

And when Richard Greenham was asked to advise a person who "for want of feeling was loath to pray," he answered that "you must not tarry to pray til you find feeling" but instead must "pray on and continue in a praier of faith though not of feeling."[50] In other words, take the next step in obedience and faith even when you don't feel like doing so. The same applies to reading your Bible: if you don't feel like doing it, that is simply all the more reason why you need to open it up and read the next verse.

Early moderns were more comfortable with this sort of advice than we often are. Sometimes we resist what can feel like a straightforward, predictable, even boring approach to spiritual formation: "Are you saying again that I should just go read my Bible? Really? Is that all you

---

49 Watson, *Heaven Taken by Storm*, 66.
50 Quoted in Ryrie, *Reformation Britain*, 46.

have?" We are often looking for something novel and immediate, imagining that if we only found the right technique or tool, then all would go smoothly and without clog or friction. We do this in other areas of life as well, imagining, for instance, that our dreams of physical fitness would finally materialize if we could only find that perfect workout routine, lifting technique, or cutting-edge supplement. Sometimes the last thing we want to hear is that there is no secret formula and that the right answer is the one we knew all along: improving cardiovascular endurance means moving a lot, and getting stronger means lifting heavy things over and over again. Likewise, in the spiritual life, if your problem is that you're disinclined to pray, then sometimes the answer is simply that you need to decide to pray in obedience to Christ and to keep on trying until, one day, you discover that by God's grace you've been praying all along and that God is forming you according to his timetable rather than your own.

Get outside Yourself

To recalibrate our spiritual dials, we need to resist the tendency to become turned in on ourselves. In chapter 6, we talked about the need for self-examination. Done well, this sort of meditation on oneself can be a vital means of growing in grace. And yet like most things in this life, there is a shadow side: too much inwardness can lead to a cramped sort of self-obsession in which an ever-increasing share of my mental bandwidth is taken up with an ever-shrinking range of solipsistic anxieties and concerns. Not only is this a common problem among Christians, it has actually been a problem for some of the very eminent Reformed pastors and theologians that we have considered in this book. For example, in his study of Jonathan Edwards, Dane Ortlund observes that "Edwards was very introspective" and sometimes exhibited "an unhealthy preoccupation with his own spiritual state."[51]

---

51 Dane C. Ortlund, *Edwards on the Christian Life: Alive to the Beauty of God*, Theologians on the Christian Life (Wheaton, IL: Crossway, 2014), 181.

This can happen to any of us, and if we sense it in ourselves, the solution is to get outside, both literally and figuratively.

First, get outside literally, as in leave your room and engage with things and people who exist beyond the boundaries of your own skull. In chapter 7, we discussed the biblical idea that the natural world is a showcase for God's glory, noting that observing and enjoying God's creation is a vital component of spiritual flourishing. Sometimes the best thing you can do to fight sin, sloth, and spiritual stupor is to rise up, breathe deeply, and actively enjoy the world God has made. Similarly, in chapter 8, we considered the vital role that Christian relationships play in helping us both grow in faith and keep persisting in it. When the sweetness of solitude degenerates into the loneliness of isolation, I should remember that "two are better than one. . . . For if they fall, one will lift up his fellow" (Eccl. 4:9–10). Both appreciating God's creation and connecting with other Christians involve directing my attention outward rather than inward, the meadow before me and the friend beside me existing as objective realities that encourage, enliven, and refresh.

Second, if you are spiritually downcast, the Christian response is to get outside yourself figuratively—to cease from dwelling on your own failures and shortcomings and to look instead to Christ. Richard Sibbes wrote that we cause ourselves "overmuch trouble, when we look too much and too long upon the ill in ourselves."[52] The reason for this is not hard to understand: given a Reformed understanding of indwelling sin, when I look inward, I always find much to lament. And if my inward focus leads me to imagine, however subtly, that my ultimate right standing before God is based on my obedience, then to the extent that I read my heart accurately, I will despair. As the Heidelberg Catechism puts it, "Even the holiest have only a small beginning of [the] obedience" God requires.[53]

---

52   Sibbes, *Works*, 1:141.
53   "Heidelberg Catechism," in Van Dixhoorn, *Creeds, Confessions, and Catechisms*, 327 (q. 114).

This is the bad news. The good news, however, is that just as a Reformed understanding of sin removes all hope of self-justification, a Reformed understanding of the gospel gives us infinitely more to rejoice over: a justification grounded on the perfect obedience of Jesus Christ freely imputed. The same Heidelberg Catechism that removes any grounds for boasting builds a strong foundation of hope in Christ alone:

> Without any merit of my own, out of sheer grace, God grants and credits to me the perfect satisfaction, righteousness, and holiness of Christ, as if I had never sinned nor been a sinner, and as if I had been as perfectly obedient as Christ was obedient for me—if only I accept this gift with a believing heart.[54]

This statement captures the cornerstone of the Christian faith and is the reason why being overly inward oriented is a danger to spiritual health.

And yet are we not called to examine ourselves? What is one to do? The advice on this point given in a letter by Robert Murray M'Cheyne is as relevant today as when he wrote it in the autumn of 1840. After urging his correspondent to practice self-examination and "learn much of your own heart," M'Cheyne added this: "For every look at yourself, take ten looks at Christ. He is altogether lovely."[55] Around the same time but on the other side of the Atlantic, Archibald Alexander sat in his study talking to his students about the Christian life. Many of those seminarians were sensitive souls and troubled by these same questions. What did Alexander tell them? As one of his colleagues recalled, he gave them advice that was remarkably similar to M'Cheyne's: "If any student went to Dr. Alexander in a state of despondence, the venerable man was sure to tell him, 'Look not too

---

54 "Heidelberg Catechism," in Van Dixhoorn, *Creeds, Confessions, and Catechisms*, 308 (q. 60).

55 Robert Murray M'Cheyne, *Memoir and Remains of Robert Murray M'Cheyne*, ed. Andrew A. Bonar (London: Banner of Truth, 1966), 293.

much within. Look to Christ. Dwell on his person, on his work, on his promises, and devote yourself to his service, and you will soon find peace.'"[56] That is advice well worth taking.

———

We began this chapter by considering the Reverend Timothy Rogers and his "inward terrors" of soul. During that time of spiritual distress, Rogers learned the meaning of Psalm 40:1 as he "waited patiently for the LORD" for some two years. Looking back, he recalled worrying that he "should never be delivered." He recalled, "I thought that I should never have any more ease in my pained Body, nor ever any more hope or quiet in my troubled soul." But he continued to wait, pray, call on the Lord, persevere, and lean on Christian brothers and sisters who encouraged him and prayed for him. He didn't know how long he would be required to wait, but he knew that God was faithful. And eventually, Rogers wrote, "that God who is Omnipotent" gave "rest to my weary Soul."[57] And as he emerged from the spiritual shadows, Rogers was determined to use his experience to encourage others, and his words and testimony still have the power to encourage us today.

When things go wrong in your spiritual life—and they will—remember that many saints have walked that road before you and have found the Lord faithful. These innumerable Christians can testify with Rogers that the God of the Bible has always been with them, even when he seemed distant:

> None have any Cause to presume, when they consider what miseries
> I felt for a long time, and how I was overwhelmed with the deepest
> sorrows, for many doleful Months together; neither have any cause

56   David B. Calhoun, *Princeton Seminary*, vol. 1, *Faith and Learning, 1812–1868* (Edinburgh: Banner of Truth, 1994), 175.

57   Rogers, *Trouble of Mind*, A2v.

to despair, they cannot be more low, more near to Death and Hell than I thought myself to be, and yet I live, and am not without some refreshing hope of God's acceptance, and can say with the Prophet, "Let Israel hope in the Lord, for with the Lord there is mercy; and with him is plenteous redemption."[58]

58 Rogers, *Trouble of Mind*, A2r–A3v.

Epilogue

THE CHRISTIAN LIFE is a growing life. Christians are growing in grace and knowledge (2 Pet. 3:18), growing into maturity (Col. 1:28), growing up into salvation (1 Pet. 2:2), and growing in conformity to the image of Christ (Rom. 8:29). Paul wrote to the Thessalonian Christians, "We ought always to give thanks to God for you, brothers, as is right, because your faith is *growing abundantly*, and the love of every one of you for one another is *increasing*" (2 Thess. 1:3). Abundant growth, steady increase, and forward progress toward that "better country" prepared by God (Heb. 11:16)—these are the marks that define the life of faith Christians are called to.

At the same time, the Christian life is also marked by suffering, inner conflict, and dying to oneself. The psalmist whose "soul thirsts for God" also finds his soul "cast down" (Ps. 42:2, 5), and the same Paul who said, "Rejoice in the Lord always" (Phil. 4:4), describes himself and his companions as feeling "so utterly burdened beyond our strength that we despaired of life itself" (2 Cor. 1:8). All this belongs to the Christian life, and the Bible consistently describes the faithful as participating in the full panorama of human experience. Growth means learning to see all of life through the prism of God's purposes such that you can "count it all joy" when you "meet trials of various kinds," confident that "the testing of your faith produces steadfastness" (James 1:2–3).

That varied richness as reflected in Scripture is the canvas on which our spiritual formation is set. In this book we have described spiritual formation as the conscious process by which we seek to heighten and satisfy our Spirit-given thirst for God (Ps. 42:1–2) through divinely appointed means and with a view toward "work[ing] out [our] own salvation with fear and trembling" (Phil. 2:12) and becoming "mature in Christ" (Col. 1:28). And whether we are rejoicing or lamenting, settled or uncertain, young or old, that process is our great life task.

Moreover, in this book we have tried to learn something about spiritual formation by looking to the Reformed tradition. We haven't done this because we wish to idolize a particular time and place or a particular group of people but rather because early modern Reformed Christians saw biblical realities clearly and wrote down what they saw. Ours has been an attempt to imitate them as they imitated Christ (1 Cor. 11:1). And if we are evangelical Christians, then their tradition of spiritual formation is a part of our own inheritance, one for which we should thank God. There are many today who have grown tired of evangelicalism, and sadly, many of them have good reason for feeling disaffected. But amid the many understandable reasons for skepticism concerning the current state of evangelical Christianity, one that should be rejected is the charge that evangelicals lack a deep understanding of spiritual formation. Reformation-minded evangelicals can celebrate a rich tradition of pursuing God among their forebears, and before we judge it inadequate, we owe it to ourselves and those who went before to at least understand it well. My prayer is that this book has been helpful in deepening that understanding.

As this book comes to a close, I leave you with one last dispatch from the world of early modern Reformed Protestantism, a snapshot of the Puritan John Janeway (1633–1657). Born into the home of a minister, Janeway was pointed toward Christ from a young age, but it was during his time at Cambridge University that he came to embrace a Puritan approach to piety and spiritual formation. According to one contemporary account of his life, "He made it his whole Business to keep up sensible Communion with God and to grow into an humble familiarity with him." Janeway "was never so well satisfied as when he was . . . engaged in what brought him nearer unto God."[1]

And what exactly was it that "brought him nearer unto God"? From a human perspective, it was taking up the practices and tools for spiritual formation that we have discussed in this book. Janeway's piety was rooted in God's word: "He studied the Scriptures much, and they were sweeter to him than his Food." He also practiced self-examination, laboring to keep "watch over his Thoughts, Words, and Actions" and taking time to review these "in a solemn manner." To help him with this, "he kept a Diary in which he wrote down every Evening, what the frame of his Spirit had been all that Day," taking special notice of ways God had answered his prayers and making "Grateful Remembrance of God's Mercies."[2]

It wasn't always easy for Janeway. He could feel dismayed by feelings of "deadness and flatness of Spirit."[3] And in a letter to a friend, he noted how easy it was for "the cares and troubles of the World" to take our minds off "from walking with God."[4] When writing about the "excellent duty of meditation," he described the practice as having a "bitter sweet" quality: "bitter to corrupt nature, but sweet to the regenerate part." Janeway recognized that taking up the means of grace could be difficult and that the Christian life could be hard, and yet he saw the work of keeping his heart as a joyful burden to carry in the pursuit of "seriousness, reality, sincerity," and "chearfulness in Religion." It was through embracing the tools of spiritual formation revealed through God's word that "the Joy of the Lord" became his "strength."[5]

---

1   Samuel Clarke, *The Lives of Sundry and Eminent Persons in This Later Age* (London, 1683), 75.

2   Clarke, *Lives*, 74.

3   Clarke, *Lives*, 74.

4   James Janeway, *Invisibles, Realities, Demonstrated in the Holy Life and Triumphant Death of Mr. John Janeway* (London, 1698), 13.

5   Janeway, *Invisibles, Realities*, 14.

Janeway did not enjoy a long life, dying of tuberculosis at the age of twenty-three. Yet during his relatively brief time on earth, he made it his mission to cultivate "a very intimate acquaintance with his own Heart: This kept him Humble, and fitted him for free communications from God."[6] And if the testimony of his siblings who gathered around him during his final moments are to be believed, the Lord granted him success in this endeavor. As his seventeenth-century biographer, Samuel Clarke, recorded,

> In the latter part of his Life, he lived like a Man that was quite a weary of the World, and that looked upon himself as a Stranger here, and that lived in the constant sight of a better world. He plainly declared himself to be a Pilgrim that looked for a better Countrey, for a City that hath Foundations, whose Builder and Maker is God.[7]

His steady use of Bible intake, meditation, and prayer had "ripened him . . . for Heaven," and as he reached the end of his pilgrimage, he left words that serve as a fitting end to this book: "My heart is full; my heart is full. Christ smiles, and I cannot choose but smile."[8]

6   Clarke, *Lives*, 74.
7   Clarke, *Lives*, 75.
8   Clarke, *Lives*, 75, 77.

Appendix

A Brief Note on Spiritual Formation, Individualism, and the Church

A HEART AFLAME FOR GOD has been largely concerned with *individual* Christian practices that foster spiritual formation and growth. Throughout the pages of Scripture—whether one thinks of the psalmist's deeply personal inner life (e.g., Ps. 77:6), Mary's quiet meditation on the remarkable workings of God (Luke 2:19), or the practice of the Lord himself, who "went out to a desolate place" to seek his Father in solitude (Mark 1:35)—the Bible presents numerous positive examples of the individual pursuit of piety.

While affirming all the above, however, we must also guard against the ever-present danger that this healthy regard for the individual as such could devolve into an unhealthy *individualism*. The danger when reading a book like this one is that we take its focus on individual spiritual disciplines as a license to practice a solo Christianity in which the individual believer pursues piety at home, on his or her own, without reference to the church. When this sort of thinking takes root in a person's mind, committing to and getting involved in a local congregation starts to appear like just *one more* spiritual discipline that I can use or not use insofar as it seems to help my spiritual formation.

If the Puritans were so confident that Bible reading, meditation, and prayer would build up one's godliness, why bother with the hassle and inconvenience of going to church? The allure of this temptation is helpfully summarized by Brett McCracken:

> If Christianity is mostly about doing your own thing with Jesus, then leaving church becomes easy to justify. If church adds something to one's personal spiritual walk, then great. But if it is a hassle or a hindrance, just ditch it. You can love Jesus without loving the church . . . or so the logic goes.[1]

We slip all too easily into this way of thinking because, in addition to sinful hearts that resist the inconvenience and friction that participating in church inevitably entails, the background noise of our twenty-first-century Western pop culture is deeply individualistic. The spirit of our age has been described as one of "expressive individualism,"[2] and as David Wells has observed, these thought patterns within the wider culture have quietly crept into evangelical thinking, distorting our Christian vision in ways we often don't fully appreciate: "The constant cultural bombardment of individualism, in the absence of a robust theology, meant that faith that had rightly been understood as personal now easily became faith that was individualistic, self-focused, and consumer oriented."[3]

Moreover, in the years since Wells wrote his analysis of evangelical culture, rapid technological change has exacerbated the problem by making it easier than ever to forgo meaningful real-life connections with other people. As the social psychologist Jonathan Haidt has documented, the ubiquitous presence of smartphones and the always-on mindset they

1 Brett McCracken, *The Wisdom Pyramid: Feeding Your Soul in a Post-Truth World* (Wheaton, IL: Crossway, 2021), 88.

2 See Carl R. Trueman, *The Rise and Triumph of the Modern Self: Cultural Amnesia, Expressive Individualism, and the Road to Sexual Revolution* (Wheaton, IL: Crossway, 2020).

3 David F. Wells, *The Courage to Be Protestant: Truth-Lovers, Marketers, and Emergents in the Postmodern World* (Grand Rapids, MI: Eerdmans, 2008), 11.

foster have effected what he calls a "Great Rewiring" of how young people relate to one another and the world around them: "The Great Rewiring devastated the social lives of Gen Z by connecting them to everyone in the world and disconnecting them from the people around them."[4]

Unless Christians identify such larger cultural currents and take deliberate counteractions, we will inevitably be swept right along with them toward a sort of me-alone Christianity that is out of step with both the Reformation heritage we've championed in this book and Scripture itself. The Bible makes clear that while God certainly calls *individuals* to new life in Christ, the individual person is called into a community composed of many others responding to the same call. Each unique individual believer is "a living stone rejected by men but in the sight of God chosen and precious," and yet God's choice of the individual stone is for a decidedly corporate purpose: "You yourselves like living stones are being built up as a spiritual house, to be a holy priesthood" (1 Pet. 2:4–5). "You" as an individual are called to join together with all the saints to "proclaim the excellencies of him who called you out of darkness into his marvelous light" (1 Pet. 2:9).

God addresses the individual but then summons him or her to the communion of saints, and the concrete manifestation of that communion is the local church. For their part, the early modern Reformed Protestants we've been looking at in this book could never have imagined a faithful Christian life apart from participating in a congregation of real flesh-and-blood believers. In his study of Puritan spirituality, historian Charles Hambrick-Stowe suggests that the Puritans' "private devotion during the week" can be largely conceived as a "preparation for" worship on Sunday, during which "the greatest concentration of spiritual activity occurred."[5] And while some have accused the Puritans

---

4   Jonathan Haidt, *The Anxious Generation: How the Great Rewiring of Childhood Is Causing an Epidemic of Mental Illness* (London: Allen Lane, 2024), 122.

5   Charles E. Hambrick-Stowe, *The Practice of Piety: Puritan Devotional Disciplines in Seventeenth-Century New England* (Chapel Hill: University of North Carolina Press, 1982), 96.

and their evangelical heirs of fostering an individualistic approach to Christianity, we must recognize that they were operating in an early modern context marked by rampant Christian nominalism and state-mandated church attendance. Under such conditions, it made good pastoral sense for Puritan writers to urge individuals to pay more attention to their own walk with the Lord and to avoid the misapprehension that bare church attendance alone could substitute for a living, vital, personal relationship with God. In an increasingly secular society like ours in which individualism runs rampant, Puritan preaching on these points might need to be rhetorically recalibrated, but their core biblical insights into the nature of the Christian life are as relevant as ever and, when rightly understood, give no support whatsoever to a solo Christianity separated from the local church.

In *A Heart Aflame for God*, we have unpacked the key spiritual practices given to us in Scripture for our growth in godliness. I have not included a chapter explicitly on corporate worship because participation in the local church is not *one more discipline* but rather the vital context in which *all* the disciplines are lived out. The working assumption across every book of the Bible is that the people of God will pursue spiritual formation in communion with one another. It is only in and through the church that we find elders "shepherd[ing] the flock of God" (1 Pet. 5:2), deacons ministering "full of the Spirit and of wisdom" (Acts 6:3), gifted preachers "rightly handling the word of truth" (2 Tim. 2:15), the Great Commission being enacted through the baptizing of disciples "in the name of the Father and of the Son and of the Holy Spirit" (Matt. 28:19), the bread and cup being given to proclaim "the Lord's death until he comes" (1 Cor. 11:26), and indeed, the whole body of Christ "speaking the truth in love" that it might "grow up in every way into him who is the head, into Christ" (Eph. 4:15). These are precious gifts and means of grace that God has given to his people, and no amount of private devotion—however helpful it might be when used rightly—can ever replace them. But when exercised within the context of such a local church ministry, our individual pursuit of godliness through the means God has appointed becomes a vital expression of and conduit for our communion with the living triune God—Father, Son, and Holy Spirit.

If you do not currently attend a local church, I would urge you to get involved with one. If you've been away for a while or perhaps have never been a regular churchgoer, taking this step might feel daunting, and it will inevitably come with some inconvenience and awkwardness. As with any corporate endeavor, participating in a local church will entail putting aside some of one's own preferences and particularities to support the group. But it's a burden worth bearing and one that Scripture explicitly calls us to: "Let us consider how to stir up one another to love and good works, not neglecting to meet together, as is the habit of some" (Heb. 10:24–25). When considering local churches in your area, look for one that takes the Bible seriously as God's inspired, inerrant word and then puts that commitment into practice by prioritizing expositional preaching—that is, preaching that seeks to explain, illustrate, and apply specific biblical texts. If you aren't sure where to start, take advantage of several helpful online directories through which you can find Bible-believing, gospel-centered churches in your area.[6]

---

6   E.g., see the Gospel Coalition's "Church Directory," https://www.thegospelcoalition.org/churches/, and the 9Marks "Church Search" tool, https://www.9marks.org/church-search/. For further suggestions on what to look for in a local church, see Ric Rodeheaver, "5 Questions for Your Church Search," The Gospel Coalition, February 11, 2022, https://www.thegospelcoalition.org/.

General Index

Scripture Index